American Ideologies

The Competing Political Beliefs of the 1970s

American Ideologies

The Competing Political Beliefs of the 1970s

KENNETH M. DOLBEARE
University of Washington
PATRICIA DOLBEARE
North Seattle Community College

MARKHAM PUBLISHING COMPANY
Chicago

MARKHAM POLITICAL SCIENCE SERIES
Aaron Wildavsky, Editor

© Markham Publishing Company 1971
All Rights Reserved
Printed in U.S.A.
Second Printing March 1971
Library of Congress Catalog Card Number: 75-136622
Paperback Standard Book Number: 8410-3043-X
Hardcover Standard Book Number: 8410-3029-4

Acknowledgements

This brief analysis is intended for the college-level introductory course in American politics or American social problems. We think it is past time for today's contending ideologies—particularly those change-seeking ideologies that have injected such a new and dangerous dynamic into American politics—to be taken seriously as subjects for analysis in such courses. Both of us have sought to do so in our respective political science and sociology courses, but have found original materials inefficient for classroom use and existing secondary sources lacking in depth and comprehensiveness. Nevertheless, both the idea and the impetus for this book came from John Applegath of Markham Publishing Company. If it does serve a useful purpose for teachers and students, despite its brevity, his perceptive capitalism may be credited.

In a more basic sense, our interest in the characteristics of American political ideas is the product of several years' exchange with students and other friends at the University of Wisconsin. They are too numerous to name, but we owe this book primarily to them, and we are both glad and anxious to acknowledge our debt to them. Several experienced teachers read this manuscript and contributed significantly to its improvement. We are grateful to Mark Greenside of North Carolina A & T; to Harvey M. Karlen of Wright Junior College, Chicago; Thomas Morrison of California State College, Hayward; and Jon Schiller of the University of California, Berkeley, for their many helpful comments. The Center for the Study of Law and Society at the University of California, Berkeley, was a congenial and helpful setting for our efforts. Perhaps necessarily, a brief analysis of complex ideologies cannot completely satisfy anyone, and we must take full responsibility for defects in our presentation. We invite reactions from readers who want to take issue with us or suggest further extensions and implications of our analysis.

Contents

1

Ideology: Alive and Well in the United States

Not long ago, American social scientists and journalists were proclaiming the "end of ideology" and the broad consensus of all Americans. From the perspective of the 1950s, it seemed that basic needs were satisfied, conflicts readily compromised, and there were no further challenges to the basic character of the American social, economic, and political order. Then the civil rights movement swept the nation, developing first into the black power stage and then into more revolutionary black liberation movements. The anti-Vietnam war and the related student protest movements exploded from the nation's campuses into the streets in 1968, escalating as steadily as did the War. The character, but not the thrust, of these movements has been modified by the increasingly far-reaching efforts at suppression undertaken by militant defenders of the status quo. The combination has revitalized—indeed, supercharged—the nation's political life. If fundamental ideological conflict was really lacking twenty years ago (or if, as seems more likely, one orthodox ideology dominated nearly all intellectual and political discourse), the situation is now totally different.

For the first time in decades, substantial numbers of Americans are challenging the fundamental assumptions on which their political system rests. They openly deny the legitimacy of existing social, economic, and political structures; they seek change of the most basic kind. Men in power have responded with a vigorous defense of orthodox beliefs and practices. Some of the general public have rallied to their support; others have been characterized as supporting established policies despite their total inactivity—the so-called "silent majority." Despite patriotic assertions of massive consensus, the fact is that profound social conflicts characterize the United States as the 200th anniversary of its independence approaches. Tensions, if anything, seem to be growing deeper and more pervasive. Conspiracy trials, police harassment, and official denunciation mark, but fail to suppress, conflicts endemic to a wide range of social problems. Riots, disruptions, and bombings continue unabated, and the call for revolution in one form or another is becoming a commonplace of political dialogue.

These conditions stem from many causes, the roots of which lie deep in the American past. In the present, however, distinctive political ideologies are both effect *and* cause. Contrasting interpretations of how and why the American political system does and should operate are now characteristic of various individuals and groups in the United States. Repression, reform and revolution draw upon comprehensive—but sharply conflicting—belief systems that link images of what might be in the future to the world today as they perceive it. In short, ideologies are a major force active in the contemporary American political dynamic.

We may disagree about the long-term meaning of today's deep gaps in political perceptions, values, and goals, but no one can deny the existence of conflict rooted in distinctive belief systems. These tensions may be transitory, a mere stage in the younger generations' adaptation to a new role in an advanced technological society, or they may be the first stage in a process of social disintegration that inexorably will lead to either a totalitarian police state or violent revolution. In either case, the contending ideologies that contribute to making our politics so dangerous and so portentous today deserve the most careful attempts at understanding. We will start by clarifying some basic terms and proceed to consider the purposes and approaches that will characterize our analysis of the ideologies now competing for support among Americans.

The Nature and Sources of Ideology

Politics, and much of social life, involves the use of power to achieve goals amidst changing circumstances. Central to this process are beliefs about the present nature of the world and the hopes one has for its future. Such beliefs and hopes, when integrated into a more or less coherent picture of (1) how the present social, economic, and political order operates, (2) why this is so, and whether it is good or bad, and (3) what should be done about it, if anything, may be termed an "ideology." Ideology, of course, plays a varied part in different times and places. Contrasting beliefs and hopes may be the driving force behind bitter conflicts. They may mobilize millions in massive movements or they may be the principal resource enabling a small but dedicated band of men to defy great nations. Or, in other settings, the dominance of one set of beliefs may be so encompassing that new ideas not only are doggedly resisted, but their advocates are either ignored or punished. Thus, whether "realistic" or not, assumptions and aspirations move men alternately to action and to acceptance.

We shall make no effort here to identify the number of believers in any particular ideology or to characterize the part that such ideologies play in their lives or in the process of politics generally. These are interesting and important questions for which empirical research may someday provide adequate answers. But our focus is on the substance—the specific principles—of the various ideologies that now contend for political impact in the United States. For our purposes, it is enough that an ideology be held by some segment of politically active people and that it have the potential of gathering support and affecting American politics. When we speak of ideologies, therefore, it is in terms of their content and not in terms of their breadth of support or their function as a source of social movements.

Despite such a focus, some of our assumptions about the nature and sources of ideologies or political belief systems are relevant to the way in which we will analyze them. The *nature* of ideology, as we shall use the term, is suggested by the definition just given: it is a system of related beliefs about how the political world does and should operate. In part, it is a series of images that seem to describe and *interpret* what happens in politics from day to day. One who holds an ideology has, in effect, a series of expectations or a map in his mind, orienting him and telling him how things work. Thus, he knows where to fit facts that he perceives and how to understand their significance. It is also a series of cues for evaluation of what he sees. Such "facts" are good or bad, or things *should* be done in certain ways, because of the standards or imperatives of the ideology to which he consciously or unconsciously subscribes. An ideology may be held with varying degrees of specificity and intensity. For some, it may be comprehensive, detailed, and integrated—that is, interconnected explanations and interpretations already exist in their minds for nearly everything that they see or feel about politics. For others, it may be fragmented and/or not strongly felt.

For those who hold to an ideology, obviously, it may serve important political purposes. An ideology provides not only cues for understanding and evaluating public affairs, but may also serve as a guide to action, as a means of self-expression, and/or as a means of relating to other people. Ideology may thus become integrated with an individual's personality. This is neither unusual nor undesirable, either for the individual or for the political system as a whole. Quite naturally, all people develop images of the world around them; they cannot help but see things in terms of their life experience, values, and aspirations. Some political activists disparage ideology as the antithesis of reason, but this may be merely because they hold a *different* ideology. All established political systems generate ideologies that explain, justify, and mobilize support for their practices. Divergent ideologies may be necessary means of enabling people to see their own individual interests more clearly. Thus, ideology may, in effect, serve as a way of developing representation for segments of the population whose real values and interests are not reflected in the preferences of those who manage the system.

The *sources* of ideology are many. People acquire their political belief systems through a complex and little-understood process in which parts are played by the individual's own personality and values, his social setting and life experiences, the effects of the education he has undergone, and the way in which he understands the events that occur in the world around him. Family and school are leading early sources of political beliefs. As young children, most people acquire from their families the basic elements of political loyalties, an image of the political world, and a sense of right and wrong in politics. These are usually reinforced by the public school system, which teaches the propriety, inevitability, and utility of American institutions and practices.

For some children, however, the everyday facts of their surroundings so challenge the idealized interpretations offered in school that they mature with conflicting commitments. The same may occur if their families are among the relatively few who hold decisive views that do not conform with dominant ideologies. Still others may begin life imbued with the usual benevolent concepts and, through a process of shedding orthodox assumptions and expectations, emerge with a whole new set of beliefs about what is and should be in American politics. Or a single dramatic condition or policy, such as racism or the Vietnam war, might so detach a person from his previous convictions that he may seek and find new explanations and aspirations for the political system he advocates.

Like other concepts and interpretive images that people carry in their minds, ideology tends to resist change. Many people retain a static view of the world in terms of assumptions and values long after forces and events have changed things. The individual clings to the familiar because a whole web of other beliefs and commitments may depend on such orientations; his own identity or the meaning he sees in life itself may be involved. The ideology itself also tends to resist change. It reaffirms its basic principles strongly, adapting to new conditions and problems only marginally, in patchwork fashion. In part, this is because a network of social and economic interests, institutions, and practices is supported and justified by the ideology.

Thus, at different levels, there are bulwarks against change in ideologies. This raises important questions for analysis: under what circumstances do individuals change their political ideologies? To the extent that such an act is rational and deliberate, what criteria should they employ in this process? And, how do ideologies themselves adapt to changing conditions and these changes among individuals? Some aspects of these questions are beyond the scope of this book, but we shall comment on others in our final chapter. The fact is, of course, that many individuals *do* experience changes in their ideologies, and new patterns of beliefs and values *do* arise to challenge orthodox ideologies. The political system may suddenly be confronted with new (and, to some, unintelligible) demands. This is why it seems to us essential to focus first on the beliefs and principles currently held by each major ideology. When their makeup is known, their prospective impact and attraction may be better understood.

The Substance of American Ideology: A Framework for Analysis

What kind of approach will provide understanding of the content of contemporary American ideologies? Naturally, the questions to be asked depend on the purposes to be served by this inquiry. Our primary purpose is to *describe* the beliefs and hopes that move people in the United States today. Secondarily, we want to *analyze* ideologies, to see what they share, and where they diverge; we must therefore compare them with each other in regard to some key components. Ultimately, we hope in this way to contribute to explanation of contemporary political behavior and to understanding of the roots of current conflicts. The reader, of course, may well seize the opportunity to go further. By putting himself into the belief system of others on an alternative basis, he will at least decisively widen his own frame of reference with regard to politics. He will empathize with the perspectives and actions of others and gain a new sense of the range of possibility in politics. By raising both factual and ethical questions, he will move closer to the day when he has personal political convictions. Thus, there are also *evaluative* purposes involved in this investigation—to give the citizen confidence in his own political beliefs and actions.

The central questions to be applied to each ideology must therefore include descriptive, analytical, and evaluative dimensions. In order to provide understanding of political behavior, basic beliefs must be exposed, fundamental assumptions must be related to underlying values, and both must be connected to resulting commitments to action. No other approach can link premises and perceptions to understanding of *why* such views are held and *what they imply* in terms of efforts to bring about change. At the same time, we must explore the values and aspirations of each ideology for their own sake, so citizens may not only see the range of what people believe but also reach sophisticated ethical judgments about the propriety or desirability of particular goals and tactics.

We shall use three distinct categories to describe and analyze each ideology: (1) the *"world view,"* [1] or general perspective on how the American economic and political systems work today, for whom, and why; (2) the *values* that are central to the ideology and the *goals* that it holds out as most desirable for the United States; and (3) the image of the process of *social change* to which it subscribes and the *tactics* that it deems appropriate in the light of its world view, values and goals, and image of change. Let us explain each of these organizing questions in turn.

(1) WORLD VIEW

Ideologies are integrated systems of belief in which definitions of reality bear a relation to a goal and methods of achieving it. First in logical sequence, though not necessarily first in order of formulation, is the nature of one's understanding of what is happening in the world around him and why. What is the nature of the social order? Is it egalitarian, or is it stratified so that some have more of the things that are valued (status, wealth, etc.) in the society? Did this pattern in society evolve because of inherent differences in the talents or capabilities of men, or is it the result of some other factors? Here we shall touch upon the extent to which the ideology sees the society divided into contending social classes (i.e., segmented by wealth, prestige, power, etc.). If society is so divided, are people aware of the divisions among them? What part does or might this consciousness play in politics? How is the economy run, and who benefits from such a system of organization? How is power distributed, and what sustains such patterns? A distinct set of perceptions about these questions characterizes each ideology, evoking a decisively different reaction.

In some respects at least, the accuracy of such beliefs is open

---

[1] We employ the term "world view" here, despite its long history and much more complex usage elsewhere in the social sciences, because we are unable to frame an equally expressive and felicitous term. We mean it synonomously with "image of social reality" or "image of power and process," and we trust no unnecessary confusion will be caused by our usage.

to empirical investigation. It is possible to define the pattern of distribution of wealth in the United States, for example, or the extent of racial discrimination in various aspects of life. Such factual descriptions can be produced, tested, and checked by research. Even then, however, differences of perspective appear: some attach great concern to the fact of inequality, while others see it as a natural manifestation of inherent differences among people or as a condition undergoing steady improvement. Looking at the same facts, some see problems, while others see progress. These differences may be due not to disagreement about the facts, but to their meaning in the context of other facts. Our understanding of the nature and significance of facts themselves reflects assumptions and preferences about the political world. In many cases, of course, no agreed "facts" are available, and we have only assumptions or outright guesses to go on. In all cases, all our perceptions (assumptions *and* facts) must be correlated in some coherent, interpretive way before they can have full significance for us. All along the line, ideology tells us what significance to see in facts, how to supplement fact with assumption, what relationship each fact has to others, and what they all add up to. This explanation of our surroundings is what we mean by the term *world view*. *What* people believe, after all, not whether or not it is accurate, is crucial for understanding their behavior.

From time to time, however, the issue of the accuracy of an ideology's world view may become important. Occasionally, the reader may find that the world view held by a particular ideology seems wholly at odds with the facts as he understands them. This may force or induce him to seek to resolve the factual issue through turning to empirical research, in which case he will have a basis for judgment about the soundness of the ideology's understanding of the world, and/or for revising his own perceptions about that same world. Regardless of the extent of convergence between his own world view and that of the ideology under examination, however, specification of that world view offers a concrete point of comparison with all other ideologies. Some of them are bound to be closer to the "reality" described by the empirical evidence—or adhered to by the reader—and all can be efficiently contrasted as to the major components of their world views. Analysis of world views thus serves both the descriptive and the evaluative purposes that we have in mind.

(2) VALUES AND GOALS

As we dig deeper into the first principles of the ideology, its fundamental commitments become apparent and a coherent relationship between its perceptions of the world and its priorities and aspirations should begin to emerge. Each ideology is attached to some values, such as equality or justice, in preference to others. The crucial questions are *the way in which such values are understood or defined* by the ideology, and *how they are ranked in priority* when they conflict with each other. Equality, for example, may be defined in exclusively formalistic legal and political terms (that is, the right to vote), or in terms of the tangible social and economic conditions of a person's existence. It may be given high status in rhetoric but low status in practice or when it conflicts (as is often the case) with property rights or commitments to established procedures. Similarly, "due process" or "law and order" may mean different things to different ideologies, and our analysis must seek to specify carefully the precise meanings intended.

The goals of each ideology reflect its perception of the *distance* between the conditions of the society today (as understood in its world view) and the values to which it subscribes. In general, ideologies seek to attain the conditions, institutions, and policies that will permit realization of their values. In some cases, this may mean defending the status quo in every respect. In others, it may require drastic changes and the development of a series of interim goals. Out of the interplay of world view, values, and goals emerges a conception of the *scope* and *direction* of social change that will be necessary to achieve the ends to which the ideology is committed.

We will try to distinguish reform and revolution as they are implied by different ideologies. The distinction lies partly in the realm of values and partly in the area of social change and tactics. In regard to values, we will see that the values and goals of some ideologies are modest extensions or reaffirmations of the basic values already dominant within the political system. For other ideologies, contemporary values must be drastically reshaped or replaced. The former may be seen as reform, the latter as revolution. In regard to images of the process of change and the tactics necessary to bring about a desired change, a similar distinction will be visible. Some ideologies adhere to the established procedures of politics. Some are prepared to undertake extra-legal methods, now or at some future time, because they see no other way to achieve their goals. Again, the former represents reform, the latter revolution.

(3) THE PROCESS OF SOCIAL CHANGE AND THE TACTICS AND METHODS OF ACHIEVING CHANGE

Each ideology develops an image of the process by which desired change can best be achieved. This sense of what is needed to accomplish change is based on its world view and its understanding of the scope and direction of change that is necessary. A given ideology's world view may posit only one or two historical determinants of change or a specific dynamic that must be followed. Thus, despite a strong desire for fundamental change, adherents of such an ideology would be constrained to wait until conditions were perceived as right for them to gain their ends. In other words, the *process* by which change is to be sought is not controlled by the *scope* of change sought; it depends also on the ideology's world view definition of present circumstances and power distribution within the society.

Tactics and methods of change may differ over time as well as between ideologies. Ordinarily, they are designed to conform with the requirements of the current stage in the long-term process of change, as understood by the particular ideology. Thus, almost no ideologies have absolute commitments to *employ* or *not to employ* physical violence, and the presence or absence of violence is not a sound way to characterize an ideology. Both reform and revolutionary ideologies may advocate violence under particular conditions, and either may feel that circumstances require peaceful means throughout the process. The point is that the use of violence must be understood in context, as a tactic that an ideology sees as appropriate under certain defined conditions and for specific reasons, and not as a universally applicable (and therefore inevitably characterizing) aspect of its system of beliefs and practices.

To be sure, there are individuals who feel that violence is abhorrent and morally condemnable; ethical pacifism has a long established and well respected place in American thought. But for most political ideologies, violence is a relative matter. The current social reality is neither neutral nor perfectly equitable. Nevertheless, some people see that reality as highly desirable and a good approximation of justice. Normally, they see war or other violence in defense of the established order as entirely legitimate. Others, however, may see existing social reality as unjust, corrupt, and destructive, and they may therefore see violence as a necessary means of achieving essential change. It is unlikely that society's existing political procedures or power distribution will help the "change-seekers" achieve their goals. It is much more likely that those in power will use violence to force obedience to the rules that sustain the existing order. Thus, official censure of violence may be self-serving or even hypocritical. To view all non-official violence as evil, no matter the provocation or the consequences, is to fall into the world view of those in power. Normally, then, violence would not be used as a basis for ethical judgment within a suitably wide frame of reference in analysis. Because violence is neither "good" nor "bad" of itself, judgment must depend on the purposes, manner, and consequences of its use in any given situation.

Each ideology subscribes to a wide variety of tactics and methods, of course, and we shall be examining more than merely the extent of willingness to employ violence. Although in most cases, tactics flow consistently from world view perceptions, values, and goals, there may be occasions on which commitments to particular tactics are so strong that they amount to one of the major values of the ideology. Or, for a variety of possible reasons, an ideology may be quite without prescriptions for the means by which change is to be secured. In these and other situations, we shall gain further insight into the nature of the ideology itself—its internal contradictions and characteristics—by comparing its tactics with its world view and its values and goals.

It will not be practical for us to follow this three-stage analytical framework precisely or rigidly. In some cases, we will supplement extensively or employ several subcategories in an effort to efficiently portray reality. But our general approach will always proceed in accordance with this scheme. Any standardized approach will result in some oversimplification, and our analysis is no exception. The remedy for this is further reading in the original works of major representatives of an ideology, and for this purpose, we have appended annotated bibliographies at the close of each chapter. We have also slighted the historical origins of the systems of thought presented. Each has a rich past, and many thinkers have contributed to the evolution of each ideology. But our focus on the contemporary character and impact of these ideologies has obliged us to curtail discussion of their origins and development. In the case of the established ideologies, we have included some preliminary paragraphs appropriate to setting a historical frame. The change-seeking ideologies, for the most part, may be seen as generated out of established ideologies, and works that explore the antecedents and evolution of both are included in the bibliographies.

We are acutely aware of another problem in presenting a synthesized interpretation of political ideologies in this fashion. How can we give each a fair hearing without abdicating our professional analytical responsibilities? Only a detailed reading of several original works and documents can give citizens a truly full understanding of the beliefs and aspirations of the various ideologies, and anything short of that is an accommodation that poses the threat of being biased by the interpreter's selections and manner of presentation. It is our specific function here to provide a comparative analysis that will enable citizens to see some crucial features of each ideology and to better understand their politics. We cannot avoid intruding between the ideology and the citizen. Under the circumstances, perhaps the best we can do is to urge the citizen to be alert and view our contributions with skepticism. We can also briefly describe some of the ways in which our views may intrude into this analysis.

In general, we have tried to allow each ideology to speak for itself as much as possible. We have used the most sophisticated spokesmen on behalf of each and tried to let their perspectives shape our presentation. We think this course assures that there will be no "straw men" erected at any point. Each ideology seems to us to have been presented by its most persuasive advocates. Nevertheless, we have felt obliged to comment from time to time about possible internal inconsistencies, lack of clarity on some points, or failure to deal with some vital questions. Moreover, we have had to make several choices in presenting each ideology, which may affect the reader's view of the ideology's viability. For example, we have selected representative authors for inclusion and quotation, extracted particular points from their works and termed these principles of the ideology, rearranged component beliefs to fit our framework, and characterized ideologies on the basis of evidence that is slim in some cases. *We* think this has been done fairly, responsibly, and objectively—but we do not expect all to agree with us on this point.

We are aware of three significant biases that have quite consciously structured our presentation. One is the conviction that it is time to take contemporary American ideologies seriously as important political forces in their own right and to cease viewing them as symptoms of psychological maladjustment, emotional immaturity, or antitechnological romanticism. In our view, people see problems and seek their solutions, principally because there *are* problems —problems that are inherent to American social, economic, and political structures—and not chiefly for sociopsychological reasons. Second, we think that citizens must strive to become critical, independent thinkers capable of analyzing and evaluating their political ideas, and the alternatives that face the United States, within the widest possible frame of reference. This means, in our eyes, that they must free themselves of the accumulated stereotypes and assumptions with which they may have become encumbered in the elementary and secondary school systems, and learn to think for themselves. Finally, we believe that the focus of their critical analysis should be on problems of change—whether changes in the *principles, policies,* and *practices* of American politics should be made and, if so, *what kind* and *by what means.* Fast-changing circumstances simply will not permit the United States to remain fixed politically. The problem (in our eyes) is one of determining which institutions are worthy of retention, and what must be changed, and selecting new forms. The sooner and more perceptively Americans take up this task, the better their chances for controlling their destinies.

We expect that the alternative ideologies presented here will raise substantial and perhaps frustrating problems of analysis and choice for readers. At some points, it may appear that there are six or seven plausible interpretations of what exists in the world and what should be done about it. The reader may begin to long for solid, factual evidence capable of resolving some of the wide divergences in world views that characterize various ideologies. To an extent, such needs may be satisfied by further inquiry or research or by purposeful use of other courses about the United States. But in another sense, a political system has no true nature *except* in terms of one's values and goals. It is what it is because we see it against a background of our own hopes and fears. Ideology, in other words, transcends facts, gives them meaning, and motivates us toward goal-seeking action. To understand the behavior of others and to gain a clear sense of our own commitments, we must learn to identify and analyze the part played by ideology with the utmost care.

American Ideologies: An Overview

We have chosen to present seven major ideologies, each in a separate chapter: capitalism, liberalism, reform liberalism, black liberation, the new left, Marxism, and conservatism. Our reasons for this approach are grounded in the characteristics of the ideologies themselves and in the nature of the American ideological scene. We have already discussed our combined analytical and evaluative purposes, in fulfillment of which we must take up each ideology as a separate belief system. But we must indulge in some general analysis of the nature and substance of American ideologies in order to justify the selection and order of presentation of ideologies in the chapters that follow.

First, some political postures that might be termed ideologies under some definitions are not included. Variants of American fascism have not been considered, for example, nor has Governor George Wallace's American Independent Party or any single-issue movement. We have deliberately excluded doctrines so little developed or seldom expressly put forward as to have little chance of generating significant political impact. No political party position is represented as such, partly because each position incorporates superficial aspects of several ideologies that are better analyzed separately and at a deeper level. Single-issue movements have been excluded because they lack comprehensiveness.

In other words, our definition of ideology as a more or less integrated belief system with a world view, values and goals, and an image of the correct process and tactics of change operates to exclude many political moods, groups, and movements. This is *not* to say that they are unimportant or unworthy of understanding. For some people, the status quo is its own justification and needs no rationale. For others, reaction or economic interest may be the sole or leading basis of political action. And it is certainly possible that the strongest and most likely to succeed thrust toward change in the American political system today comes from the reaction of men in power and their supporters against the claims and pressures of one or more of the change-seeking ideologies. Our purpose is not to analyze all, or even most, of the determinants of action in politics, but to attempt to understand those ideologies that are comprehensive in nature and that explain the political world and justify particular forms of change. Thus, we focus exclusively on those comprehensive patterns of belief that offer a full and considered rationale for a particular relationship of institutions, policies and practices in the United States.

Second, we see a continuing intimacy between economic and political thinking in the United States that defies their separation. One cannot develop a political ideology without making some assumptions about the present and proper nature of the economic order or about the social structure to which it gives rise. To think about power, which is the central focus of politics, is to speculate about its sources and distribution. That leads immediately to wealth, status, and other resources of power, many of which have their origins in the nation's economic order—the organization of the economy and the patterns of distribution and social class structure that it establishes in the society. We have dealt with this intertwining of economic and political thinking by seeing political ideologies as including an economic strand and seeking explicitly to define the nature of each ideology's economic assumptions. At the outset of our presentation, we have abstracted capitalism from liberalism as fully as possible and presented each separately—recognizing, of course, that they are complementary, that is, each completes the other.

Finally, we have arranged the ideologies to first set up the economic and political mainstream—capitalism and liberalism. Then we follow them with their contemporary challengers, but without regard for any particular left-right spectrum, which we consider more confusing than revealing. Capitalism and liberalism represent the mainstream because they are the established, enduring, "orthodox" ideologies that have dominated the thinking of American political and other leaders throughout the twentieth century. There have been clashes among them on occasion, sometimes of such magnitude and bitterness as to suggest that they contain conflicting premises or goals. But, properly understood within a wide frame of reference, they do not. Their antagonisms are exaggerated by an active mass media and viewed out of proportion by many observers because of inattention to really contrasting viewpoints. In fact, they have many fundamental things in common, and they share so many basic values and assumptions that deep-seated conflict among them is unlikely.

Shared elements of the mainstream ideologies. The basic perspective of these ideologies toward the American system is one of acquiescence and approval. They take the existing class structure and the contemporary economic order of the United States as fixed or "given" and they raise no fundamental challenge to the characteristics, principles, or practices of either. They share an image of the American political process as "pluralist"—a bargaining, compromising process among many legitimate interests in which accommodations reached are in the interest of the people as a whole. Needless to say, such benevolent images are not shared by all ideologies.

Those who advocate the established ideologies insist that existing rules and procedures must be followed precisely because only in this manner can legitimate ends be attained. Their argument that bargaining and negotiation are the only proper ways to gain an end and that there is room for all to work through existing institutions is compatible with the pluralist assumptions. This image of the efficacy of existing institutions is similarly not shared by all ideologies.

Perhaps most important, capitalism and liberalism share basic values. Both emphasize individualism and the "natural" rights of the individual to serve his own needs as he sees fit. They see the economic marketplace as the chief instrument through which individual self-seeking will lead to the greatest good for the greatest number. A network of legal rules supports these commerical processes and limits interference from the state or other outside sources. This insistence on the market and on the materialist values that accompany it has provoked rejection from those who challenge the capitalist and liberal ideologies. They deny that the market is operable today and contend that the values associated with it are not only outmoded but destructive of the good life, properly conceived.

Capitalism and liberalism parallel and complement each other so completely, and American thinking is so thoroughly suffused with their overlapping effects, that it is a difficult and somewhat arbitrary act to separate them. But there are two strands—one economic, the other social and political—and major American theorists tend to focus chiefly on one or the other. Thus, the effort to treat them separately may yield greater understanding of each. *Capitalism,* of course, is an ideology that is concerned with how and why the economy should be organized. As the economy is never divorced from the state or the society the principles of capitalism relate to the manner in which the state should be organized and conducted, and these principles overlap substantially with liberalism. *Liberalism* is an ideology that concerns how and why the polity should be organized and operated. Since the polity's organization and activity, however, must be based on some assumptions about how the economy does and should operate, liberalism substantially overlaps capitalism. Capitalism and liberalism are interdependent. Both proceed from some shared assumptions about the nature of man, the nature of society, motivational forces in the world, and progress, etc., and the two ideologies grew up together (each influencing the other) in the same historical era. In the United States, the two ideologies have dominated two hundred years of development, and they are intricately intertwined. This complementary relationship will become clearer as we examine each in turn.

The margins of the mainstream: Reform liberalism and conservatism. Neither of these ideologies has come close to enjoying the status and dominance accorded capitalism and liberalism. But they have each been recognized as worthy of a hearing, as having potent advocates, and as being semi-legitimate expressions of the viewpoint of a significant segment of opinion. Occasionally, each has been put into practice as the guiding principle behind a statute or a program of the national government. Frequently, through their proponents, both are given a voice in the institutions of government through which they continue to promulgate laws that reflect their views— again, in the semi-legitimate manner of an authorized court gadfly. But their expression and achievement always occur within the general context formed by the congruence of capitalism and liberalism, and they have learned to operate within that frame of reference.

Reform liberalism is a term intended to include those thinkers who start from essentially the same premises as other liberals but seek somewhat greater emphasis on equality and a somewhat reduced role for property rights, materialism, and individual self-interest. Many of the so-called "old left" of the 1930s are included in this category, thinkers who recoiled in revulsion at communism, adjusted to the incrementalism of the system in pragmatic fashion, and set their sights at defending freedom of speech against men such as Senator Joseph McCarthy. Also included are some of the early democratic socialists whose program consisted of several social insurance plans that have been implemented in the last thirty years. Reform liberalism accepts the basic outlines of the American economic and social system, including its emphasis on individualism and legalism. Its adherents are distinguishable from orthodox liberals by their willingness to try new programs for social improvement, by their somewhat greater concern for equality in the tangible socio-economic (rather than merely formal or legalistic) sense, and by their distaste for merely materialistic standards.

Conservatism is more than the opposite of reform liberalism. It consists of two quite distinguishable strands, the second of which amounts to a truly distinctive set of ideas in the American context. The first strand, individualist conservatism, is equivalent to nineteenth century liberalism, with its insistence on a completely free market and a strict policy of laissez-faire on the part of government. This ideology, stemming from the classical economist's belief that a totally free market would ultimately be self-regulating and provide the greatest good for the greatest number, holds that individuals and corporations should be free to do whatever they wish with the power flowing from their economic possessions without government interference. In this version of liberalism, property rights are given complete ascendancy over equality—which is seen as formal, political equality (equality of opportunity to take part in the quest for economic success) only. Senator Barry Goldwater and other "rugged individualists" who also believe in a firm American posture against the encroachment of communism fall within this category. As it is used in newspaper headlines, the term "conservative" usually refers to this set of nineteenth century liberal ideas.

The second strand of conservatism has a closer tie with classical conservatism, which is a type of ideology only rarely expressed in the United States. This type of conservatism proceeds from the view that the needs of society are superior to those of individuals, that the society is a continuing organism independent of the individuals who comprise it at any time, and that government should be conducted by an elite of talent who take the masses' wishes into account but actually decide matters on the basis of what is right and proper for the society's advancement. This is a distinctive mode of thought (not subject to some of the characterizations made earlier) which we shall investigate in detail later. For the moment, it is enough to point out that, in practice, both forms of conservatism espouse the validity and preferability of older values and ways of doing things. They are both antimajoritarian and grudging about the use of government for social purposes, and they both value property over equality in distinctive fashion. As a result, they become associated in many causes and may be seen together for the sake of efficiency.

The Heart of the Challenge: Black Liberation, the New Left, and American Marxism

These ideologies represent the major thrusts toward change in the 1970s. They do not share the generally benevolent view of the American system as open, inclusive, and capable of flexibly delivering all legitimate goals to those who take part in it. Instead, they see a more or less closed system that is run by and for the benefit of a relative few and is committed to racist standards and policies. An integrated arrangement of rules, rhetoric, and repression operates to prevent modification of the system's basic priorities, which center on the material achievements of the American economy, particularly perpetuation of the present pattern of distribution of benefits. Advocates of these ideologies, defining equality and justice in broad social and economic terms, find such values denied at every turn by American institutions and practices. In their eyes, individualism and market values must be replaced by emphasis on community and cooperation.

The scope of change necessary is very great, reaching to the fundamentals of the economic and social order as well as to the basic distribution of power in the political process. The means by which such changes are to be secured, however, are the subject of considerable and continuing disagreement. To some, persuasion and traditional politics, spiced with occasional protests and demonstrations, seem the only route to success. Others see no alternative to full-scale upheaval, but disagree as to the timing, tactics, and alliances necessary to its achievement.

These three major change-seeking ideologies provide much of the dynamics of American politics today. Their proponents are raising questions and challenges not heard with such force, depth, or comprehensiveness for decades, perhaps at any time. Even if they should lose some of their current impetus or support, their impact may be dramatic. For one thing, they create a situation where more moderate change-seeking ideologies may acquire new support and influence over public policies. For another, they raise the immediate prospect of generating a reaction which, in defending the status quo with an increasingly rigid determination, may effect a fundamental change in the character of the American system. Such a reaction could gradually, perhaps unthinkingly, convert it into an unprecedented form of electoral fascism in which an anticommunist, militarist, materialist orthodoxy would become the official American ideology. In a final chapter, we will try to identify some of the cutting edges of conflict that separate the various contending ideologies and to speculate on the crucial questions and problems that must be settled before the great issues of the American future can be resolved. By that time, the reader should be a more competent analyst in his own right, ready to deal critically with any analysis or prescription in the light of his own well-grounded views.

Annotated Bibliography

Bell, Daniel. *The End of Ideology*. Glencoe, Ill.: Free Press, 1960. The classic argument about ideology's demise as a fighting force capable of moving modern men.

Boorstin, Daniel. *The Genius of American Politics*. Chicago: University of Chicago Press, 1953. Argues that the American experience is so unique that no philosophy has been developed, nor is one necessary.

Chamberlain, John. *Farewell to Reform*. Gloucester, Mass.: John Day, 1932. Progressivism and liberalism in the early twentieth century.

Commager, Henry. *The American Mind*. New Haven, Conn.: Yale University Press, 1959. History of political ideas in the 19th and 20th centuries.

Grimes, Alan P. *American Political Thought*. New York: Holt, Rinehart and Winston, 1960. A good standard source on the evolution of American political ideas.

Hartz, Louis. *The Liberal Tradition in America.* New York: Harcourt, Brace & World, 1955. A major argument concerning the lack of conservative *and* radical traditions, resulting from dominance of liberalism.

Hofstadter, Richard. *The American Political Tradition.* New York: Knopf, 1948. Critical analysis of twelve major figures in American political development and of the ideas that motivated them.

Lynd, Staughton. *Intellectual Origins of American Radicalism.* New York: Vintage Books, 1969. Good revisionist account of the early radical ideas and their submergence/ surfacing processes since.

Minar, David W. *Ideas and Politics.* Homewood, Ill.: Dorsey Press, 1964. Good standard account of the evolution of ideas.

Parenti, Michael J. *The Anti-Communist Impulse.* New York: Random House, 1969. An analysis that finds the roots of American foreign policy in anti-Communist ideology.

Schumpeter, Joseph. *Capitalism, Socialism, and Democracy.* New York: Harper & Row, 1942. A major study of the relationship between social and economic change and the role of economic ideologies and/or systems.

2

Capitalism

Capitalism is the private ownership of the means of production and allocation of the resources, goods, and services of the society through the mechanism of prices set by competitive markets. No doubt, many people understand capitalism essentially as a term descriptive of the American economy. But capitalism is much more than a descriptive term for most Americans. It is an ideology, because those Americans who subscribe to capitalism make value-based assumptions about the nature of man and the desirability of certain procedures and their expected results. Such a network of assumptions about man, about ways to reach particular goals, and about the desirability of those goals converts capitalism from a descriptive term to a prescriptive and justifying ideology.

Modern capitalism may be dated from a comprehensive statement of the principles of economics by eighteenth century economists Adam Smith,[1] David Ricardo,[2] and Thomas Malthus.[3] They saw a

---

[1] Adam Smith (1723–1790) was both moralist and economist. His major work, *The Wealth of Nations,* is available in a variety of editions and still serves as a major source of basic capitalist ideology.

[2] David Ricardo (1772–1823) followed Smith's principles, applying them particularly to the value of land as a key factor of production. See *Works and Correspondence of David Ricardo,* Sraffa, ed. (Cambridge: University Press, 1951).

[3] Thomas Malthus (1766–1834) is well known for his *Essay on Population* which, like Smith's work, has been reprinted in many editions. His major theme is that population increase is a drag on wages and leads to cyclical starvation.

nation's economy as dependent upon three "factors of production:" land, labor, and capital. Land is vital for the production of food, for the development of various natural resources, and as the geographic site of other productive facilities such as factories. Labor is needed to work in factories, till the land, and provide other services. Capital, money or its equivalent, is essential for investment in machines and other implements of production. When supply of these factors is matched by demand for their use, they argued, profits, wages, and rents are produced, and the economy is more fully able to meet demands upon it.

These classical economists believed that the various factors of production would be kept in balance by means of the economic market. We will explore contemporary assumptions about the market in detail shortly, but its basic nature and purpose should be familiar to all. Smith felt that if all individuals sought to serve their own self-interest, an impersonal process of equating supply with demand would result. This would lead to maximum use of all factors of production and maximum possible distribution of the best possible products at the lowest possible cost. In short, the market was the instrument whereby the greatest good for the greatest number was to be realized. All men were to have an equal right to take part, to pursue their own self-interests as they saw them, and the result would be socially beneficial. The best men, of course, were those individuals who were better suited for (or more diligent and self-disciplined at) the competitive practices of the marketplace—for these were the men who made the greatest good for the greatest number possible.

Smith and the others saw capital as the essential ingredient for making profits, providing employment opportunities, and achieving progress. They acknowledged, however, that these results would lead to a rise in the value of land and the rent derived from its use, and, in turn, reduce profits, lower wages, and produce food shortages. The weight of the burden would be borne by "the iron law of wages," in that income could not for very long rise above the minimum level necessary for the physical survival of an ever-expanding population. In contrast, the landlord and the capitalist would be left sufficiently well off to begin a new cycle from a somewhat more advanced position, i.e., achieve progress. The grim pessimism of this version of economic life led to the famous characterization of economics as "the dismal science."

The American economic experience, despite repeated swings from boom to depression, has been interpreted in much more optimistic terms. In this chapter, we will first set forth the basic framework of assumptions and beliefs that characterize the American capitalist ideology. Next, we will describe two major dilemmas faced by capitalist ideologists in the twentieth century and explore the major modifications that have arisen in response to them. Finally, we will try to see how capitalist ideology has evolved as a result of these modifications.

World View

(1) THE BASIC ASSUMPTIONS

Capitalism begins from the premise that man's needs for food, shelter, and protection against environmental dangers, etc., are primarily *individual* rather than community needs. The individual is therefore seen as seeking to serve his personal needs first, and he becomes the unit around which subsequent analyses and assumptions are built. Man is acquisitive by nature; he first tries to fulfill his minimum current needs and then aspires to assure against future hardship or privation. The unending nature of the quest for greater and greater security against want or danger provides the dynamic force behind social life. In economic terms, it translates itself into the profit motive: individuals seek to maximize their personal returns—their net reward—from all transactions in which they engage.

The profit motive is an essential component of capitalism; it is the basis of all subsequent assertions and the prospect of attaining desirable goals. Every man, whether destitute or millionaire, must seek to gain the largest possible net return from every transaction to which he is a party. If he does not, the market will not work effectively as a regulator of supply and demand, and there will be neither efficiency in the allocation of goods and services nor progress for the society as a whole.

Second only to the profit motive, and also proceeding from the individualist focus, is the principle that man is by nature competitive. He is attentive to the behavior of others and aspires to excel in a variety of attainments. In the economic world, this means that producers will find it natural to vie with each other for customers, and no man will be content with even a high level of achievement. The combination of competitiveness and profit motivation assures constant individual self-seeking, which will ultimately mean progress for the entire society. Those who are unsuccessful in the competitive race may even be viewed as somehow unfit or unsuited for the natural rigors and demands of the real world.

The chief economic and social problem with which a capitalist society must contend is that of regulating the supply and demand for the various factors of production. Adherents of capitalism assume that there is a natural harmony among these factors, and that they tend to regulate themselves. But either too much or too little of any one factor may upset their natural harmony and prevent realization of a profitable production level with stable and full employment. An oversupply of labor, for example, will drive wages below the level necessary to provide the resources with which to purchase the products of the economy, and perhaps even below that needed to sustain life. Too little capital will mean the absence of investment necessary to provide employment opportunities and perhaps an excessively high price of products. Too much capital will mean an unprofitable investment situation and, perhaps, unserved needs on the part of consumers.

(2) THE CRUCIAL ROLE OF THE MARKET

The chief regulative instrument of supply and demand, and ultimately of the factors of production themselves, was and is the free and competitive market. From Adam Smith to the present, assumptions about such a market have been fundamental. The market's proper operation depends upon prices being determined independently—solely by the individual decisions of producers and purchasers, with both groups competing. There must be many sellers, each aware of the others' practices and each seeking competitively to undersell the other and still make a profit. At the same time, there must be many purchasers, each with knowledge of each others' bidding and of the quality and prices of the sellers' products. No seller or buyer can be large enough to exercise an appreciable influence on prices. In this way, nobody controls prices, and everybody must adapt to them. This leads to the impersonal and nearly perfect equilibrium that is consistent with the natural harmony of the various factors.

Much capitalist writing centers on the utility of the market for these purposes. Perhaps none has summarized the principle as succinctly as the United States Department of Commerce in its 1965 pamphlet entitled "Profits and the American Economy:"

> Price is the mechanical arbitrator in our market system.
>
> In our capitalistic economy, we adhere to the belief— indeed we have established safeguards to insure—that the pricing process is completely impersonal. This means that normally the free play of demand and supply produces a price on which the buyer and seller agree, and a bargain is struck. To the extent that a price is reached by means that are *not* impersonal—to the extent that either the buyer or the seller can dictate or influence the setting of the price—to that extent our system of controlling the efficient use of resources is not working properly.[4]

Many desirable results flow almost automatically from the proper working of the free market system. First, maximum efficiency in allocation of scarce resources is realized. Capital is directed toward profitable uses. Thus, all available capital is put to work in the most productive way possible, and all relevant natural resources are used. Such widespread productive activity means employment for the maximum possible number of workers which, in turn, means that they earn the wages necessary to buy the economy's products. The resources of the society, in other words, are in full use in the most productive way. They are producing what the community wants, and competition induces continued efforts to improve products, lower costs, and attract new buyers. This makes for economic change and progress that is always maximally efficient. When consumer desire for one product slackens and causes a reduction in both price and production levels, the employer reduces his labor costs by discharging some workers and leveling off at a new but profitable balance of costs and prices. Discharged workers do not suffer because other employers who are experiencing a rising consumer

---

[4] U.S. Department of Commerce, "Profits and the American Economy" (Washington, D.C.: U.S. Government Printing Office, 1965), p. 13.

demand for their products need labor to produce larger quantities. Or the labor rate can be reduced to a level that the employer can afford, just as the employer, on occasion, was forced to reduce his prices to his purchasers.

A second result is a high degree of stability or equilibrium at this efficient level. The aggregate of demand always equals the aggregate of supply, except for marginal adjustments from time to time as consumer demand shifts from one product to another or the ratio of savings to consumer expenditure shifts. As we have just seen, the former case is a characteristic of progress and temporary dislocations are quickly cured. The latter case is dealt with by the natural forces of the market in much the same way. When capital is needed to produce new products, potential consumers are induced to save (and ultimately invest) by the offer of high interest rates. When the need for capital drops, interest rates go down, and the consumer is likely to shift toward use of all his earnings in consumption again. Thus, consumer demand would have been interrupted only temporarily by the thrifty tendency towards savings, and the long-run effect would be beneficial because the savings were used to finance the manufacture of new products. As long as consumer demand kept up, there could be no major depression. Indeed, capitalism does not consider that a serious prospect as long as the natural forces of the market are at work. Only when "artificial" forces (unions, or government regulation of prices, wages or trade) enter is the market inadequate as a natural regulator of the economy.

Third, the market achieves a kind of consumer sovereignty. Demand is the key, and because it shapes supply, the consumer is enabled to get what he wants by "voting" with his purchase money for the products of his choice. Thus, not only are all the factors of production used fully and most efficiently, but at the same time, the consumer is enabled to specify what will be produced. This "sovereignty" of the consumer is also celebrated in the Department of Commerce's characterization:

> The dollars you spend in the marketplace for your needs, your wants, and your preferences are, in a very real sense, your "votes" for allocation of our resources to the production and distribution of the goods and services you buy. These votes are a *demand* and they dictate to producers

what they must *supply.* If a producer interprets these votes correctly, he earns profits. If a producer does not interpret these votes correctly and produces too much or too little, or at a price that is too high or too low, or at a level of quality uncalled for or inadequate, he will soon realize his mistake, thanks to the absence of profits.[5]

Finally, this whole process takes place exclusively through private decision-making and with an irreducible minimum of coercive requirements. Nobody is forced to do anything if he is normally endowed with competitiveness and the profit motive and his wants are roughly similar to those of others in the society. If he is highly unusual in either of these categories, he might be economically coerced, that is, unemployed or unable to obtain particular kinds of goods. But there would be no government coercion applied to structure his behavior, and he would never face the prospect of losing his liberty or being physically coerced concerning his choices. Indeed, one of the highest achievements of the market arrangement is the elimination of government involvement. Assuming that the market is in operation, the government's role is that of complete laissez-faire, except for such necessary supports as defense of the society from enemies, enforcement of contracts and collection of debts, and maintenance of general domestic order. Intrusion by governments would not only apply coercive power to individuals, but would also upset the natural workings of the market and destroy its achievements.

The achievements of the free market and of the capitalist system itself are perceived as very great. Indeed, everything desirable about the American standard of living and/or way of life is often attributed to the nature of the capitalist system. This too is well illustrated in the official words of the United States Department of Commerce:

> As American citizens, we are convinced that the sum total of these private decisions not only proves profitable to those who make the decisions but also brings great benefit to the entire national economy.

---

[5] *Ibid.,* p. 11.

. . . Our country has only 6% of the world's population, occupies only 7% of the world's land area, and yet produces and consumes something over 40% of the free world's goods and services.

Finally, we would do well to remember that our private enterprise system is the world's mightiest economic engine. It has generated the highest profits, wages, and family income in man's history. It has achieved a broadly based distribution of goods and services with many benefits to our citizens. It has given the United States of America the highest standard of living the world has ever known.[6]

This review of the basic world view of capitalism is admittedly oversimplified and, as we shall see in subsequent sections, outdated in the minds of some 20th century advocates. But it nevertheless represents the core of the thinking of many Americans, and can be seen in a variety of sources. A group of Harvard economists, for example, made an exhaustive study of the ideology of American business, drawing on advertising, speeches, publications, official testimony of business leaders, and trade association pamphlets. Their detailed findings as to the essential beliefs closely resemble what we have presented here in distilled form.[7] Robert Heilbroner, a leading economist, employed the addresses given by the presidents of the great American corporations in a distinguished series of annual lectures to develop the same basic characterization.[8]

Values and Goals

Just as capitalism's world view proceeded from a focus on the individual, so does its value system place paramount emphasis upon *individualism*. This individualism stresses the moral responsibility and opportunity of each person to serve his own needs as he sees

---

[6] *Ibid.*, pp. 40–41.

[7] Francis X. Sutton, Seymour E. Harris, Carl Kaysen, and James Tobin, *The American Business Creed* (Cambridge: Harvard University Press, 1956).

[8] Robert Heilbroner, *The Limits of American Capitalism* (New York: Harper & Row, 1966).

fit. It is his responsibility to act purposefully in his own behalf; he should not be concerned for others, nor should he expect others to serve his needs for him. Of course, he is accountable for his actions and will experience their consequences, whether good or bad. The other dimension of individualism is the insistence upon full opportunity for individual choices and action. Autonomy, self-reliance, and private self-seeking must be given full play: this is the meaning and substance of freedom. To the extent that there are restrictions on individual choice, whether that of businessman or consumer, freedom has been diminished.

Individualism carries with it a special set of emphases concerning the relationship of the individual to the society. Because the good society is synonymous with the most prosperous, and because it can only be attained through all individuals' determinedly seeking their own private interests, that activity constitutes the individual's sole obligation to his society. Thus, because of the exclusive moral duty to serve one's own private needs and the conviction that such is the way to progress for all, questions of the justice of social or economic arrangements either do not arise or are deflected. The sum total of many such private decisions, and only such action, will carry the society inevitably to its next higher stage. No moral or ethical distinctions are made between types of production, types of services rendered, or particular forms of consumption; all are equally worthy if they return a profit and are chosen freely by individuals.

The value placed on individualism in this form is closely related to one of the major goals of capitalism: *self-realization in the sense of fulfillment of the self-interest of the individual person,* and the resultant moral and material progress of the society. Only through the growth and development achieved by successful competition and by the satisfaction of having achieved one's goals amidst difficulties does an individual reach a sense of fulfillment. His character has been molded, tempered, and uplifted by the struggle he has been through, and he emerges a far better man morally *and* materially. The society in which many such men are produced is indeed fortunate, for the talents they have applied and the strength of character they have developed are the basic fibre of that society and assure its continued improvement.

A second major value, again closely related to individualism, is *materialism.* It is the dominant (and sometimes the only) standard by which the achievements of individuals or of the economic system as a whole are to be measured. The emphasis in American capitalism on a high standard of living, defined as the possession of specific material goods for private consumption purposes, is indicative of the extent to which this value has become its chief measuring standard. Materialism is sometimes expressed as an emphasis on productivity, which in turn becomes one of the highest virtues to which a system may aspire. Capitalism makes few, if any, distinctions about the types of material goods or the nature of the productivity that is valued. It is enough that individuals be able to serve their wants by amassing material goods of their choice and that total productivity (presumably of the kinds of goods that individuals demand) be high —high enough to fill all wants.

Several other values combine with materialism and individualism to fill out the capitalist value system. For the individual, an active life based on a practical grasp of the "realities" of the economic world is in order. The good man will have confidence in the economic system and in his capacity to make it work in his behalf. He will take risks, seek new opportunities, and look pragmatically to the future. If he does, he will be rewarded exactly in proportion to the quality of his foresight, the nature of his talents, and the extent of hard work he invests in his own cause. For the society, steadily increasing productivity and utter freedom for individuals to serve their own interests in this manner will amount to progress. *Progress,* defined as increasing levels of goods and services, is both a value and a goal. It is good, and must continue. Channels of opportunity should be kept open so that all or most individuals may feel the values of capitalism and act accordingly. In this way, the underlying dynamic that makes for broad societal progress will be kept at work.

Behind this constellation of values, and vital to giving them meaning, is the concept of *private property.* The idea that an individual can "own" something, to the extent of being absolutely entitled to exclude others from its enjoyment, is fundamental to capitalism. This exclusive entitlement to land or moveable goods is what makes individual self-satisfaction and achievement possible; it permits others to compare one individual with another and judge their relative talents, and it enables an individual to provide for, not only his own wants, but those of others in his family. Unless man can realize something tangible from his labor, he will have little incentive to work. The opportunity to acquire private property, which can then be used either to acquire more or to achieve other goals, is the crucial inducement that makes the individual's self-seeking a rational act.

Social Change and Tactics

Capitalism envisions its goals of individual self-fulfillment and general material progress of the society as being attainable automatically, through the "natural" operation of private forces. The principal mechanism is the free and competitive market, in which profit-maximizing individuals seek their private ends. The simple beauty of this arrangement is that all men, merely by doing what comes most naturally to them (seeking material satisfactions), will advance the society as a whole through steady stages of progress. Transformation of technological advances, changes in values, and world developments into market forces will inspire and suggest responsive behavior by all participants in the nation's economic and social life.

Operation of the market, because it is crucial to the process by which social change occurs, must be protected from external and "artificial" forces. This means that government should observe a strict laissez-faire policy, avoiding all "interference" with the operations of the market. Government has, of course, the important task of enforcing the contractual and other arrangements with which the business of the society is carried on. In discharging these necessary functions, government should take care that its revenue matches its expenditures lest it influence the market by creating an unbalanced or "artificial" excess of demand.

In addition, it is the government's task to defend the integrity of the market against challenges from domestic or foreign enemies. Although we will explore these aspects of the state's role more fully when we examine liberalism's commitment to particular economic practices, we note here that property rights are among the most fundamental constitutional rights. The state is obligated not only to defend individuals' possessions against the claims of other individuals, but also against the claims of majorities. The people are held to be powerless to change the status of property rights except under very limited circumstances. Further, in order for the market to be effective, it must extend throughout the society. Advocates of other, noncapitalist, economic systems must be persuaded, educated, legally required, or, if necessary, coerced by whatever means are required to conform with the capitalist practices. The same principles apply wherever the effective power of the state reaches: it is always preferable to have capitalist economies in foreign countries, regardless of the cost to national well being in those countries or the level of force required to maintain such practices.

When these principles are operating, capitalism is essentially self-regulating and its method is no more than the free and unrestricted activity of many individuals in pursuit of profit. Those individuals who are not yet persuaded of the propriety of this form of economic organization have either not been offered an opportunity to see how it will benefit them or are in the grip of some false alternative ideology from which they should be rescued. Wherever possible, they should be firmly confronted with the merits of the capitalist system. Both rhetorically and militarily, capitalism acts upon its vision in messianic ways.

Two Dilemmas of Mid-twentieth Century Capitalism

Although the basic framework of an ideology might sometimes seem oversimplified or outdated, this may not affect the adherence of its advocates. But the challenges aimed at American capitalism in the mid-twentieth century led many who were sincerely devoted to capitalism to reexamine and revise some of their beliefs. In the United States, these challenges stemmed from inescapably obvious facts and events that had widespread social consequences. It is little wonder that for some people, orthodox capitalist ideology has been bent in new directions. But many people, including leaders of business and government, remain firm adherents of the basic framework that we have just reviewed. A summary of two of the major challenges to capitalism in the United States will give us an idea of the scope and depth of the problem. We will consider, first, how the Great Depression of the 1930s and the apparent failure of the market affected capitalist ideology and, second, the effects of the rise of the new economy based on supercorporations, vast governmental expenditures, and the apparent nonexistence of the market.

(1) DEPRESSION AND THE APPARENT FAILURE OF THE MARKET

After the Depression, neither economists nor ideologists could continue to talk exclusively in terms of "normal" conditions of high, stable prices and full employment. Nor was it enough to posit cycles or the rhythmic rise and fall of business activity in which the economy would be self-correcting if left alone. The stark social fact was that several million newly unemployed persons were desperate; they were facing hardship and even death from starvation. In the face of this kind of reality, business, labor, and farmers exerted heavy pressure to force the government to "do something" to get the economic engine going again. Capitalist ideology offered no solution, of course, because it held that the economy would correct itself and that government involvement was bad. As the New Deal went ahead with its "pragmatic" and "problem-solving" approach to economic recovery, it found itself seeking to use industrywide agreements to prevent ruinous competition and permit the return to profitable prices at one stage and, at another, to promote competition and prevent domination of product areas by one or a small number of producers. No principles seemed to emerge as to *how* government should act, but the basic conclusion that government had the responsibility to do *something* under conditions of hardship was firmly established.

The Depression had the further effect of peremptorily calling attention to a social fact that was often ignored or dismissed in American capitalist ideology—that of sharp inequality in the distribution of economic rewards in the United States. At the time when the great industrial machinery of the United States was being developed, substantial segments of the American population were living on marginal subsistence levels. From the Civil War on, the plight of such people had moved reformers to seek government assistance of some kind to supplement the private philanthropies that clearly were no longer able, if, indeed, they ever were, to carry the burden. This social concern had become so troublesome to some advocates of strict laissez-faire capitalism that they had responded with the famous doctrine of "Social Darwinism." This doctrine held that those who were low in economic attainments were economically unfit and therefore should be allowed to starve or die in the interest of improving the moral character and competitive quality of the population. Nevertheless, the reformers succeeded in getting some social legislation passed in the early decades of the twentieth century. But their successful uses of governmental powers (e.g., to require minimum wages or to prevent excessive prices where sellers had a monopoly) were not reflected in capitalist ideology, which continued to assert the virtue of laissez-faire and the inevitability of widespread distribution of wealth to all. With the reality of the Depression, however, it was no longer possible to insist that poverty was attributable to the failures of individual poor people or that there were only marginal differences in the level of material wealth possessed by the working and middle classes.

Both the fact of the Depression and the extent of inequality to which it called special attention drastically undermined confidence in the free and competitive market as an allocative device. Of course, the Depression might be attributed to excessive government interference with the market (as some at first sought to do). But the more usual reaction was a gnawing uncertainty about the market's capacity: apparently, it could no longer be relied upon to do its assigned job. Further, the market had apparently not actually spread income and wealth as widely as it should have during sustained periods of prosperity. If depressions and poverty were unavoidable and inevitable under market economy conditions, one of two results seemed to follow. Either economic life was going to be full of hardships and have a high potential for social unrest, or some new way of supporting the market and preventing drastic cycles would have to be found.

(2) THE NEW ECONOMY: CONCENTRATIONS OF POWER
AND WAR EXPENDITURES

The facts of American economic life also challenged the orthodox capitalist ideology from another perspective. Publication in 1932 of Adolf Berle and Gardiner Means' *The Modern Corporation and Private Property*[9] ultimately had profound impact on per-

---

[9] Adolf A. Berle and Gardiner C. Means, *The Modern Corporation and Private Property* (New York: Macmillan, 1932).

ceptions of the nature of the American economy. Drawing on stock-holders' reports, sales and assets figures, government calculations, and other empirical data, the authors argued that there were really two very different economies in operation in the United States. One was made up of millions of sole proprietorships, partnerships, and small corporations and functioned much in accordance with the assumptions of the marketplace. The other, by far the most significant because it included most of the major industries, was composed of a relative handful of giant corporations. These supercorporations dominated the economy in terms of assets, sales, and profits, dwarfing other forms of business entirely. Berle and Means showed, for example, that in 1930, 130 companies trading on the New York Stock Exchange had gross assets of more than one hundred million dollars, but together, these companies held 82% of all the corporate assets traded on the exchange.[10] The 200 largest non-banking corporations received 43% of all income earned in 1929 by all non-banking corporations.[11] Further, the authors argued, since this concentration was proceeding steadily, the economy would soon be completely dominated by concentrations of power of this magnitude.

The second major point in the Berle and Means presentation was that the size of these corporations—and the resultant large number of stockholders—none of whom owned a substantial portion of stock—made it impossible for stockholders to exercise control over the corporation's policies. They showed that all but a handful of the large corporations had wide diffusion of stock ownership, with voting rights spread among tens of thousands of people in some cases. Under such circumstances, stockholders' meetings could be little more than ceremonies in which uninformed laymen ratified the actions and choices of the company's management. Most people would simply return proxy votes supporting the management's slate of nominations for the Board of Directors and relate to the company only in terms of cashing dividend checks. All the decisions involved in actually running the company would be left in the hands of the officers and directors.

The implications of these two major findings were very serious for capitalist ideology. The existence of giant corporations that

---

[10] *Ibid.,* p. 29.
[11] *Ibid.,* p. 30.

dominated major industries meant that they could, and often did, establish prices at which they would buy materials or sell products. Where one or two companies account for a very large share of a particular type of product, such as in the automobile industry, they can dictate the sales price. Competition can be eliminated by tacit agreements among producers, minimizing the risk of losing gigantic investments in plants and production machinery that characterize the industry (through long and destructive competitive price-cutting). The size of the investment behind these giant corporations also prevents potential competitors from entering the field. A similar advantage accrues to the large corporation in regard to acquiring materials: it can effectively set suppliers' prices because of the sheer size of its purchases, because it is often the only buyer, or because it can threaten to go into the supply business itself.

The giant corporation thus foreclosed the possibility of a free and competitive market. It set prices, instead of responding to impersonally determined reflections of supply and demand. It did not compete with other producers through pricing, nor did it respond to consumer demands. Indeed, it could hardly be expected to respond to consumer demands when the complexity of many products required years of research and design, plus careful advance planning of material acquisition, production, and marketing arrangements. If necessary, the giant corporation was more likely to rely on the power of advertising to create "artificial" consumer demands in the image of the product it found to be practical and profitable to manufacture. Under such circumstances, the "market" lost much, if not all, of its relevance and function.

The implications of the divergence of stock ownership from the capacity to control the corporation were equally fundamental. The owners of invested capital, it could be assumed, would seek to maximize profits—and thereby do their part to keep the market operating properly. But if the corporate management were actually in control, they might, not being owners, respond to a wholly different set of priorities. They might be more interested in maintaining themselves in power, or in doing any of a number of other things, than in maximizing profits. If they were, of course, the market would be undermined from this direction too. There would also be substantial units of power loose in the economy, acting on essentially arbitrary bases and threatening unpredictable consequences.

The concerns expressed by Berle and Means as a result of their analyses made headway chiefly among economists, in government, and in a few leading business circles in the 1930s. They received confirmation from the increasing visibility of the supercorporation in the 1940s and 1950s, however, and acquired new adherents in the business community. More popular expressions of many of the same concerns may be found in the several writings of the Harvard economist-politician John Kenneth Galbraith. In *The Affluent Society*,[12] for example, he stresses the dangers emanating from the unrecognized power of the large corporation. An exclusive insistence upon production of material goods, he argued, was merged with corporate manipulation of consumer "wants" through advertising. This led, in his eyes, to a kind of "social imbalance" in which no attention is paid to more general, nonconsumable public needs such as schools, hospitals, and recreation facilities.

At the same time as the giant corporations were creating the new economy that Berle and Means (and ultimately others) described, a second development threatened to turn capitalist ideology on its head. This was the huge spending by the United States government to prosecute World War II. Vast stores of food, equipment, and supplies had to be produced and transported overseas. The national government became a giant revenue-raising engine and an even greater engine of economic recovery. At one point, the national government absorbed nearly half of the Gross National Product in furtherance of the war effort. These vast purchases not only restored the American economy, but put many businessmen on notice that sales to the government could be highly profitable. In the post-war decade, some defense suppliers and contractors found that this could also be a *steady* source of demand for their products. The point is that government has acquired a major role as a taxing agent for the purpose of purchasing the products of a particular segment of the economy—almost a complete reversal of the traditional capitalist ideology. It also serves to maintain the general level of demand, so that profits remain high. In short, events have forced at least some adherents of the ideology to try to incorporate

---

[12] John Kenneth Galbraith, *The Affluent Society* (Boston: Houghton Mifflin, 1957).

a variety of permanent government expenditures into revised versions of capitalism.

Modernizing the Ideology: Capitalism in the 1970s

At the start of this chapter, we made the point that our concern is with capitalism as an ideology, not as a purported description of actual practice. We are analyzing beliefs, not activities. But the facts of the real world, if salient enough, may affect beliefs. That is what seems to have occurred in the case of capitalist ideology. Evidence of the great divergence of reality from the orthodox capitalist model has forced various modifications. Two problems stand out: (1) the free and competitive market, having been exposed as either inoperative or undesirable, must be replaced by some allocative device that promises to work and to distribute income on a reasonable basis; and (2) government, having been found a vital source of economic stability and profit, must be integrated into the new scheme.

Not all adherents of capitalism make such adjustments, of course; the grip of an established ideology is not released so readily. But over the last two or three decades, the ideology has been sufficiently revised to warrant substantial exploration. We will examine two major directions of the revision: (a) Keynesianism and a permanent supportive role for government, and (b) "People's capitalism" and the "managerial ethic." These are not mutually exclusive, but are rather closely related themes in the modification of capitalist ideology. The first deals principally with a new role for government, the second with changes in relationships between people and other economic entities such as corporations. Both are current in the United States and, together, they serve as overlapping or alternative justifications of American capitalism today.

(a) KEYNESIANISM AND A PERMANENT SUPPORTIVE ROLE FOR GOVERNMENT

In 1936, the British economist John Maynard Keynes published an analysis and prescription concerning depressions that promptly became adopted (in simplified form) by many Americans as a new rationale for the role of government in the economy.[13] In the course of a complex and abstract economic argument, Keynes made two crucial points. First, he denied that depressions were abnormal and that the "natural" condition of the economy was an equilibrium of high productivity, full employment, and stable prices. He saw alternative periods of depression and inflation as the natural order and held that the economy *could* stabilize at a *low* level of productivity and a *high* level of unemployment.

Second, through an analysis too complex to recount here, Keynes concluded that an excess of savings was the key to depressions and that savings were not subject to the demand-and-supply workings of the free market. The danger he saw was that people might hold their money out of consumption, causing a drop in actual purchasing power and ultimately a drop in prices, production, and eventually employment. He contended that employment and overall consumer demand would remain high if savings were fully used, either in purchasing goods and services or in investment.

At this point, government entered Keynes' prescriptions. By exercising its powers to tax, borrow, and spend, government could tap income that would otherwise become unproductive savings or release income to bolster purchasing power. Or it could borrow or otherwise spend to supplement private investment and maintain productivity and employment. In simpler terms, when the economy is heading downward toward recession or depression, the government should decrease taxes, incur a deficit between revenues and expenditures, and invest in public works or other employment-generating activities. When the economy is heading upward toward inflation, it should increase taxes, run a surplus, and cut back its own expenditures and investments. Over the long range, assuming that there are alternating deflationary and inflationary trends, the government's budget would be in rough balance.

Keynes' arguments had a profound impact on depression-conscious Americans, and they were rapidly adapted into both ideology and practice. The reversal in the role of government—from an implacable enemy to an indispensable ally—did not sit well with some businessmen. But for many, the essentials of private decision-making in the economy seemed to have been preserved, while new assurances

---

[13] John Maynard Keynes, *General Theory of Employment* (New York: Macmillan, 1936).

about stability and full employment had been gained. The name of Keynes is probably either unknown or derided by most Americans, but the legitimacy of such an economy-managing, stability-assuring role for the national government is doubted by only the most rigidly orthodox capitalists.

The modification of capitalist ideology that acquiesced in a Keynesian definition of government responsibility has also come to terms with other means of promoting economic security. The Depression-initiated web of social security legislation, beginning with unemployment compensation and retirement insurance and continuing with aid to families with dependent children and medical care for the aged, has achieved a legitimacy of sorts. It is rationalized as a means of reducing or eliminating individual hardships. Other forms of government assistance that fall into the general category of "welfare" are also legitimated as either necessary to prevent excessive individual suffering or desirable as a means of providing opportunity for all to take part in the competitive economy.

American capitalism has not enthusiastically embraced the new role of government in either of these two forms. But it has come to terms with them on the grounds that the excesses or inadequacies of the market should be moderated. Perhaps another basis for this adaptation is the fear that failure to accept a limited government role can only lead to a larger one. Both of these grounds are illustrated in passages from an address by President Thomas B. Watson of I.B.M.:

> Much as we may dislike it, I think we've got to realize that in our kind of society there are times when government has to step in and help people with some of their more difficult problems. Programs which assist Americans by reducing the hazards of a free market system without damaging the system itself are necessary, I believe, to its survival. . . .
>
> To be sure, the rights and guarantees that the average man believes in and insists upon may interfere, to some degree, with our ability to manage our enterprises with complete freedom of action. As a result, there are businessmen who either ignore or deny these claims. They then justify their views by contending that if we were to recognize or grant them, the whole system of free enterprise would be endangered.

This, it would seem to me, amounts to an open invitation to exactly the kind of government intervention that businessmen are seeking to avoid. For if we businessmen insist that free enterprise permits us to be indifferent to those things on which people put high value, then the people will quite naturally assume that free enterprise has too much freedom.[14]

In addition to the substantial, if reluctant, incorporation of the market-supplement role of government into capitalist ideology, there has occasionally been celebration of this new principle under the label of "welfare capitalism." In effect, making a virtue and an achievement out of what began as necessity, this argument holds that the harshness of market economy has been so fully contained by government assistance and assurances that capitalism has become a mass-oriented system. In other words, the economic system not only spreads material affluence widely, but also provides revenue for the government. This revenue is then applied to the use of the people through various forms of social and economic improvement programs. It is said that "cradle to the grave" security is provided by government and real poverty has been eliminated for all but a handful of untrainable or unmotivated persons. In part, the vast sums annually expended by government are seen as confirmation of its "welfare" role, even though the majority of such expenditures is in the form of purchases from business or salaries to employees.

Within the framework provided by the new role of government, of course, it is assumed that many of the established practices of orthodox capitalism will take place. Indeed, the part played by government is not intended to replace, but rather to make more effective, the basic freedom and independent choice of individuals within the system. In some respects, the government may be seen as a detached referee whose function it is to promote the fairness of the contest taking place. Galbraith is responsible for the famous image of "countervailing powers" which sums up the primary role of private forces as regulators of the economy.[15] Galbraith believed that every economic force, when applied, would attract or create a

---

[14] Cited in Heilbroner, *op. cit.,* p. 34.
[15] John Kenneth Galbraith, *American Capitalism* (Boston: Houghton Mifflin, 1952).

counterforce to contain it, and that there would therefore not ordinarily be uncontrolled power loose at any time. The confrontation of labor and management provided him a convenient illustration, and he generalized from this to other areas. The important point was that there were private forces capable of exerting a preeminent self-regulating control in most instances. This meant that the regulatory role of government should be limited to those special cases where, for some reason, the private system did not generate the necessary countervailing forces or where inflation made them less effective. When rationally applied, as Galbraith found to have been the case since the 1930s, this principle had the effect of assuring widespread prosperity for all amid stable economic conditions.

The breakthrough accomplished by Keynesianism was its provision of an *economic* (as opposed to a social, moral, or political) rationale for the use of government. The type of things that Keynes held government should do were not, after all, very different from what governments had always been doing—that is, taxing, borrowing, and spending. The specific purposes for which these acts of state were now to be designed, and the scale on which they were to be applied, were distinctive. And the consequences, in terms of reliance upon the same government that had heretofore been exclusively the source of intervention or interference, were profound. Among other things, as we have seen, Keynesianism brought with it an umbrella that legitimated several other forms of government assistance to individuals. It also legitimated public works in economic terms and blunted attacks on them as mere unwise spending. The net result was to place the government squarely within the revised principles of capitalist ideology. This left as the major question only the nature of the relationship between the government and the economy (particularly, which was to dominate the other), not whether there should be any contact between the two centers of power.

(b) PEOPLES' CAPITALISM AND THE MANAGERIAL ETHIC

The second theme in the modification of capitalist ideology concerns the emergence of new forms of private relationships within the economy as opposed to the new role of government that was the subject of the last theme. It is composed of two main strands. One is the argument that new forms of ownership and control of economic power have developed so that the giant corporation is not the threat it once might have seemed to be. The other is the argument that the managers of the great corporations have developed a special type of professionalism and public spiritedness that makes them relatively benign and socially responsible entities.

A. A. Berle's *The American Economic Republic*[16] illustrates both of these. Faced with his own landmark finding that the managers of large corporations were apparently free of stockholders' control, Berle at first found the primary source of restraint on them in public opinion. This principle also assumed, of course, that public opinion would occasionally manifest itself—and make real its threat to corporate autonomy—through regulatory action on the part of government. The overall effect would be to render the corporation approximately as socially responsible as any other person in the society. In time, corporate managers would develop a kind of "conscience" and employ their powers moderately and without danger to the rest of the economy or society.

Berle finally integrated this principle of managerial behavior into a more comprehensive image of the new "economic republic." He added the vital dimension of active popular involvement and control—ultimately a kind of "peoples' capitalism." He argued that the people had really assumed control of the corporate economy through a number of means, and that it therefore was obliged to (and did) respond to their preferences. This control was exercised through a wide diffusion of stock ownership which, while it did not give rise to direct control over specific corporations (that would have been contrary to his own prior analysis), assured that managers would not be directed by a few wealthy persons and would be free to act subject to their own socially responsible inclinations. The people also shared widely in the wealth produced by this corporate economy, both by virtue of the spread of ownership (and dividends) and through the general level of affluence that it created. Reduced inequality would contribute to increased political awareness and capability, and an attentive public would use its political power through the vehicle of the government to impose restraints upon

---

[16] Adolf A. Berle, *The American Economic Republic* (New York: Harcourt, Brace & World, 1963).

corporate activities of which it disapproved. Only occasional exercises of such power would be necessary to keep managers tuned carefully to the trends of public opinion.

This last prospect—socially responsible managers seeking avidly to conform their behavior to the principles and preferences of an attentive public—is, for Berle, the key to the progress and the ongoing democratization of the American economy. He terms this "the transcendental margin," declaring that it is the means whereby standards of justice, equality, and morality are steadily being integrated into the American economy. The motivations that animate the economy are no longer, in his eyes, merely individual self-interest. Instead, they are popularly shared communitarian and humanitarian values; the economic system becomes a means to ends that are no longer merely material, but transcendental—morally and spiritually ennobling and uplifting.

This glowing image has not found its way into capitalist ideology in its entirety, but the ideology has endorsed a substantial part of it. Certainly, the idea of a "peoples' capitalism," in which ownership and control are spread democratically and highly professional managers respond to popular preferences expressed in public consensus or government action, has achieved widespread acceptance in the United States. So has the belief that this economy has generated *and distributed on an essentially egalitarian basis* an affluence unimagined elsewhere in the world. Only a handful of the unmotivated or the willfully ignorant, it is assumed, can have failed to enjoy a share in this unique productivity. In this view, American capitalism has modernized itself naturally and taken on the forms that are most profitable for, and most desired by, the American people.

Berle's emphasis on popular controls over the economy are less frequently echoed than his assertions about the socially responsible character of the new professional managers. Many writers have detailed the ways in which the new business ethics have diverged from the old standards.[17] This "managerial ideology" is an important new strand in mid-twentieth century capitalist ideology.[18] It is

---

[17] For three major illustrations, see James Burnham, *The Managerial Revolution* (New York: Doubleday, 1956).

[18] A full account may be found in Sutton, *et al., op. cit.*

associated with the larger corporations and the business community surrounding them, rather than with the myraid smaller businesses where the traditional capitalist ideology is more current (and more likely to be confirmed in market and other economic conditions). It holds that the American economy has been through vast transformation, that it is now indeed a new economy, that its technological sophistication mandates large size, and that the economy today is really a collective effort in which all are playing parts for the common good. The problems it sees are exclusively technical. In other words, we all want to achieve maximum affluence for the largest number and are dedicated to that end. Only some technical questions about how best to achieve that goal, rather than deep, value-based issues of who should get how much or who should control the economy, remain to be solved.

Summary: Capitalism in the Late Twentieth Century

These two types of modifications of capitalist ideology have thus added new elements concerning the role of government and the nature of private relationships and motivations. What is new and different is a change from the view of government as almost exclusively a threat. Capitalism has not come full circle to the point of viewing government as a fully legitimate participant in the economy. But it has acknowledged that there are stabilizing purposes for which government can and should be used and that government expenditures and other policies provide a means for the advancement of business enterprise. Government's new role is not without constant controversy, of course: there is ample room for disagreement about the propriety of any particular use of government, about its timing, sufficiency, etc. There are also divergences within capitalist ideology about the extent to which government and the economy should be seen as antagonists or partners. Nevertheless, the main thrust of the ideology today acknowledges government in a way that was unknown prior to the New Deal.

Another addition to capitalist ideology is the aura of benignity and egalitarianism that now forms part of the image of the American economy. Its new size and concentration involve not threat, but opportunity; monopoly, oligopoly, technology, impersonality—all are for the best. Depressions are no longer real possibilities because government is managing and stabilizing the business cycle. Productivity is higher than ever and affluence is well distributed throughout the population. Individual security and opportunity are assured by government-sponsored programs of various kinds. Wide agreement on the purpose of economic activity assures socially desirable behavior by the big corporations, which are subject to popular control in a variety of ways in any event. Together, welfare capitalism, peoples' capitalism, and the new business ethic of the professional managers have produced the prospect of ever-expanding affluence and individual satisfactions in the United States.

These two modifications have come to full flower in the post-World War II years. They represent much greater optimism and pride in achievement than the prewar version of the ideology. But for the most part, they remain merely a gloss upon the basic world view, values, and goals of capitalism. What is *not* different, or at least only marginally changed, are the broad assumptions about man as a competitive, profit-seeking individual, and the need to allow full freedom in the economy and society. The values of individualism, materialism, and the rights and prerogatives of private property are unchanged or only marginally affected. The free and competitive market is still taken to be the standard, from which deviations are to be accepted only after a showing of special need and circumstances. Individuals perform their social duty by serving their own self-interest. Those who do not succeed in the competition bear the primary responsibility and should suffer the consequences and, through the limited assistance properly made available to them, should seek to prepare themselves for productive roles in the system as soon as possible. Conversely, those who do well have earned their rewards and should not be expected to share their achievements with others.

This amalgam of economic beliefs, with the new interpretations engrafted upon the established principles, makes up the economic half of the mainstream of American ideology. It is closely integrated with the political half, which we shall describe in the next chapter. Indeed, the congeniality between the two segments of the mainstream of American ideology is so great that they are frequently blurred together. A strict analysis, however, reveals that one set of assumptions and beliefs deals chiefly with economic matters and the other with political arrangements. The two are mutually supportive belief systems, however, for each makes sometimes unstated assumptions about the other. For example, capitalism assumes a government of limited powers which practices laissez faire policies. Liberalism constructs such a government because it assumes the effective working of the capitalist economic system, particularly the free and competitive market. Both ideologies rest on the same basic values—individualism, materialism, private property, and individual self-seeking as a primary element in the definition of freedom.

Annotated Bibliography

Barber, Richard J. *The American Corporation: Its Power, Its Money, Its Politics*. New York: Dutton, 1970. A thorough current analysis of the role of supercorporations and the economy they dominate.

Berle, Adolf A. *The American Economic Republic*. New York: Harcourt, Brace & World, 1963. A recent summary of Berle's thought, emphasizing the themes of peoples' capitalism and managerial ethic.

Berle, Adolf A., and Gardiner C. Means. *The Modern Corporation and Private Property*. New York: Macmillan, 1932. The classic study of concentration and control in the corporate economy. Reissued in paperback and updated by the authors in 1967 by Harcourt, Brace & World.

Burnham, James. *The Managerial Revolution*. New York: John Day, 1946. A classic study of the trend toward control by corporate managers and their standards of operation. Subsequent writings develop a generally conservative view of capitalist evolution.

Drucker, Peter. *The Concept of the Corporation*. New York: John Day, 1946. One of several thoughtful works, again from a conservative perspective.

Galbraith, John Kenneth. *The Affluent Society*. Boston: Houghton Mifflin, 1957. A summary of the views of the celebrated liberal economist prior to his governmental service and subsequent move to stronger reformist analysis.

Heilbroner, Robert. *The Limits of American Capitalism*. New York: Harper & Row, 1966. A brief argument by a prolific liberal economist concerning the basic values and scope of capacity of American capitalism.

Reagan, Michael D. *The Managed Economy*. New York: Oxford University Press, 1963. One of the best short analyses combining business ideology with evidence about government activities regarding the economy. Contains an excellent bibliography.

Shonfield, Andrew. *Modern Capitalism.* New York: Oxford University Press, 1965. An excellent comparative analysis of trends in public-private power relationships in Britain, France, Germany, and the United States.

Sutton, Francis X., Seymour E. Harris, Carl Kaysen, and James Tobin. *The American Business Creed.* Cambridge: Harvard University Press, 1956. An exhaustive but highly readable analysis of the beliefs of American businessmen.

3

Liberalism

Decades of highly varied use, both as justification and as denunciation, have robbed "liberalism" of much of its specific meaning. In its early classic usage, liberalism—much like capitalism, its sibling —implied primacy for the individual and strict limitations upon governments to ensure full freedom for the individual to serve his needs as he saw fit. In the twentieth century, growing concern that changing economic and social conditions made it impossible for many individuals to do so led to a near reversal in liberalism's attitude toward the use of government. Given such flexibility and such a course of evolution, it is small wonder that the term liberalism carries many meanings for different people. A brief survey of the origins and evolution of liberalism will provide a setting for understanding the contemporary version and the challenges it faces.

Liberalism's individualist beginnings may be traced to an earlier time, but its emergence as a comprehensive set of political principles is usually associated with John Locke, a seventeenth century Englishman. Locke published his major work, *A Second Treatise of Government*,[1] in 1690, shortly after the English Parliament had replaced one line of kings with another in the Glorious Revolution of 1688. Locke's perspective was that of the mercantilist financier and businessman, caught in the middle between lords and peas-

[1] John Locke, *A Second Treatise of Civil Government*. Citations here are to the Hafner Library of Classics edition, Thomas I. Cook, ed. (New York: Hafner Publishing Co., 1947).

ants and striving to maintain an independent status. No such social group had existed under the social and economic conditions of feudalism, and legitimating and protecting their right to do business seemed a large task.

The central theme of Locke's ideas was the right of individuals to be secure in their property—which in turn required strict limitations on the potentially threatening power of government, then dominated by nobles and the king. Locke defined property as that body of goods, land and rights to which individuals gained title through mixing their labor with unimproved resources and producing something which had greater value than in its original state. The sole purpose of government was to protect these natural rights of individuals. It had no broader social functions and was limited by the individuals who created it through a contract that spelled out the authority of officeholders and the limits on the scope of their powers. Locke summed up the individual-government relationship in these words:

> The reason why men enter into society is the preservation of their property; and the end why they choose and authorize a legislative is that there may be laws made and rules set as guards and fences to the properties of all members of the society to limit the power and moderate the dominion of every part and member of the society; for it can never be supposed to be the will of the society that the legislative should have a power to destroy that which everyone designs to secure by entering into society, and for which the people submitted themselves to legislators of their own making.[2]

As capitalism became more prominent, liberalism also evolved, in effect, applying capitalist principles to the organization and operation of government. Liberalism emphasized individualism and saw economic self-interest as the principal motivational force in social life. Moreover, the free and competitive market was the vital means —and the only means—to the good life. Government was a danger, constantly threatening to interfere with the natural processes of the market. In general, economic life was central and politics was strictly a secondary sphere. All individuals were primarily concerned with

[2] *Ibid.*, p. 233.

their economic needs and goals. Men who succeeded in the economic world could bring great benefits to society; those in politics could serve best by doing nothing or by heeding the instructions of the economy.

With industrialization, urbanization, and rapid population increase, both the needs and the consequences of economic life began to impose new demands upon the state. Business and industry began to employ government subsidies, supports, and protections of various kinds. Segments of the public sought regulation of some of the activities of business and protection for individuals against some of the economic hardships that resulted from the new conditions. Liberalism responded to these changing economic circumstances, much as did capitalism, by developing a rationale for occasional government actions, ostensibly to support and promote the workings of the market. Thus we come to the mid- and late twentieth century.

The World View of American Liberalism

(1) THE DOMESTIC SCENE

When liberals look at the United States, they see a mixed but essentially capitalist economy, which they accept unquestioningly as the major achievement of American social life. Capitalism, operating through the market as supplemented and aided by government, has succeeded in creating a unique affluence that has, in turn, been spread broadly throughout the society. By alert use of the economy-managing tools, government can both maintain stability and growth in the economy and help to steadily reduce the number of poor people in the society. A generally middle-class social structure, in which agreement on fundamental policies and practices is widely shared is the result.

Not only does liberalism's world view assume that the political system's task is to support and promote the operating capitalist economic system, but it views the political process itself through capitalist economic concepts. Politics is seen as a free market for the exchange of demands, support, and public policies. Each individual has his specific wants and equivalent purchasing power—one vote. He "buys" the policies and candidates of his choice in the competitive market on election day. If the products he seeks are not available, the demand will soon create the supply. Officeholders act as brokers, adjusting government policy products to the wants of enough consumers to obtain the votes of a majority. In this fashion, participating individuals control major government policies, which in turn may be understood as flexibly responding to changing popular preferences *and* representing the public interest. In realistic and modern language, this is democracy.

In a complex industrial society such as the United States, special conditions must be maintained to keep this market truly free and competitive. By and large, however, these conditions have been met. In particular, three combined legal and social processes assure this. First, opportunity for all individuals to voice their wants and demands is maintained through adherence to the civil rights of freedom of speech, freedom of press, and freedom of association. Constitutional protection of these rights enjoys the support of most leaders and is guaranteed in practice by the courts. The judicial process effectively and neutrally balances the needs of the society for self-preservation against its simultaneous interest in maintaining open political processes.

Second, competing political parties offer voters choices representing the realistic alternatives that a potential majority of the population might actually want. This is made possible by regular elections of party officials and delegates, by the natural desire of politicians to win office, and by a necessary internal process of compromise between extremes of popular preference within the party. This electoral system is consistent with the social heterogeneity of the population, the diversity of their interests, and the varying levels of participation in politics that are natural to them. At the close of a major study of voting behavior, for example, the research team concluded that classical democratic theory placed too much emphasis on the participation of all citizens and allowed the achievements of the system as a whole too little weight:

> We need some people who are active in a certain respect, others in the middle, and still others passive. . . . Low interest provides maneuvering room for political shifts necessary for a complex society in a period of rapid change. Compromise might be based upon sophisticated awareness of

costs and returns—perhaps impossible to demand of a mass society—but it is more often induced by indifference. Some people are and should be highly interested in politics, but not everyone is or needs to be. Only the doctrinaire would deprecate the moderate indifference that facilitates compromise.[3]

Finally, an elaborate network of voluntary associations (or interest groups) provides supplementary representation for many individuals. These groups reflect the social reality and diversity of ethnic, religious, occupational, economic, and regional interests within the nation, and their interaction is the principal dynamic of between-elections politics. A leading political scientist characterized the importance of interest group activities in this way:

> At bottom, group interests are the animating forces in the political process. . . . Whatever the bases of group interest may be, the study of politics must rest on an analysis of the objectives and composition of the interest groups within a society. . . . The chief vehicles for the expression of group interest are political parties and pressure groups. Through these formal mechanisms groups of people with like interests make themselves felt in the balancing of political forces.[4]

Liberalism sees this interest group activity as the leading characteristic of American politics, the means whereby the contemporary political "market" is kept open and responsive to popular preferences. Liberalism's image of politics in the United States is sometimes labeled "pluralism" [5] or "pluralist democracy" [6] by its spokesmen. Americans are seen as such joiners that every significant interest is

---

[3] Bernard R. Berelson, Paul F. Lazarsfeld, and William N. McPhee, *Voting* (Chicago: University of Chicago Press, 1954), pp. 314–315.

[4] V. O. Key, Jr., *Politics, Parties, and Pressure Groups* (New York: Knopf, 1942), pp. 23–24; Cited in Daniel Bell, "The Adequacy of Our Concepts," in Bertram Gross, ed., *A Great Society?* (New York: Basic Books, 1966).

[5] See, for example, Theodore Lowi, *The End of Liberalism* (New York: Norton, 1969), or William Kornhauser, *The Politics of Mass Society* (Glencoe, Ill.: Free Press, 1959).

[6] Robert A. Dahl, *Pluralist Democracy in the United States: Conflict and Consensus* (Chicago: Rand McNally, 1967).

represented by one or more groups which press their claims upon each other and upon the government. The political arena is a vast array of competing groups engaged in a continuing process of building alliances, appealing for popular support, bargaining, pressuring, and negotiating. Finally, officeholders weigh the conflicting claims, mediate compromises, and produce policy. Then the scene shifts to implementing agencies, the courts, and the electoral realm again, and goes on in slightly revised form. The structure of power in the institutions of American government is highly conducive to interest groups' impact, for the many committees, agencies, levels of government, etc. assure that every group has access at some point and thus a chance to make itself felt at some stage of decision-making. Again, this process amounts to a definition of democracy. Another leading political scientist says:

> It is a markedly decentralized system. Decisions are made by endless bargaining; perhaps in no other national political system in the world is bargaining so basic a component of the political process. . . . With all its defects, it does nonetheless provide a high probability that any active and legitimate group will make itself heard effectively at some stage in the process of decision. This is no mean thing in a political system.[7]

Interest-group politics produces some vital returns for the American political system. Participants feel integrated into the system, learn to become effective politically, and also learn tolerance for each other's views. Those who rise to group leadership become particularly committed to protecting the rights of others because they realize that their own future opportunities to be heard may be at stake. Groups balance each other and individuals within them feel conflicting pressures, keeping the whole political system closer to the middle of the road. Thus, stability is enhanced, democratic values are promoted, and representation is provided—all at the same time and through an entirely natural American process.[8]

---

[7] Robert A. Dahl, *Preface to Democratic Theory* (Chicago: University of Chicago Press, 1963), p. 150.

[8] For a full statement, see David B. Truman, *The Governmental Process* (New York: Knopf, 1951).

This is not to say that advocates of liberalism believe all problems have been solved, for they see the ideology as acutely tuned to unserved needs in many dimensions—from broader sharing of wealth and opportunity among the poor to provision of more public goods, such as hospitals and roads, to greater sensitivity to the needs of the human spirit. But the key to solving these problems is a productive, stable economy. When such unserved needs are seen against the background of the past and in terms of the practical problems of achievement amid many other demands and needs, the American political system must be understood to be highly responsive and to have delivered effectively in recent decades.

(2) THE INTERNATIONAL SCENE

American liberals see the United States as uniquely favored among the nations of the world. No other country has approached the standard of living generated by the productivity of the American economy. Nor do other peoples exhibit the political maturity of the American people or enjoy the broad scope of democratic freedoms and popular government control that is characteristic of the United States. These American achievements, however, both impose responsibilities upon the United States Government and cause it difficulties in its relations with the rest of the world. The power of the United States can be a great force for good in the world, as can the example of our political institutions and processes. Our sole interest in the rest of the world is continued peace, stability, and opportunity for American business to trade with, and invest in, other countries. But hostile forces prevent these altruistic goals from being realized.

Communism is the principal obstacle to world peace and orderly development. The form of government actually created by those who profess to endorse the disarmingly attractive goals of communism is a totalitarian dictatorship that denies free expression, eliminates democratic choice in elections, and manages the lives of its citizens. These self-perpetuating elites are compelled by their ideology and self-maintenance needs to seek expansion of their domination and to try to undermine the United States. Writing in 1969, Arthur Schlesinger, Jr. characterized the roots of communist behavior from the cold war to the present as follows:

Marxism-Leninism gave the Russian leaders a view of the world according to which all societies were inexorably destined to proceed along appointed roads by appointed stages until they achieved the classless nirvana. Moreover, given the resistance of the capitalists to this development, the existence of any noncommunist state was *by definition* a threat to the Soviet Union. . . . So long as the United States remained a capitalist democracy, no American policy, given Moscow's theology, could hope to win basic Soviet confidence. . . . So long as the Soviet Union remained a messianic state, ideology compelled a steady expansion of communist power. (Italics in original.) [9]

The disillusionment of some older American liberals with communism as it evolved in Stalin's Soviet Union has had an important influence on liberalism generally. What results is a specially rigid posture or "hard line" against the evils of communism and, in particular, against Soviet or Chinese expansionism. Communist nations' actions are often perceived as united and controlled by a single central source. Similarly, Third World social reform movements are perceived as Communist where, in fact, they may be nationalist, socialist, or merely opportunistic independence movements. In the late 1960s, some liberals began to see separate centers of power within the communist world and to treat them independently. But nearly all shared the view that the only way in which American security could be assured was to be ready at all times to employ massive military power to hold back communist expansion. The form of the continuing conflict with communism might vary, from the chiefly ideological, to the small war over Third World territory, to the brink of nuclear confrontation. But only American firmness and military readiness can dissuade communist adventurism and permit the competition to remain a "cold war." It then takes the form of a battle for mens' minds, in which the allegiance of the Third World nations is the prize. During the time purchased thereby, space exploits, military assistance, and economic aid will help to maintain American predominance. With the open door for American business thus main-

---

[9] Arthur Schlesinger, Jr., *The Crisis of Confidence: Ideas, Power and Violence in America* (Boston: Houghton Mifflin, 1969), p. 136.

tained, the Third World may be enabled to develop in a stable and perhaps capitalist fashion.

Occasionally, either indigenous or Communist-inspired local movements arise to threaten the status quo. The United States repeatedly has been obliged to defend established governments, either economically or militarily. This necessity of defending the non-Communist ("free") world against encroachment from any source has led to some actions that are probably not desirable for their own sake. Vietnam is one of these; but experience teaches that peace and stability can sometimes only be obtained at the risk and cost of small wars. Liberalism has taken the lessons of Munich and other pre-World War II appeasements of Hitler's Germany to heart and sees the avoidance of ultimate nuclear war as requiring a firm military posture today. The major flaw in Vietnam, in this view, was error in calculating the chances and means of achieving a desirable result. In reviewing what went wrong in Vietnam, Arthur Schlesinger, Jr. declares:

> The tragedy of Vietnam is the tragedy of the catastrophic over-extension and misapplication of valid principles. . . . I do not see that our original involvement in Vietnam was *per se* immoral. What was immoral was the employment of means of destruction out of all proportion to rational purposes. The wreckage we wrought in Vietnam had no rational relationship to a serious assessment of our national interest or to the demonstrated involvement of our national security.[10]

Values and Goals

Liberal values may be analyzed in two categories. First are the values that concern creation of the good life or the good man. Because liberalism views the economic world (and, within it, the free market) as primary, natural, and fulfilling, these values are much like the basic values of capitalism. Second are the values associated with the kind of political process that will succeed in defending both the economic and the political markets from such artificial forces as

---

[10] *Ibid.*, pp. 174–175.

concentrations of power, particularly from concentration of power in government. These values closely resemble liberalism's domestic world view images of the American political process. Descriptions merge with prescriptions, and the "is" (as perceived) sounds very much like the "ought" that is desired. What starts as an objective description becomes a celebration of achievement; such is the power, and the defensiveness, on occasion, of a dominant ideology. Almost any high school civics text, and most college American government texts, readily illustrate this process.

(1) VALUES PRIMARILY ASSOCIATED WITH THE QUALITY OF PRIVATE LIFE

The beginning value of liberalism, as noted, is individualism. Individuals are entitled to serve their own interests in order that both they and the society may develop and progress. Their entitlement is absolute, part of their birthright; it belongs to them solely by virtue of their existence as persons and not through the benevolent grant of any outside source. Thus it is appropriate to speak of "rights" of the individual, such as the right to hold property, the right to take part in politics, or the right to personal liberty.

To assure freedom and the openness of the political processes, the individual must be protected against encroachments upon his rights from those sources of power in the society that might reduce the area of personal freedom surrounding him. Individual rights are secured against government by framing them into legal descriptions and expressing these as prohibitions in the basic contract by which government is created. The Bill of Rights of the Constitution is the leading example of the expression of individual rights by American liberalism.

The principal rights of the individual, however, represent independent values in themselves. In effect, liberalism sees a comprehensive package of rights surrounding the individual. But these rights are valued in order of priority—they are not all of equal significance to liberal ideology. Two rights or values which have long contended for top place in the liberal priority ranking are *property* and *equality*. Property is essential to permit men to retain the fruits of their labor and to enable them to be truly independent individuals. Equality has usually been defined as an equal right to take part in the contest for advantages that the market institutionalizes. It is also seen as necessary to enable citizens to take part as equivalent units in the political marketplace. But on occasion, the rights of some to retain the advantages gained through the free and competitive market may conflict with the rights of others to compete on an equal basis. Any effort to truly equalize the opportunity of some to compete may result in the reduction of the freedom and property rights of others. In actual practice, property rights have usually triumphed. Equality has always had strong supporters and has come to be increasingly prominent in the last decade; nevertheless, it is probably accurate to say that progress has been more in the realm of rhetoric than of reality.

Liberalism has juggled these two potentially conflicting values, generally succeeding in harmonizing them. This is no easy task, for the two can be quite contradictory. In the 1960s, for example, the efforts of blacks to advance the value of equality by means of civil rights legislation, such as open housing laws, ran up against the claim of some whites for observance of the value of the property right of owners to sell houses to whomever they pleased. The clash occurs over and over again in this subject area: in public accommodations laws, in fair employment laws, and in claims for "compensation" or "reparations" for blacks. Property rights as a paramount value are manifested also in resistance to controls on pollution, to zoning regulations, to taxation, and to social legislation generally. Equality manifests itself in demands for "one man, one vote" election arrangements, for full citizenship for blacks, and for "participatory democracy" in neighborhood governments.

Equality has been expanding in meaning, particularly in the last two decades, and its challenge to property rights is increasingly forcing this potential conflict within liberal ideology out into the open. Equality was at first understood to mean only the formal or legal equality of opportunity to take part in political affairs, such as the right to vote. Even then, its scope was limited to property owning males. The right has been expanded to include all citizens, although it was extended to blacks only after the Civil War and to women as recently as 1919. But two types of further expansion in the concept of equality have also occurred, converting it into something perhaps better called "human rights." First, the concept has acquired more than a formal or legal dimension, reaching as well to the tangible reality of the existence or nonexistence of the right for people in the circumstances in which they live. Black citizens in the South, for example, had a formal right to vote long before they were allowed to participate in the real sense in elections. Second, the concept has been expanded from its original role of assuring participation in public affairs to include the social and economic conditions of people. For many liberals, equality now means the rights of people to have some minimum share in the economic prosperity of the American society. Government's obligation to assist individuals in regard to economic security *and* opportunity is very clear. With such developments in the understanding of human rights or equality, the tension arising from the conflict, property between equality rights is becoming increasingly evident.

(2) VALUES PRIMARILY ASSOCIATED WITH THE POLITICAL
PROCESS THAT IS CAPABLE OF DEFENDING THE ECONOMIC
AND POLITICAL MARKETS

To keep these markets open and competitive, concentrations of power, particularly in government, must be prevented. One way is to limit government through legal prohibitions; another is to foster a social process that will give meaning to such limitations. Thus, one major value is the principle of limited government. Government has been erected by many individuals to serve and protect their rights. Its powers stem from the voluntary grant of those individuals, and it has no other powers. It is thus a government of limited powers, capable only of doing what it has been set up to do. In short, it is a servant, subject to dismissal for failure to perform its task adequately or for taking on tasks not assigned. The question of whether it is empowered to do particular acts is one that may be resolved by reference to the basic creating instrument, in this case the Constitution. The virtue of this is that the acts of government may be challenged at any time by a single individual, and the process of public action must stop while the authority of government is determined in court.

Another major value of liberalism, also expressed as one of the natural rights of individuals, is the individual's right to be secure against arbitrary government interference with life, liberty, or property. This is the right to *due process*. It means that government power may not be applied to limit or take the individual's life, liberty, or property *except through due process*—i.e., in accordance with the procedures established by law for such action. The distinction is between regular, accepted, authorized ways of operating and arbitrary, discretionary, or whimsical uses of power by government officials. Before a man may be jailed and deprived of his liberty, for example, there must have been a properly enacted law on the books prohibiting his act, and he must be shown to have committed that act so clearly that a jury of ordinary citizens finds after presentation of all the evidence in an open trial that he did so. In this way, liberalism seeks to accomplish two things: First, it achieves another dimension of protection for the freedom of the individual. Second, it renders the actions of government into more of mechanical exercise and less of a personal or discretionary vehicle for men to employ.

Underlying the values just discussed, and making possible their realization, is the strong liberal faith in *legalism*—the capacity to express rights and prohibitions in contractual terms and to enforce them through legal and judicial means. Elaborate legal mechanisms are seen as enabling the avoidance of society-splitting conflicts and the securing of individual rights even under circumstances where people care deeply about conflicting goals. "The law" takes on a special quality of its own in liberal ideology, becoming something more than the acts of men and, therefore, worthy of special respect and regard. Answers to deep value conflicts are said to lie within the reservoir of wisdom represented by the law. Its neutrality is asserted, and neither the circumstances of its enactment nor the disputes of learned lawyers and judges over its proper interpretation are permitted to legitimate others' denial of validity to particular laws which may appear to them unjust or selfish. Only where law receives such independent regard is it possible to realize the values of individualism, property, equality, due process, and limited government in the manner that liberalism endorses.

But the major value to be served through law, and through the interest group type of social process, is the creation and maintenance of *fair procedures* for decision-making. Every man's opinion and preference in politics is just as good as any other's, just as all wants are equal in the economic marketplace. There is no way to choose between possible alternative policies on moral or ethical grounds. Indeed, it would be dangerous to try to do so, for bitter disputes would arise. One man's version of morality may be utterly repugnant to another's. Far better to have an utterly impartial process of decision-making, similar to the economic market, where impersonal decisions (and not judgments on the *merits* of claims) determine results. Justice and fairness are thus defined in terms of consistency and neutrality of decisional standards, not by the advantages conferred or purposes served by the decision itself. In effect, liberalism places its confidence in the *method* by which decisions are made rather than in the people who make them or in the inherent quality of the decisions themselves. A complicated system of checks, balances, division and limitation of powers, resting ultimately on majority-rule elections but with multiple opportunities for individual impact, becomes in itself the solution to the problem of conflict. Deep value conflicts that are likely to excite and divide people and threaten stability, not all conflicts, are avoided in this way. At least some basic issues are muted, while others are held and resolved within the more "responsible" leadership echelons.

This brings us to liberalism's values regarding the social system that will support effective limits on power. The basic premise may be seen in the words of Robert A. Dahl, a leading political scientist:

> The fundamental axiom in the theory and practice of American pluralism is, I believe, this: Instead of a single center of power there must be multiple centers of power, none of which is or can be wholly sovereign.[11]

These multiple centers of power, in social terms, are to be found in the interest groups into which the society is divided and in the method by which such groups are consulted in decision-making. The good system, in which natural self-interest is harnessed (much as occurs in the case of individuals), produces the greatest good for the greatest number.

The pluralist process achieves this, according to liberalism. In effect, all groups share an investment in maintaining the fairness and openness of the process through which they seek to attain their ends. Each wants to be able to be heard when it is seeking something, and in order to assure such opportunity, it must help at all times to defend the rules of the game by which the polity is conducted. These rules involve fair hearings for all, tolerance for all views, and regular

---

[11] Dahl, *Pluralist Democracy,* p. 24.

procedures for making decisions. Above all, parties to this process should be willing to try to see the other side's problems and to be willing to compromise somewhere short of their own goals—and, also, short of absolute disaster for the other side. When each group knows in advance that its needs and interests will not be totally ignored or eradicated by the other if that side should win, the debate loses some of its bitterness.

The merits of this system are enormous. It channels goal-seeking, promotes compromise, and makes for flexibility and progress. Not only does it mute conflict and stabilize politics, but it leaves officeholders free to act wisely and in the public interest. The established legal procedures and the pluralist social process that supports and defends the rules of the game acquire the status of an independent political value. For liberalism, the rules become a kind of test of loyalty to the entire process: those who adhere may continue to play; those who do not are beyond redemption and properly may be punished. In the words of a former Supreme Court justice:

> Procedure is the bone structure of a democratic society. Our scheme of law affords great latitude for dissent and opposition. It compels wide tolerance not only for their expression but also for the organization of people and forces to bring about the acceptance of the dissenter's claim. Both our institutions and the characteristics of our national behavior make it possible for opposition to be translated into policy, for dissent to prevail. We have alternatives to violence.[12]

It is vital that the rules be enforced and that conflict be reduced or absorbed in this manner because agitated masses may otherwise threaten stability. The authors of a major voting study, applauding low levels of interest and knowledge among the electorate as functional for democratic politics, ask:

> How could a mass democracy work if all the people were deeply involved in politics? Lack of interest by some people is not without its benefits, too. True, the highly in-

---

[12] Abe Fortas, *Concerning Dissent and Civil Disobedience* (New York: Signet, 1968), p. 60.

terested voters vote more, and know more about the campaign, and read and listen more, and participate more; however, they are also less open to persuasion and less likely to
change. Extreme interest goes with extreme partisanship and
might culminate in rigid fanaticism that could destroy democratic processes if generalized throughout the community.[13]

They call for a balance of stabilizing groups and multiple other at-
tachments, so that citizens are not led to excessive involvement in
politics:

> For political democracy to survive, (certain) features are
> required: the intensity of conflict must be limited, the rate
> of change must be restrained, stability in the social and
> economic structure must be maintained, a pluralistic social
> organization must exist, and a basic consensus must bind
> together the contending parties.[14]

This concern is broadly shared, particularly among liberal social
scientists. Many see the group structure as the principal bulwark
against extremist actions by masses. Civil liberties, it is believed,
depend on the more sophisticated support of elites, many of whom
will have learned the rules of the game in their interest group activities. They also depend on competition between elements of elites.
These principles are well summarized in the words of a leading
sociologist:

> Civil liberty requires considerable social autonomy of *both*
> elites and non-elites. This means specifically that elites and
> non-elites must have the following characteristics:
>   (a) There must be extensive self-government, private
>   as well as public, and individuals must belong to
>   several self-governing units.
>   (b) There must be extensive opportunities for elites to
>   formulate policies and take action without *ad hoc*
>   interference from the outside.
>   . . . social pluralism is a social arrangement which performs
> this function. A plurality of independent and limited-function

---

[13] Berelson *et al., op. cit.,* p. 314.
[14] *Ibid.,* p. 313.

groups supports liberal democracy by providing social bases
of free and open competition for leadership, widespread participation in the selection of leaders, restraint in the applica-
cation of pressures on leaders, and self-government in wide
areas of social life.[15]

The other major return to be realized from a multiplicity of
groups and strong support for the established procedures is the provision of some autonomy and discretion for governing elites. Liberals
assert that there are difficult decisions to be made, and only a few
people are qualified to make them. Continuity, insulation, and expertise will be important attributes of decision-making elites. Pluralist
democracy is also seen as providing these opportunities through its
many layers of authority and its development of a kind of "subcul-
ture" of elites. The latter is an essentially self-perpetuating group of
specially adept persons who carry the principal responsibility for
keeping the system on an even keel, making the crucial decisions, and
setting the agenda for mass political actions. In the words of political
scientist V. O. Key, Jr.:

> The longer one frets with the puzzle of how democratic
> regimes manage to function, the more plausible it appears
> that a substantial part of the explanation is to be found in
> the motives that actuate the leadership echelon, the values
> that it holds, in the rules of the political game to which it
> adheres, in the expectations which it entertains about its own
> status in the society, and perhaps in some of the objective
> circumstances, both material and institutional, in which it
> functions.[16]

(3) GOALS

The goals of liberalism may be succinctly stated. In general,
they are that as many individuals as possible realize as many of their
private preferences as possible. This means, first, that the American
economy must generate material prosperity on an ever-increasing

---

[15] Kornhauser, *op. cit.*, pp. 230–231.
[16] V. O. Key, Jr., *Public Opinion and American Democracy* (New York:
Knopf, 1961).

level and, second, individual freedoms inherent in the rights of property, equality, and due process must be maintained. The American system is seen as being in constant and steady motion toward greater and greater realization of these goals of individual freedom and self-fulfillment. Material possessions and the less tangible rights to take part in the political affairs of the nation are steadily expanding, and, soon, very few people will remain unintegrated into the mainstream of an increasingly affluent and harmonious society.

Some specific goals that liberal ideology holds out for the political system as such are really intended as means to such private and individual ends. The chief goals of political activity are stability and the avoidance of disruptive conflict. In order to achieve stability, the basic framework of procedures must be defended and violations promptly punished. At the same time, however, the procedures must be sufficiently flexible to give promise of successful attainment to the individual goals of most people, and the policies formulated by government must move marginally in the directions preferred by unsatisfied groups of people possessing significant fragments of power. Stability is thus a product of insistence upon maintainings of established rules while delivering at least some of the goals sought by individuals who might otherwise be tempted to break the rules. *Liberalism offers half a loaf to many, whole loaves to very few; but it hopes that there are even fewer who receive nothing at all, and that everybody will find it preferable to continue to work within the system than to challenge it.*

Other goals are taken to flow more or less naturally from the unconfined efforts of many individuals toward their private ends. Progress, for example, is both a desirable goal and one which may be anticipated from individual effort. The freedom from restraint that is achieved in the liberal system will permit a maximum of inventiveness and experimentation, not just in technological and economic affairs, but also in literary, social, artistic, and political matters. The result will be attainment of levels of material comfort, aesthetic enjoyment, and political civility unknown in other societies. And in this case, the people will share very widely in all of these attainments because part of the definition of progress is the broad and increasing distribution of all the desired products and achievements of the system. Continuing movement toward realization of these goals will

foster increased recognition of the virtues of our system and promote harmony and national pride within the society.

Not least among goals of this kind is the goal of finally triumph-
ing over communism in the battle for mens' mind. The material
achievements of our economy and the associated levels of individual
freedom, social harmony, and national pride that they generate will,
in time, demonstrate to the attentive world that our economic and
political institutions are better—more worthy of emulation—than
those of the Soviet Union or China. Such a showing, coupled with
the maturation of both Communist and Third World nations, will
result in increasing acceptance of democratic methods and a lasting
peace.

This is not to say that there will be an easy time for the United
States in the continuing conflict with communism. The proper role of
government is, of course, the protection of the market and of the
growth of the economy, abroad as well as at home, so there are
bound to be clashes. Anticommunism and the promotion of business
interests are taken for granted, although liberalism sees itself as
moderate in these respects. For example, a recent work by Arthur
Schlesinger, Jr. states the proper balance of goals:

> I would regard anticommunism as a moral necessity for any
> believer in democracy. After the last thirty years of world
> history, one hardly need insist that liberalism and commu-
> nism have very little in common, either as to the means or
> ends of government, either as to principle or practice. But
> it is essential to distinguish between *rational* and *obsessive*
> anticommunism: between anticommunism as an element in
> a larger position, . . . and anticommunism as a total posi-
> tion.[17]

Nevertheless, the liberal implementation of this principle retains a
firm, if not hard, line with regard to serving the American national
interest in international affairs. Schlesinger offered the following
guidelines in 1969 for future American foreign policy:

> We should undertake military intervention only (a)
> when the national security of the United States is directly

---

[17] Schlesinger, *op. cit.,* p. 161.

and vitally involved, (b) when the people whom we think we are supporting display a capacity for resistance themselves, and (c) when, in addition, there are reasonable prospects for success.[18]

Social Change and Tactics

Liberalism's world view, values, and goals merge and find expression in its image of how change comes about. To begin with, it assumes that all legitimate interests are heard under conditions of fairness, mutual tolerance, and realistic assessment of others' needs and power. In such a context, reasonable men can arrange a compromise that nearly all will consider acceptable. Then the problem of change reduces to one of implementation—of finding the rationally best means to generally shared ends. Thus, pragmatism and rationalism in both policy making and administration characterize liberalism's approach to change.

This emphasis on pragmatism and rationalism carries several implications. Liberalism regards all absolutes with profound skepticism, including both moral imperatives and final solutions produced through factual analyses. The criteria for a sound decision involve the manner in which it is reached more than the substance of what is done; the solution that is appropriate is one that is realistic in the sense of being responsive, *first,* to the established or evolving pattern of power and preference in the society and, *second,* to the merits of the problem involved. Insistence upon any particular solution is the mark of an ideologue, one who does not understand liberalism's method. In Schlesinger's words, "those who rush around ladling out moral judgments quickly arrogate to themselves an alarming and repellent sense of their own moral infallibility." [19] Further, liberalism's effort to avoid extremes causes it to see the decision that strikes the middle path between polar positions as best. Because it acknowledges no particular solution to be intrinsically best or ethically superior, liberalism is uniquely able to shift its ground, balance demands and pressures, and emerge with a compromise that can be universally accepted. On occasion, action may be delayed until such

---

[18] *Ibid.,* p. 191.
[19] *Ibid.,* p. 89.

polar positions are taken and the middle path is identifiable. Finally, decisions must be generally applicable to all who are similarly situated or neutral. They must not be deliberately discriminatory, even with benevolent intent. This principle ("If we do it for one, we must do it for all") flows from the previously discussed emphasis on consistent, impartial standards of decision-making that do not take results into account.

These standards for decision-making emphasize not only mechanical characteristics of the process by which they are made but, also, technical aspects of the decisions themselves. Because of the importance of such technical characteristics—the specific implementing means whereby the shared ends are to be achieved—liberalism sees a special role for intellectuals and their principal home, the universities. Social scientists, in particular, have rational and administrative skills that serve to effectuate and interpret liberalism's policies. The kind of change that is best from liberalism's perspective is one for which empirical data point the way, suggesting improved techniques for attaining agreed goals.

In the years since World War II, the universities have come to serve more and more as bases for research in both the natural and social sciences. This is a natural outgrowth of liberalism's emphasis on maximum use of rational and technical skills, and the desire to be of service animates the universities as well. In his famous *The Uses of the University,* Clark Kerr (then head of the University of California) declares, "Knowledge is now central to society. It is wanted, even demanded, by more people and more institutions than ever before. The university as producer, wholesaler, and retailer of knowledge cannot escape service." [20] At the same time, of course, Kerr recognizes that the university's directions "have not been set as much by the university's visions of its destiny as by the external environment, including the federal government, the foundations, the surrounding and sometimes engulfing industry." [21]

Emphasizing the uses of pragmatic, rational, relativistic means of dealing with problems helps liberalism avoid confrontation with potentially insoluble conflicts. By stressing the established rules, seeking a middle path, avoiding absolutes, balancing contending

---

[20] Clark Kerr, *The Uses of the University* (New York: Harper & Row, 1966), p. 114.
[21] *Ibid.,* p. 122.

forces, and relying on technically sophisticated means, the peaceful continuity of the society is furthered. Conflict must be avoided where possible—particularly class, religious, or racial conflict—because of the prospect that it cannot be managed, or its results foretold.

Perhaps ironically, liberalism's efforts to deflect and avoid the merits of issues lead to a complementary emphasis on flexibility and change. To avoid confrontations, it is desirable to try to satisfy every group that is pressing a claim and has some political power to apply within the system. It is relatively easy to do so when it is less essential to actually debate the merits than to establish that the group is powerful and unsatisfied. Today's public policy has no necessary ethical or moral standing; it is merely the product of yesterday's configuration of power, which is now out of date. The policy should therefore now be modified to register the new pattern of power. In the long run, assuming the political processes remain open, this means a steady process of incremental change. On occasion, it may be necessary to act to reopen temporarily closed units of the political process, but this can usually be accomplished without serious difficulty because of the widespread agreement on the propriety of the familiar rules of the game of politics.

One of the major accomplishments of such a continuing process of change in the character of governmental activity is that it preserves the primary initiative toward change for the private sphere. Government responds to thrusts generated by individuals and groups whose changing power and interests reflect shifting trends in technological, social, and economic affairs, rather than taking the initiative to shape the society in somebody's image of what it should be like. This, in general, should be the role of government. It is both more natural and more likely to encourage the individual diversity and achievement that, in the aggregate, spell progress for the society.

As we have noted, however, there are firm limits to what individuals may do when it comes to the rules of the game of politics or to the economic market which those rules are designed to protect. Violators of the rules of the game in domestic politics are legitimately subject to harassment and legal or physical coercion. The system is sufficiently important to justify violent tactics to defend it when necessary. The use of violence by change-seekers is untenable, for it not only seriously threatens the integrity of the system but creates the danger of provoking system-destroying violent reactions from others. Nonofficial violence, in other words, is always wrong, regardless of context, provocation, or consequences; official violence, however, may be necessary to prevent or repel challenges to the system.

This attitude toward violence is even more visible in international affairs. The needs of the economy apparently include trade and investment in foreign countries. Communism, socialism, nationalism, and general social unrest threaten to interfere with such opportunities. Social change and unrest in foreign countries frequently involve violence. Because the American government's role is the protection of the market economy, such violence, or even peaceful change deemed inimical to American interests, may set the stage for use of military violence. Other goals are also involved, of course, such as defense of "the free world," self-determination of peoples, and preservation of democratic liberties; but these may be less central than the basic protective function of government. In any event, liberalism sees violence as a legitimate tactic in international affairs even more readily than in domestic matters. In an amoral world, the only lasting standard is one's own national interest, and under most circumstances, only military force can ultimately assure that it is served.

Liberalism and the Challenges of the 1970s

Advocates of dominant ideologies do not welcome challenge, particularly when the ideologies have been highly successful in their own terms. Capitalism encountered two serious but factually undeniable crises—the Great Depression and the rise of the integrated corporation-government economy. In both cases, a healthy liberalism helped it adapt to the new realities. Liberalism's crisis is still not acknowledged as such by many of its spokesmen, in part, because they do not see such tangible evidence of the irrelevance or contradictions of their beliefs amid developing circumstances. The crisis dates only from the mid-1960s, but already, it seems likely that it will be more severe than the crisis that capitalism experienced and, ultimately, will have a more drastic impact. For one thing, since the current challenge is directed at both capitalism *and* liberalism, neither can draw upon the other. Moreover, escalating social tensions may make it impossible to develop any practical adaptations within the liberal framework.

Essentially, liberalism is now charged with being not much more than a rationalization for unwillingness to solve pressing problems and/or a facade for maintaining an economic and social status quo that is unjust and destructive. Problems such as race relations, poverty, pollution, and war are laid at liberalism's door, and its utility as a basis for political practice is continually questioned, sometimes through violent means. The nature of these allegations and the alternatives offered will be explored in subsequent chapters. But liberalism is not defenseless against such challenges to the viability of its doctrines and the legitimacy of the political system that embodies them. It is an ideology in crisis, but it shows a vitality appropriate to its longevity as part of the American mainstream. This spirited defense serves to highlight some important aspects of liberalism and of the present conflict of ideas in the United States.

Liberalism's response to its challengers is an integrated defense of the established political system and practices, particularly of the values and purposes that they serve. It demands that its challengers recognize that most people do not agree with them and asserts that the great diversity of interests in the United States means that those who challenge liberalism are no more than a tiny minority. They should therefore realize that their chances of achieving their goals are dependent upon preservation of the established procedures.

The other side of liberalism's emphasis on following those procedures is what happens if they are *not* followed. When they *are* followed, the result, by definition, is right, appropriate, or at least the best possible under all the relevant circumstances. Bitter conflicts are channelled into arenas where they can be safely ventilated, compromised or absorbed; the mechanism remains flexible and responsive, and a large and heterogeneous society is enabled to go on living together. The resultant change may be neither swift nor fully satisfying to those who seek new and unfamiliar goals, but it *is* change, and it is accomplished peacefully and with the consent of all concerned. If the established procedures are *not* followed—if change is not carried out peacefully and with consent—fatally disruptive agitation and conflict may ensue. Finally, if force, rather than law and due process, becomes the final arbiter, the reactionary Right will wipe out the gains made through decades of patient effort on behalf of the underprivileged. Wide distribution of economic rewards, observance of civil rights, and meaningful political participation will be ended in the wave of reaction and repression that will follow a takeover by those who hold the major resources of power in the society.

Liberalism's adherents are not unaware of the costs of placing such paramount emphasis upon established methods and procedures. They acknowledge the three major points that are often made in criticism of its procedural fetish: (1) the established procedures did not spring full-blown from either a divine or a neutral source: they were created by powerful men who were satisfied with their achievements (and probably concerned to defend them). Therefore, they permit only such behavior and types of change as those men were willing to allow and did not see as a threat to their positions and possessions. (2) The social and economic realities that lie behind the laws and procedures of any nation at any given time do not represent an ideal world, but rather a particular structure of advantages for some and hardships for others. Some people may justifiably consider this situation reprehensible and desperately in need of change. Following the established procedures, assuming they permit the desired change at all, will mean delay and incomplete attainment of goals. (3) Established laws and procedures must be enforced only through the acts of policemen, prosecutors, judges, and other public officials. Since public officials are charged with the duty of making judgments, their selfish interests and perspectives on ethics are likely to reflect the more advantaged segments of the population and, thus, favor the status quo. A decision of a court, then, may be tainted by the preferences of the person who made it—neither a neutral product embodying justice nor a solution designed to be responsive to the problem.

Liberals are aware of all these facts but, nevertheless, place their faith in the established methods and procedures, particularly, in the machinery of the law. This is not because the legal method is foolproof or really mechanical (indeed, official violation of procedures is recognized as perfectly possible), but *because there is no better way. Any other method* of resolving disputes raises the prospect of the assertion of one brand of morality upon other people, or the use of power on behalf of a cause or a goal essentially self-selected by those who happen to hold the power. Because there is no way to choose who is right or whose solution is best, the only way to solve the dilemma of action is to accept whatever emerges from a recognizable and agreed set of procedures. The citizen may not like a law, but he ought to obey it until it is changed through the regular procedure. To ignore the established procedure is to raise the prospect that others will do the same—in which case the next prospect is the mutual use of force to achieve goals. Presumably, the side that first mobilized the overpowering force would be victorious. The fabric of civilized society is very fragile, and every effort must be made to keep conflicts within the framework where they can be dealt with without causing upheaval.

This condemnation of nonofficial violence is made with particular vigor in an unusually blunt little book by former Supreme Court Justice Abe Fortas.

> Violence is never defensible—and it has never succeeded in securing massive reform in an open society where there were alternative methods of winning the minds of others to one's cause and securing changes in the government or its policies. In the United States, these avenues are certainly available. Our history, and specifically the remarkable story of the present social revolution show that the alternatives of organization and protest . . . are open and effective. They may be long processes. They may be difficult. But they can produce lasting results.[22]

Not only is violence undesirable from the point of view of the system and of the change-seekers themselves, but it also poses the threat of reaction:

> This sort of assault is ultimately counterproductive. It polarizes society, and in any polarization, the minority group, although it may achieve initial, limited success, is likely to meet bitter reprisal and rejection of its demands.[23]

Liberalism also sees the established procedures as already providing a potentially incendiary level of individual freedoms and opportunity to seek change in established policies. Exercises of free speech and dissent frequently create highly volatile situations, even

---

[22] Fortas, *op. cit.*, pp. 76–77.
[23] *Ibid.*, p. 62.

riots. Defense of this set of opportunities provides liberalism with a further justification for requiring efforts toward change to conform to the prescribed limits. Freedom of speech, press, assembly, and the right to vote are regularly celebrated as providing ample chance for minorities to become majorities or to mobilize sufficient support to cause changes in public policies. Indeed, much of the energy of liberals is expended in defending these opportunities against those who would entirely prevent any efforts to change the status quo. Thus, liberalism sees itself as holding firm to a middle path that succeeds in maintaining an open political process against attacks from both left and right.

A second dimension of liberalism's response is an affirmative counterattack based on the inherent superiority of middle-line solutions. Neither left nor right extremes, but a popularly grounded, problem-sensitive middle course offers a realistic means of achieving the multiple goals of Americans. In one sense, extremists share the same oversimplified view of politics. Schlesinger says,

> the New Left and, less clearly, the New Right share a common view: that is, that the American democratic process is corrupt and phony, that it cannot identify or solve the urgent problems and that American society as at present organized is inherently incapable of providing justice. . . . the New Left and the New Right are agreed in their condemnation of the central institutions of American power, whether real (the national government), semimythical (the Establishment) or mythical (the power elite). However much they detest each other, the two extremisms have common methods and common targets. . . . For all their vast differences in values and objectives they end as tacit partners in a common assault on civility and democracy.[24]

But liberalism (here, the "New Politics") understands the existing system, and knows how to make it produce the greatest good for the greatest number. Again, Schlesinger tells why the middle path is superior:

> The New Politics acknowledges the existence and urgency of the questions that fill the extremists with apoc-

---

[24] Schlesinger, *op. cit.,* pp. 250–251.

alyptic despair. But it believes that these questions can be met and resolved by democratic means. . . . No one should ignore the fundamental difference between, on the one hand, the determination to master and use the existing political system and, on the other, the determination to reject and overthrow that system. A test question would be whether the Vietnam War is seen as the result of particular decisions taken by particular men in a situation where other men might have taken other decisions; or whether it is seen as the predetermined expression of an evil system that would have imposed an imperialistic policy on whatever body of men sat in the councils of state.[25]

Thus, drawing on both dimensions of response, liberalism, in essence, says that it has *not* merely elevated form over substance or been more concerned with *how* things are done than about *what* is done. Instead, it has found a way to tread the very delicate line between stability and change; it achieves all that can be done on behalf of the deprived of the society while retaining the consent of a substantial majority and avoiding serious, perhaps fatal, conflict. The merits of the problem receive every possible consideration, and action taken to solve such problems is all that can be done in the context of the situation and given the real risks involved. To some, the costs of adhering to established procedures may be particularly salient and the costs of failing to do so less obvious. But failure to understand the crucial importance of recognized and neutral (liberal) standards raises the prospects of the most drastic costs possible to civilized society.

A primary source of support for liberalism's unwillingness to violate its own standards even in an intensely pressured situation comes from its image of the social and economic worlds as distinct and not really a proper subject for political action. Although conditions of life are not ideal or even tolerable for many people, and a relative few hold most of the resources and benefits available, such conditions are the product of private activities over time. Imperfect as they are, they represent individual striving under conditions that are freer and less coercive than would be the case if government tried to specify exactly what the results of social and economic activity

---

[25] *Ibid.,* pp. 251–252.

should be. Thus, liberalism takes existing social and economic patterns as established and hopes to make marginal improvements that will steadily expand equality in all its dimensions. The operative principle is to permit all to join and enjoy, rather than to seek to reconstruct, the basic economic and social order in the United States. Liberalism insists that this is more practical, humane, and just than any other approach to politics today.

Liberalism thus deemphasizes the role of politics as a means of redressing grievances and attaining ethically superior ends; it stresses instead the primacy of private economic life and individual striving. In so doing, it takes direct issue with the developing emphasis among its challengers upon community. As we shall see, all of liberalism's challengers adhere to some version of community, either in the sense of rejecting the individualism and self-interest emphases of capitalism-liberalism as outmoded or, in a more affirmative commitment, to cooperation, sharing, and mutual assistance among men. Self-interest and profit motivation and a system built to serve such ends do not command the loyalty of adherents of the challenging ideologies. Procedures, pragmatism, and realism are not important to them; they hold instead to more idealistic, humanistic, and fraternal visions of what life could be like. They see men not as atomized, self-seeking units, but as mutually supporting and fully participating members of a larger universe, capable of creative development in many dimensions besides material achievement. This contrast lies at the heart of the split between the mainstream ideologies of capitalism and liberalism and all the others. The latter display great diversity, of course, but they are united in their rejection of what they see as the incapability of capitalism-liberalism to embody moral aspirations for an uplifting social life. We shall now move to an analysis of the change-seeking ideologies.

Annotated Bibliography

Dahl, Robert A. *Pluralist Democracy in the United States: Conflict and Consensus.* Chicago: Rand McNally, 1967. An extended essay developing and applying the pluralist image to American national politics.

Fortas, Abe. *Concerning Dissent and Civil Disobedience.* New York: Signet, 1968. A brief and forceful defense of liberal procedures from a legal perspective.

Girvetz, Harry K. *The Evolution of Liberalism.* New York: Collier Books, 1963. An authoritative historical analysis, with suggestions for future liberal policies and practices.

Kennan, George F. *Realities of American Foreign Policy.* Princeton, N.J.: Princeton University Press, 1954. A good short statement of the role of national interest and realism in foreign policy.

Kennedy, John F. *The Strategy of Peace.* New York: Harper & Bros., 1960. The proper stance for liberalism in foreign policy.

Kerr, Clark. *The Uses of the University.* New York: Harper & Row, 1966. A good statement of the integration between the state and education that results in the liberal state.

Lerner, Max. *America as a Civilization.* New York: Simon and Schuster, 1957. A two-volume celebration of the achievements of liberalism.

McCarthy, Eugene J. *A Liberal Answer to the Conservative Challenge.* New York: MacFadden, 1964. A response to the individualist-conservatives, setting forth the merits of liberalism and progress.

Moynihan, Daniel P. *Maximum Feasible Misunderstanding.* New York: Free Press, 1968. A liberal's critique of those who would create conflict by seeking to force change in established structures.

Roosevelt, James (ed.) *The Liberal Papers.* Garden City, N.Y.: Doubleday Anchor Books, 1962. Standard collection.

Schlesinger, Arthur M. Jr. *The Crisis of Confidence: Ideas, Power and Violence in America.* Boston: Houghton Mifflin, 1969. Staunch defense of liberal principles against the challenges of the late 1960s and 1970s.

4

Reform Liberalism

Reform movements have regularly been generated by specific problems or needs felt by segments of the American population. In many cases, such as the granger, populist, progressive, labor, and civil rights movements, they have been partially successful in gaining their policy goals. To a lesser extent, they have also affected the dominant ideologies. For the most part, however, such movements have been blunted by being thus partially incorporated (or "coopted") by liberalism's flexible style. Nevertheless, beliefs in the need for reform within the general framework of established ideas and practices are an enduring strand of American ideology.

We use the category "reform liberalism" to encompass contemporary versions of reform ideology. Today's reformers are set apart from capitalist-liberals chiefly by matters of degree, but these differences are quite capable of generating tensions between them. Reform liberal beliefs are *liberal* in their base, because they are rooted in individualism, civil liberties, faith in the reason and capacity of all men, perception of a pluralist political process in the United States, and acceptance of continuing unresolved tension between the values of equality and property. They are *reformist* in character, because they seek the realization (or modest change) of long established values, and by means which accept the procedures and affirm the validity of the established political process. The distinctions from orthodox liberalism are visible in the reform liberal conviction that politics can be purposeful—it can be the means toward societal solution of shared problems and attainment of qualitatively different and more important ends than those sought by liberalism. Reform liberalism also is distinguished by the beginnings of shifts in the priorities assigned to familiar liberal values, and the beginning of an analysis which finds the causes of problems in the character of the political system itself.

Reform liberalism is perhaps best characterized by an acute concern for contemporary social problems—poverty, war, racism, deterioration of the physical and natural environment—coupled with the conviction that the established ideologies cannot or will not cope with them adequately. Reform liberalism also is impatient with what it sees as patchwork solutions tardily arrived at by current capitalist-liberal methods—"solutions" that succeed only in perpetuating those features of the status quo that helped create the problems in the first place. It holds that capitalism-liberalism are not really living up to the generally sound values which they espouse, and that the selfishness or obtuseness of leaders has blocked the generally responsive and adequate political system from taking actions of the necessary kind. *Revitalization of the basic values* (with some changes in emphasis) and *reopening of the political processes* (with some modernizing improvements) are thus the keys to reform.

Reform liberalism is particularly critical of what it sees as capitalism's and liberalism's complacent, business-as-usual approach to problems. Over time, it has thus developed a continuing tension with these dominant ideologies: it complements them, as it strains to improve them. The resulting conflict-ridden but mutually sustaining relationship reveals much about the real priorities and limits of all three ideologies, and reform liberalism represents one of the major directions in which capitalism and liberalism may evolve. We will examine the distinguishing features of reform liberalism in each of our three categories of analysis, and look at one major reform liberal ideology—democratic socialism—in integrated fashion. Finally, we will briefly explore the sometimes acute dilemma of ideologies that are critical of many of the consequences of capitalism and liberalism, but nevertheless act entirely within their framework and on the basis of the same values.

World View

(1) THE CONTEMPORARY ECONOMIC ORDER

Reform liberalism sees a highly technological economy of super-corporations, with government as a kind of junior partner assigned the task of stabilizing, promoting growth, and ameliorating the most severe hardships suffered by individuals. It accepts American capitalism, at least in this form, as basically desirable or in any event permanent. But it is not content with what it sees as an excessive private capacity to maximize profits or otherwise employ corporate power at the cost of public needs and convenience. Nor is it acquiescent in the present balance of initiative in private hands, which it sees as producing chaotic consequences for economic growth, equitable distribution of income, and the quality of life in the nation.

Contemporary capitalism tends to celebrate Keynesian welfare capitalist and government economy-managing achievements, but reform liberalism sees a misapplication of Keynesian principles which has the effect of serving the wrong values and/or creating danger of depression. A new, post-industrial economy is envisioned—one in which highly complex and technological industrial giants must manage their markets and shape the society to their needs. They require from government the absorption of risks, assurance of stability and predictability, promotion of growth, and maintenance of demand; these needs make it imperative for such industries to convert government into the agent of the productive enterprises and not of popular goals and needs. Two major consequences follow.

(a) Some see this corporate domination of government as bringing with it a *redistribution of power*. In *The New Industrial State*,[1] for example, Galbraith argues that power has really drifted into the hands of the experts within the industrial economy, the "technostructure." Neither stockholders, owners, nor top managers —and certainly not legislators—can exercise control over the technostructure. By virtue of their skills, they cannot be controlled externally; the motive forces for the economy and society thus stem from the values which they hold uppermost. Galbraith sees their basic

---

[1] John Kenneth Galbraith, *The New Industrial State* (Boston: Houghton Mifflin, 1968).

goals as autonomy and assured earnings. To assure attainment of these individual goals, the corporate economy must be successful. This, in turn, requires that societal goals be increased production, a higher standard of living, technological progress, and economic growth.

(b) Others see the abundant productivity of the new economy as creating *unprecedented new problems*. Despite great abundance, there are fewer and fewer jobs, a shortage of demand, and unjust patterns of distribution. The abundance that could be shared widely is not really shared at all. To make matters worse, government's frantic effort to maintain full employment by promoting growth only postpones the day when Keynesians will finally face the fact of abundance. Robert Theobald, for example, argues that Keynes himself saw that when the stage of abundance was reached, societies would have to change their values and adjust distribution to principles of equity and justice. He quotes and endorses Keynes as follows:

> When the accumulation of wealth is no longer of high social importance, there will be great changes in the code of morals. We shall be able to rid ourselves of many of the pseudo-moral principles which have hag-ridden us for two hundred years, by which we have exalted some of the most distasteful of human qualities into the position of the highest values. We shall be able to dare to assess the money-motive at its true value. . . . All kinds of social customs and economic practices affecting the distribution of wealth which we now maintain at all costs, however distasteful and unjust they may be in themselves . . . we shall then be free, at last, to discard.[2]

The dangers that Theobald foresees are (1) increased unemployment because of automation and cybernation and (2) government efforts to promote full employment that merely reemphasize private consumption, chain men to meaningless jobs, and ignore public needs. He summarizes his analysis in these words:

---

[2] Robert Theobald, "Policy Formation for New Goals," in Robert Theobald, ed., *Social Policies for America in the Seventies* (New York: Doubleday, 1968), p. 165. (Quoted from T. M. Keynes, *Essays on Persuasion* [New York: Harcourt Brace, 1936], pp. 369–70.)

We saw that although there were major unfulfilled public needs, these would not be met unless changes in the socio-economic system took place. In addition, we saw that continuation of the drive for the maximum rate of economic growth would be not only ineffective in meeting our goals but also increasingly destructive of Western values, for it would not avoid a rising rate of unemployment, and would not even succeed in averting a worldwide slump.[3]

Reform liberalism thus sees and condemns an ongoing process of adapting men to the needs of the productive mechanism in the society, rather than vice versa. Public needs are not being served, even though the economy could do so with ease if it were properly organized. Unnecessary unemployment and economic hardships are being experienced. The basic causes are unperceived changes in the character of the economy, outdated ideas about the proper relation of government to the economy, and faulty premises about how man's true needs can best be served.

(2) THE DOMESTIC POLITICAL PROCESS

Reform liberalism sees the American political process as essentially pluralist in character, that is, many groups exist and through aggressive and sophisticated efforts, all can make themselves heard under conditions of fairness. Elections offer further opportunities for participation and impact on the direction of government policies. But reform liberalism also sees an increasingly complex society developing bureaucracies, technical expertise, and other unresponsive accumulations of power that insulate official decision-making from popular preferences. Although most stop short of explicit class conflict analyses, reform liberals do see unequal distributions of political power and uncontrolled powerholders (chairmen of Congressional committees, old political party leaders) sitting astride the channels that are assumed to be the means of communicating popular wants to officeholders. If these obstacles were removed, however, the political system would be sufficiently responsive to achieve their goals. The failure of capitalist ideology to provide for socially responsible plan-

---

[3] Robert Theobald, *Free Men and Free Markets* (New York: Doubleday, 1963), p. 111.

ning and goal setting through government action and the blockages that exist in the liberal political system mean that the nation is incapable of coping either adequately or democratically with its problems. These problems are so severe that failure to take remedial action that will reach their causes (and not just their superficial symptoms, such as riots or poverty) may threaten the stability and even the continuity of the American polity. No current program is sufficiently drastic, innovative, or on the massive scale necessary to solve these problems. Today's policies are hopelessly trapped in the assumptions, precedents, and self-imposed limitations of the increasingly irrelevant past.

Reform liberalism sees liberalism as experiencing a hardening of the arteries as the result of excessive time in power. This is visible in many ways. One is a kind of super-realism, in which the moral dimension is excised from politics and officials become capable of legitimating practically anything they desire in the name of efficiency or realism. Citizens are urged to be quiescent and to trust in the wisdom of the experts—in short, to see politics as the art of the possible, rather than as an arena of hope and aspiration. Reform liberalism challenges current images of democracy in particular, arguing that democracy has been redefined to fit whatever empirical studies of politics find to exist in the United States. Too little emphasis is placed on citizen participation, on what might be possible through enlightened leadership, and on the growth of individuals through sharing in power. Too little real concern is felt for the reality of the civil liberties that lie at the center of the democratic political process. And, most serious of all, too little attention is paid to citizens' demands for change; entrenched liberal elites delay, deflect, and ultimately deny opportunities for change in the status quo.

In many cases, reform liberalism joins battle with liberalism over specific policy questions. What separates the two ideologies is often the *depth of analysis of causation* employed, and sometimes the timetable for solution. Liberalism sees unfortunate situations requiring cure but attributes them to the poor judgment of men in office or to the multitude of problems they face and the other legitimate needs they must serve, and it will do the best it can as soon as practical to solve the problem. Reform liberalism sees crucial social problems of such importance as to challenge the sincerity of one's claim to believe in equality or other human values and attributes such prob-

lems to *more systematic causes* such as regular patterns of recruit-
ment of men into office, shared ideology among officeholders, or the
economic interests of decision-makers. The solution of these problems is an immediate necessity, even if it means loss of other desirable goals or the production of political tensions. Except under the
most extreme conditions of official obstinacy or willful disregard for
established procedures, however, reform liberalism does *not* endorse
illegal actions. It believes in a full use of all the major civil liberties,
broadly defined, but stops short of resort to other forms of pressure
for action.

(3) THE INTERNATIONAL SCENE

Reform liberalism sees liberalism as obsessed with anticommunism, and as hopelessly outdated in its perceptions of the nature and
varieties of communism in the world. For these reasons, the United
States is committed to a disastrous, counterrevolutionary posture in
the world that constitutes a severe danger to world peace. Where
liberalism sees unity in the Communist world, reform liberalism sees
diversity; where liberalism suspects Communist inspiration behind
local insurgencies, reform liberalism sees nationalism rooted in social
injustice; and where liberalism seeks to promote capitalism and
stability, reform liberalism seeks economic viability and popular self-
determination.

Again, reform liberalism's assignment of causes for American
difficulties in international affairs is more systematic and somewhat
deeper than liberalism's, but it does not reach to the level of basic
values or economic imperatives. One major critique of American
policy toward the Third World, for example, attributes U.S. policy
to an ideology shared among "National Security Managers." [4] This
ideology holds that the United States has a duty to suppress revolutions wherever they occur on behalf of peace and stability in the
world; according to this analysis, "the prevailing official view is that
there is no way for a great country to relate to a small one other than
as manipulator or exploiter." [5] Thus, the United States pursues an

---

[4] Richard J. Barnet, *Intervention and Revolution: America's Confrontation with Insurgent Movements Around the World* (New York: New American Library, 1968).

[5] *Ibid.,* p. 262.

undesirable policy because its policy makers have faulty perceptions of the world around them. By implication, replacement of such men would make for a clearer view and a more flexible policy.

A similar kind of analysis distinguishes reform liberalism's attitude toward military expenditures in the United States. The armed forces and their allies in industry are seen as having usurped initiative and control from Congress and other popularly responsive institutions, in effect constituting themselves into a military-industrial complex in which the balance of initiative lies with the military. Their self-maintenance needs, together with the liberal emphases on anticommunism and patriotism, have caused them to exceed their proper bounds—aided of course by the eagerness of businessmen and Congressmen to secure the contracts to build their expensive weapons. But there is nothing fixed or inevitable about this predominance, and either Congress or the people are capable of recapturing control over the defense establishment at will.

Thus, the superrealism with which reform liberalism charges liberalism is evident in both domestic and international policies and practices. Operating exclusively in terms of national interest standards and obsessed with the need for security against real and imagined dangers, liberalism has abandoned the moral dimension in politics completely. Reform liberalism insists that politics cannot and should not be amoral, that there are bounds beyond which no government can go without vitiating its claim to integrity and democracy. Repeated incidents of espionage, duplicity, and subversive activity with regard to other nations serve to escalate the tensions between the reform liberal and the liberal position in international affairs. Reform liberalism is neither naive nor ignorant about communism; it simply sees both a greater necessity and a livelier prospect of being able to practice peaceful coexistence.

Values and Goals

VALUES

Reform liberalism essentially endorses the basic values of capitalism and liberalism, but it reserves the right to modernize them and perhaps to adjust the order of priority in which they are held. Impatience with patchwork solutions contributes to this questioning, both about the sincerity of capitalist-liberal commitments and about the order in which they should be ranked. First, reform liberalism questions the sincerity of the capitalist-liberal commitment to equality in the sense of both broad sharing of power and broad distribution of wealth. It asks whether liberalism means what it says about political equality when the one-man, one-vote principle encounters so much delay, political parties are run from the top down, the Congress is controlled by committee chairmen and the seniority system, and effective citizen participation is short-circuited. It asks whether capitalism is honest in its stated goal of widespread distribution when wealth remains tightly concentrated among the top one or two percent of the population and millions live in poverty. For most reform liberals, it would be enough if capitalism and liberalism were to live up to their oft-stated values, and if the system could be made to work for all.

Second, however, reform liberalism tends to put forward an alternative priority ranking among the basic capitalist-liberal values. Equality is raised to share the top position with property rights, or even to have primacy over property rights. In the "human rights" sense, equality is defined in terms of the actual social and economic circumstances of peoples' lives, not just in terms of the right to take part in public affairs or the opportunity to compete in the economy. Two other differences in value rankings or definition are closely associated with this development. (1) Reform liberalism is no less individually oriented than capitalism-liberalism, but it emphasizes the moral, humanistic, and qualitative dimensions of individual achievements and circumstances rather than the more strictly material side. Concern for the ecology, aesthetic amenities, and public facilities that make individuals' lives enjoyable wins out over concern for the individual's possession of tangible goods in excess of those that are necessary for satisfaction of his needs. (2) Reform liberalism is committed to the established rules and legal procedures of politics, and particularly to democratic civil liberties, but it does not overlook the importance of the substance of what is done through these processes. Indeed, just because reform liberalism looks so carefully at the content of the policies produced and compares them with the depth and urgency it sees in the problems that exist, it has become impatient with the current value priorities and the slow and uncertain style of capitalism-liberalism.

The net result of these changes in the priority ranking and/or definition of well-established liberal values is to reduce the harshness of the capitalist-liberal emphasis on competition, effort, and privately generated solutions to problems of societal use of resources. In its place, there emerges a stronger emphasis on communitarian action to solve shared problems, and particularly a more legitimate role for government as the conscious agent of popular will. Two other values begin for the first time to compete for high position in this context. One is the social side of the value of freedom: in the past, it had been assumed that freedom meant the opportunity to gain individual goals, particularly the possession of property that would permit one to be independent, and thus was linked closely to capitalism. Reform liberalism speculates that a more qualitative understanding of freedom would hold that it is not complete unless a multitude of aesthetic and humanistic opportunities are actually available and that they can only be made available through a conscious social use of government to provide them. The other is an increasingly internationalist view of the problems and obligations of the American economy. Capitalism and liberalism assume the nation as the unit, with the external world important chiefly for purposes of resources and trade; they also place a high value on nationalism, patriotism, and integration into a single national community. Reform liberalism, on the other hand, tends to see the American economy as interdependent with that of the rest of the world, to take on a larger share of moral responsibility for other nations' economic circumstances, and to give a lower priority to protecting American security through military power, militant anticommunism, and intervention.

GOALS

The goals of reform liberalism move beyond liberalism's hopes for steady extension of existing benefits to wider and wider populations. Where an ideology develops a world view that stresses the social problems of the present, it is likely to speculate also on innovative ways of solving them. Reform liberalism is committed to significant enlargement of the public sector (schools, housing, recreation facilities, transportation, etc.), as well as to gaining control over the military-industrial complex and restructuring foreign policy. But its goals extend farther, to a qualitatively different set of aspirations. The proper goals are, in Galbraith's words, "those that serve not the production of goods but the intellectual and artistic development of man." [6] A meaningful leisure and a socially determined rate and process of development are other reform liberal goals; they should replace the work ethic and the chaotic and essentially regressive manner in which the economy now evolves.

For a time, one of the major goals of reform liberalism was a constitutionally guaranteed individual right to an income sufficient to provide an acceptable standard of living. This proposal was geared not to replacement of the welfare system, but to the need to replace the work ethic, distribute surplus, and enable new and more humanistic activities to develop and it was forcefully advocated by Robert Theobald in a series of books. He saw it as a remedy for the loss of jobs as the result of cybernation, a means of setting new values in the society, and releasing man from economic bondage. Individuals would be freer and, because purchasing power would be better spread among the population, the economic market would also work better. In Theobald's words:

> The only way of preserving both free men and free markets is to recognize that the economic system needs to divorce the productive function from the distributive function and therefore allow each to work in a way which will be of maximum benefit to society. . . . Once the obligation to provide market-supported jobs for all was lifted, the frantic search for ways to stimulate sales and thus employ surplus productive capacity would no longer be necessary. The level of production could then be determined by desired levels of consumption, rather than consumption being forced by the existence of unused productive capacity. We would, therefore, have the power to determine economic policy on the basis of our social goals rather than continuing to be forced into social actions because of what are, at present, economic necessities.[7]

---

[6] Galbraith, *op. cit.*, p. 376.
[7] Theobald, *Free Men*, p. 132.

What is distinctive here is the desire to reshape values through policies that qualitatively differ from those that now exist. The ultimate goal is not incompatible with liberalism; indeed, the kind of life envisioned by reform liberals might very well be endorsed by liberalism. But the interim goals and the innovations in policy that are characteristic of reform liberalism indicate a bolder, more imaginative, and less constrained approach to reaching the good life.

Another characteristic goal of reform liberals that illustrates the qualitative difference from liberalism is the firm insistence upon reviving the moral and uplifting dimensions of politics. Officials and citizens alike should realize that politics cannot be amoral, for one's morals inevitably enter his perceptions and judgments in many ways; they shape what he sees, his self-interests, his commitments, and his ideology. Nor *should* politics be amoral: political actions are never neutral, and criteria of citizen judgment should include explicit examination of the moral quality of government action. Not to do so results in such morally vicious acts as the Vietnam war. But the realization that politics is a real route toward noble ends should be simultaneous with the reintroduction of morality. Through understanding and extension of the traditional civil liberties, substantial accomplishments on behalf of the underprivileged are possible; many vital gains have been recorded in the United States through effective struggle in the past. Arnold Kaufman's *The Radical Liberal* shows the mixture of realism and hope that characterizes reform liberalism in addressing this very point:

> What has been won is due to the genius with which America's powerful and privileged elites have, since the Civil War, been able to buy off discontent through peripheral remedy of grievances. Yet enough peripheral movement equals substantial social change.[8]

What is required, according to Kaufman, is recognition of the importance of the goals available through existing political processes, and that many "half-loaves" add up to more than a whole loaf. With the return of morality and idealism, the rejuvenation of the political system may be possible in short order.

---

[8] Arnold Kaufman, *The Radical Liberal* (New York: Atherton Press, 1968), p. 53.

Social Change and Tactics

The impatience that reform liberalism feels for capitalist-liberal capacity to deal with today's acute problems does *not* carry it outside the established rules and procedures. Essentially, the reform liberal position is that if (a) the selfish or obstinate individuals located in key positions of power could be replaced by better men, *and* (b) the people could be alerted to the dangers that face them, either directly or through the wise actions of such new leaders—the political system would be capable of solving all existing problems. Reform liberals envision a larger role for government in the immediate future: they see it as setting new and better goals, involving greater economic planning, rationalizing popular wants with productive capacity, and drastically redirecting resources toward problems of race, poverty, the cities, etc. But they see such changes coming about through the existing political mechanisms, principally by means of rational education and persuasion of the general public and its informed action to install and support new leaders through the elective process.

Reform liberalism is aware that the sweeping nature and drastic scope of the changes called for imply difficulty in attainment. It recognizes that established powerholders are not likely to be enthusiastic about such changes, particularly when they mean the reduction of existing privileges and a new role for government in the society. Nor is the task of persuading the public, and then of enabling that public to find and electorally install the right kinds of new leaders, expected to be an easy one. But reform liberals persevere in such methods despite the prospect of long delays, in part, because they see no better route. Violence, under some circumstances, does speed up the process of change, but it carries grave risks of counterviolence and chaos. Besides, democratic civil liberties hold such a high place among the values of reform liberalism that no other path seems valid.

In short, when it comes to the process of change, reform liberals are very much like liberals: they endorse the established procedures because they fear the alternative. They seek to persuade those leaders who are amenable to their views and research findings. They call for greater popular participation, such as in new political parties and interest groups, as one means of reducing the influence of obstinate present leaders. They stoutly defend the liberties of free speech, press, and assembly that contribute to making change possible. And they fear that prescriptions for change that involve non-liberal tactics or go outside the established procedures may lead to worse conditions than now exist—so they operate sincerely and consistently within the rules and practices of liberalism.

To some extent, the process of change envisioned by reform liberals may be a product of their conviction that mass-based change movements are either unlikely to develop or undesirable. Or perhaps reform liberalism merely exaggerates liberalism's faith in rationality and persuasion. But it is clear that reform liberalism places its confidence in a process of change that is rooted in education and the universities and is essentially elite-focused. In some cases, this reliance is explicit. In others, there is a kind of "necessity will provide" emphasis which seems to lead in the same direction.

The process of change envisioned by Galbraith, for example, is entirely dependent on the intervention of a new set of values through the vehicle of the technostructure and "the educational and scientific estate." The latter, as the supplier of the productive agent for the economy, is a vital source of power and potentially the key to the society's future values and purposes. It is the new agent of change:

> As the trade unions retreat, more or less permanently, into the shadows, a rapidly growing body of educators and research scientists emerges. This group connects at the edges with scientists and engineers within the technostructure, and with civil servants, journalists, writers and artists outside. Most directly nurtured by the industrial system are the educators and scientists in the schools, colleges, universities and research institutions. They stand in relation to the industrial system much as did the banking and financial community to the earlier stages of industrial development. . . . In the mature corporation, the decisive factor of production, as we have seen, is the supply of qualified talent. A similar complex of educational institutions has similarly come into being to supply this need.[9]

---

[9] Galbraith, *op. cit.*, p. 282.

The colleges and universities are under strong influence from the industrial system to merely celebrate its achievements and serve its needs ("One is led to inquire whether education remains education when it is chained too tightly to the wheel of the industrial system"),[10] but potential leaders can learn new values and goals there. Individuals must simply "opt out" of existing values and frames of reference. The new values can then be communicated by the mass media and through the political activity of the new educational and scientific elite. Once the determination exists, the channels may be found or made and the political system redirected and revived to serve the new goals.

Other specifications about change sound more mass-based and democratic, at least initially. Some call for a combination of particular interest groups, a coalition built around specific goals and operated under specified principles. This is essentially an effort to use the pluralist framework and extract maximum rewards from that effort, apparently on the ground that no other tactics are really effective. In *The Radical Liberal,* for example, Kaufman calls for:

> A new politics of radical pressure that synthesizes in mutually reinforcing ways welfare politics, coalition politics, and participatory democracy—a politics of radical pressure which operates on the principle that when one of these three vital constituents of a total liberal strategy is formally absent or defective, everything, short of rebellion, required to provide informal substitutes for them ought to be done—but done *effectively.* . . . Morally and politically, the development of a more deliberative process of coalition politics, the growth of participatory institutions, and the completion of the welfare state are concomitant enterprises—none more important from a theoretical point of view than any of the others, all three absolutely indispensable conditions of a good American society.[11]

The coalition would be held together by policy commitments such as compensation for blacks, support for the black power movement, higher education for all in universities converted into bastions of social criticism, and morality in foreign policy.

---

[10] *Ibid.,* p. 322.
[11] Kaufman, *op. cit.,* pp. 72–73.

Less specific but similar images of the process of change are those that assume public belief systems can be changed through rational persuasion by the more alert and educated individuals. Somewhere, somehow, some individuals must free themselves from existing values and attitudes and then proceed to do the same for others. But political movements built from masses of the citizenry are not the preferred vehicle. Robert Theobald showed exactly this conflict when he first emphasized that "the critical problem of our time is that of powerlessness" on the part of "the poor, the aged, students, the Negro, those in poor countries;"[12] but he goes on to disclaim intent to transfer power to such people, arguing instead for an elimination of power and its replacement by willing consent on the part of all. It may be that, pragmatically, he merely seeks time in which to reshape values through particular policies (such as his guaranteed annual wage) which may be justified on other grounds:

> Proposals that fail to appear conservative of existing values have no opportunity of success, and proposals that will not be trail-blazing have no relevance. The task is to discover those measures that appear conservative and will be trail-blazing.[13]

What seems to be emerging here is not so much political inexperience as an affirmative judgment that the best route to desired ends is through converting policy makers and other powerholders to the new values and priorities. Whether that "best" is due to the practical difficulties in promptly mobilizing masses or to a feeling that this would be dangerous or undesirable on other grounds is not clear. Perhaps it is a natural outgrowth of the fact that reform liberalism principles are espoused chiefly by middle-class intellectuals. But it does call into question reform liberalism's expressed concern for greater participation, and raises the question of whom the more open political processes that are desired are intended to serve, and it reinforces the impression of reform liberalism as a "within the system" ideology.

---

[12] Theobald, "Policy Formation," p. 163.
[13] *Ibid.,* p. 158.

Comprehensive Reform Liberalism: Democratic Socialism

So far, we have analyzed reform liberalism as a generic term encompassing several slightly different strands of political thinking. In doing so, we deliberately ran the risk of falsely implying that ideologies in this category were fragmented or unintegrated in order to emphasize their similarities and differences with their principal target, liberalism. We shall now analyze one reform liberal ideology, democratic socialism, as an integrated set of beliefs presenting a comprehensive program.

Democratic socialism synthesizes and modestly extends many of the principles we have just noted, but never goes beyond the boundaries of reform liberalism in any significant regard. It accepts the contemporary welfare state as a point of departure for gradual progress toward full popular control of the economy. It places its highest priority on equality and the established civil liberties and rejects all tactics not consistent with liberalism's democratic procedures, visualizing the American political process as offering ample opportunity for persuasion and successful change through electoral means.

WORLD VIEW

Democratic socialism sees the United States of the late twentieth century as characterized by ferment, conflict, innovation, violence, a measure of madness—but nevertheless at a point where significant gains are possible. A welfare state of sorts has been accomplished, and some milestones of individual liberty and material well-being can be identified. According to Irving Howe, editor of the journal *Dissent,* this is partly the product of previous struggles between classes:

> The welfare state is importantly the result of social struggle on the part of the labor movement. If the working class has not fulfilled the "historic tasks" assigned to it by Marxism and if it shows, at least in the advanced industrial countries, no sign of revolutionary initiative, it has nevertheless signifi-

cantly modified the nature and softened the cruelties of capitalist society.[14]

The achievements of the welfare state, according to democratic socialists, have been brought about by knowledgeable action on the part of coalitions of groups—each, in turn, pressing for its fair share of economic rewards available through the American system. The kind of political process envisioned is the familiar pluralist one, but the democratic socialists see no reason why such a process need be static. There is danger that dominant elites will be able to deflect thrusts from below, but such a result is far from certain. Democratic socialists deny that mass needs or wants have been satisfied and insist that the established framework can still be pressed to yield great additional returns for many people. Pressing for more through the system need not result in blunting or coopting (buying off through appearing to accept) such demands. The proper coalition, animated by the appropriate moral urgency, can achieve new waves of progress if people will be "realistic" about the means of getting from here to some desirable future point.

This opportunity is partly attributable to some internal contradictions in the current character of the welfare state. Rapid transformations and dislocations now characterize the American economy, as it shifts to a technological and automated basis. At present, the transformation of the economy (and hence the society) is proceeding in an unplanned, arbitrary, and chaotic fashion—with disastrous results for all but the few whose wealth enables them to protect themselves. New forms of large-scale organization are inevitable, and unimagined accumulations of economic power are being built. But this inevitable thrust toward change is also inherent in the character of the promises made by the welfare state. Commitments to eradicate poverty, for example, carry certain promises about the future, and contribute to expectations about what that future will be like. Because the political processes are essentially open, a demand thus raised will become a major factor in the ensuing political dynamic.

---

[14] Irving Howe, "Notes on the Welfare State," in Jeremy Larner and Irving Howe, eds., *Poverty: Views from the Left* (New York: Morrow, 1965), p. 293.

VALUES AND GOALS

The major operative value of democratic socialism is the preservation and enhancement of democratic civil liberties. There is a unity between democracy, understood in terms of such civil liberties, and socialism. Socialism, in the modern sense, involves popular control over the economy—and there are various means by which such control might be institutionalized. The achievement of socialism has nothing to do with totalitarianism or authoritarianism, but is rather the natural extension of the reality of democracy to all spheres of life. According to Irving Howe:

> To preserve democracy as a political mode without extending it into every crevice of social and economic life is to allow it to become increasingly sterile, formal, ceremonial. To nationalize an economy without enlarging democratic freedoms is to create a new kind of social exploitation. Radicals and liberals may properly and fraternally disagree about many things; but upon this single axiom concerning the value of democracy, this conviction wrung from the tragedy of our age, politics must rest.[15]

Observance of the civil liberties is thus the primary commitment of democratc socialism, because these rights are the means by which individuals may hope to secure their ends and, thus, are the key to social change. Within this framework, the secondary goal of popular control over the economy may be realistically anticipated.

Democratic socialists do not strongly emphasize the goal of nationalization of the economy. This is not because they do not hold such a goal as primary but because, in the American context, there are both better ways to phrase the goal and a perceived inevitability about arriving at nationalization or its equivalent if the commitments of the welfare state are seriously pursued. Democratic socialists see uncontrolled power flowing from aggregations of economic resources, together with serious consequences of actions occurring within the

---

[15] Irving Howe, "New Styles in 'Leftism,'" in *Steady Work: Essays in the Politics of Democratic Radicalism, 1953–1966* (New York: Harcourt Brace & World, 1966), p. 78.

private economy. Thus, the impulse to assert popular control through government may be seen as merely another application of democratic principles of participation and control over sources of power that threaten individual freedom. Furthermore, the end result of the promises implicit (and explicit) in the nature of the welfare state must inevitably involve such popular control over the economy. Anything short of such a relationship will amount to a denial of welfare state promises.

SOCIAL CHANGE AND TACTICS

The process of change envisioned by democratic socialism is a natural and evolutionary one. When the inherent or implicit dynamic of the welfare state's promises is combined with popular perception of the limitations and consequences of capitalism, democratic socialists believe that an irresistible force for change will be generated. Thus, the crucial task of democratic socialists is to link the acknowledged problems of the society to the imperatives and characteristics of capitalism, pointing out how different procedures and policies could lead to better results for most people. Any serious effort to eradicate poverty, for example, would eventually have to confront the reality of the poor's lack of skills in a technological economy. The amount of economic growth that would have to be promoted in order to create enough prosperity to assure jobs for the poor would require fundamental change in the relationship of government and economy; if it were successful, the number of newly employed poor might spur new labor organizing and give new impetus to a left-wing political coalition. As things stand, government efforts to stimulate growth are beneficial chiefly to the middle-class contractor or entrepreneur. Keynesianism, to democratic socialists, is increasingly conservative in character, actually creating a kind of social-industrial complex. But liberalism's patchwork efforts may readily be exposed as the illusory "solutions" they are.

The inevitability of popular recognition of the failures of capitalism is a central component of democratic socialist images of change. The future of political democracy itself is involved in the choice of how (or if) the new aggregates are to be controlled: the only future for democracy, according to Michael Harrington, lies in creating means whereby the people can manage the economy.

From the very beginning, the socialists knew that modern technology could not be made just by dividing it up into tiny parcels of individual ownership. It is of the very nature of that technology to be concentrated and collective. Therefore, the socialists assigned a new and radical meaning to democracy. The people's title to the social means of production would be guaranteed . . . through votes. The basic economic decisions would be made democratically.

In this context, the nationalization of industry is a technique of socialism, not its definition. It is one extremely important way of abolishing the political and social power that results from concentrated economic ownership. It also facilitates directing economic resources to the satisfaction of human needs.

. . . The one set and undeviating aspect of socialism is its commitment to making the democratic and free choice of citizens the principle of social and economic life.[16]

Democratic socialism thus holds an optimistic view of the capacity of unsatisfied groups to press the welfare state for delivery of its promises, ending ultimately with the transformation of that welfare state into socialism, defined as a truly integrated politicoeconomic democracy. But it does not fail to recognize that there are many obstacles, although it maintains that these are frequently exaggerated. It rejects the claim that the material benefits provided by the welfare state have so trapped people in acquiescence and material tranquility that there is no longer any serious popular desire for fundamental change. Individualism and humanism are too strong to permit acquiescence in either mass society or technological grounds for such conclusions; instead, democratic socialism argues that such theories are antihistorical and assume that, somehow, the movement of history has been arrested at this particular stage. To act in accordance with such a view, furthermore, is to impose self-limitations and create a self-fulfilling prophecy. The end of social transformation has not been reached, and the sincere radical must commit himself to the long-range task of the creation of a social structure that promotes and supports humane values.

---

[16] Michael Harrington, *The Accidental Century* (New York: Macmillan, 1965), pp. 278–279.

Despite some early intimations that socialist intellectuals should carry the burden of bringing understanding to the public and generating change in that manner, democratic socialists promptly came to the conclusion that the need for action was so pressing that socialists should form coalitions with other like-minded groups and get about the business of extending the welfare state as far as its flexibility would permit. In *The Accidental Century,* for example, Michael Harrington was not optimistic about finding political support among the poor or labor; instead, he envisioned a constructive minority of educated middle-class students and intellectuals—perhaps the core of a new political party. Three years later, however, in *Toward a Democratic Left,*[17] Harrington talked less of specifically socialist solutions and more of the need and opportunity to build a new, broadly based major party of the Left. To the core previously envisioned, he would add labor, the poor, and members of civil rights movements to construct a large coalition mobilized around the issue of controlling corporate power and ultimately questioning the myths of free enterprise. He anticipates that liberalism's inability to provide real solutions to the visible and pressing problems of the day will become increasingly obvious. He warns that the far left is equally unable to provide solutions: "A hazy apocalypse is no substitute for an inadequate liberalism." [18] The new majority coalition is both possible and necessary to see that the use of government to which we have reluctantly become accustomed is not diverted to the mere maintenance of the status quo or to the advantage of corporate enterprise. In particular, central public planning and widespread citizen participation at various stages of policymaking and implementation are proposed. Public choices about the rate and direction of economic development would be facilitated by a series of reports on current conditions in America and the alternative prospects for the future. These are beginning routes, it seems clear, to the ultimate restructuring of basic values to supplant materialist and acquisitive motivations by concern for the human and spiritual qualities of individuals—and thus to socialism. These goals can be effectuated by exerting mass-based political pressure through a revitalized

---

[17] Michael Harrington, *Toward a Democratic Left* (New York: Macmillan, 1968).

[18] *Ibid.,* p. 17.

majority party. The basic strategy remains one of forcing the welfare state to make its promises good.

Though we have sought to avoid repetition by emphasizing only the distinctive aspects of democratic socialism, it should be clear that it sees many of the same problems and adheres to the same values as the other reform liberal ideologies. It is somewhat more explicit in assigning capitalism the blame for many current social problems, and similarly about the need to bring the economy under popular control. The envisioned process of change appears to rest more firmly on mass-based action. But, like the other reform liberal ideologies, democratic socialism's complaints are limited to the charge of failure to live up to sound values and goals, and it perceives the established political process as essentially open and capable of delivering the new goals it seeks. The traditional civil liberties lie at the core of the good political process, and if they are scrupulously followed (as, for the most part, they are today), desired changes can be achieved. Thus, even though its goals include radical transformation of the economic system itself—as fundamental a change as may be contemplated in social life—democratic socialism envisions attaining such ends through the existing political framework. With such principles, it belongs squarely within the reform liberalism category, sharing both the strengths and the problems of those ideologies.

The Dilemma of Reform Liberalism

In many ways, reform liberalism makes severe criticisms of capitalism and liberalism. In the face of serious, society-splitting social problems, it charges, these ideologies make complacent assumptions about the benignity and efficiency of the American economy, the responsiveness of the political system to demands for change, and the sufficiency of current values and priorities. Reform liberalism sees instead a faltering economy, a stagnant political system with faulty policies, and outdated and excessively materialistic values dominating action. Without some sweeping changes, reform liberalism foresees drastic, perhaps ruinous, consequences for the United States. Because the industrial system now dominates the government and is forcing people to shape themselves into the kinds of beings needed for the benefit and perpetuation of that system, the only real prospect is a constantly accelerating worsening of the situation.

The kinds of goals contemplated are also substantial, even though they are presented in terms of a return to, or true realization of, the familiar values of liberalism. A different priority among those values is contemplated, with equality rising to unprecedented levels and other humanistic values receiving attention along with the more established material standards. Morality, idealism, and participation are to be revived. And many policies—most of which have been in effect for a sufficient number of years to have developed supportive constituencies from among those who benefit economically or otherwise from their provisions—are to be drastically reshaped.

The nature of the critique of capitalism and liberalism that reform liberalism makes and the kinds of goals it advocates suggest that by contrast with those ideologies, change will be dramatic— and difficult. But the *means of change* that reform liberalism sees as adequate to its needs are exclusively those of the established political system—the same procedures that, apparently, have given rise to the intolerable situation that reform liberalism now seeks to alter. This is the central dilemma of reform liberalism. Because it accepts so many of the premises and values of capitalism and liberalism, it is apparently forced to endorse also only limited means of achieving relatively marginal goals. Two examples may suggest dimensions of this dilemma. (1) Reform liberalism complains about the patchwork solutions of liberalism, alleging that the marginal changes possible within the capitalist-liberal framework succeed in treating some symptoms but perpetuate the real causes of problems. But all it really asks for are *many* such changes, on a wider front and on a more continuing basis, apparently in the belief that enough instances of such changes over a sufficiently sustained period of time will bring about the qualitative transformation that is sought. (2) Reform liberalism's conviction that the existing structure of civil liberties is complete, operative, democratic, and fully protective of the rights of all to bring about desired change holds it to only limited (and perhaps containable) types of efforts toward its goals. It cannot justify going outside the established procedures, both for reasons of principle and because it sees such acts as self-defeating.

These self-imposed limits in the scope of change sought and the means by which it is sought stand in rather sharp contrast to the critique made earlier and the description of current American problems presented. One example of such contrast may be seen in John Kenneth Galbraith's prescriptions for achieving control of the military-industrial complex. After detailing the scope of military dominance over the economy and specifically over Congress and the dangers associated with such conditions, Galbraith offers suggestions. He says:

> My instinct is for action within the political framework. This is not a formula for busy ineffectuality. . . . if sharply focused knowledge can be brought to bear on both weapons procurement and negotiations; if citizen attitudes can be kept politically effective by the conviction that this is the political issue of our times; if there is effective organization; if in consequence a couple hundred or even a hundred members of Congress can be kept in a vigilant, critical, and aroused mood . . . and if for the President this becomes visibly the difference between success and failure, survival and eventual defeat, then the military-industrial complex will be under control. It can be made to happen.[19]

Reform liberalism's self-imposed contraints appear to flow, in part, from acquiescence in liberalism's principles, in part, from assumptions about the efficacy of existing procedures, and in part, from a judgment that any other route would be self-defeating. Like liberalism, reform liberalism defines the real danger to progress as coming from the potential reaction of the right, if aroused, and if the veneer of civility provided by the democratic procedures is once removed. The unhappy result is a posture that continues to condemn liberalism for failing to achieve reform but, in many respects, shares the commitments that prevent liberalism from doing more. In one sense, the dilemma is that of democracy itself: where a political

---

[19] John Kenneth Galbraith, *How to Control the Military* (New York: Signet Books, 1969), p. 84.

system is responsive to the wishes of the people, reformers who are also democrats must await broad popular conviction that reform is needed before it can be instituted—even if they believe sincerely that such reform is long overdue. But the key to this dilemma is the premise on which it rests. If the political system as presently constituted is *not* responsive to the wishes of the people, or if they have been in some way prevented from understanding their true interests, must even the truest democrat be bound to follow the procedures of that system? May he not be free to base his tactics on the principle of what works best to gain the democratic ends he seeks? The issue of the nature of the current political process thus becomes a crucial element in an ideology's system of thought, as we shall see in the ensuing chapters.

Annotated Bibliography

Alinsky, Saul D. *Reveille for Radicals.* Chicago: University of Chicago Press, 1946. A major work showing how to use the system to produce results amounting to significant redistribution; a model of reform tactics at work.

Bachrach, Peter. *The Theory of Democratic Elitism.* Boston: Little, Brown, 1966. An incisive summary of the way in which empirical researchers have consciously or unconsciously employed pluralist ideology to redefine democracy into what they found to exist.

Barnet, Richard J. *Intervention and Revolution.* New York: New American Library, 1968. A powerful analysis of errors in American foreign policy, tracing them to the ideology in the minds of policymakers.

Chamberlain, John. *Farewell to Reform.* New York: Liveright, 1932. A useful summary of the experience of a major reform movement.

Galbraith, John Kenneth. *The New Industrial State.* Boston: Houghton Mifflin, 1968. An important analysis of the shifting character of the economy and the shifts of power and purpose that follow.

Harrington, Michael. *Toward a Democratic Left.* New York: Macmillan, 1968. A classic within-the-system statement from a democratic socialist.

Hicks, John D. *The American Nation.* Boston: Houghton Mifflin, 1941. Sets background of American history from 1865 to 1940 with attention to the role of reform movements.

Kaufman, Arnold. *The Radical Liberal.* New York: Atherton Press, 1968. Good sketch of how the reform liberal will distinguish himself from orthodox liberals, by a philosopher-activist of the "New Politics."

Ridgeway, James. *The Closed Corporation: American Universities in Crisis.* New York: Random House, 1968. A series of allegations about the perversion of universities by the operations of the liberal state.

Weinstein, James. *The Corporate Ideal in the Liberal State.* Boston: Beacon Press, 1968. A valuable study of the penetration of the state by business under the guise of reform.

Wolff, Robert Paul. *The Poverty of Liberalism.* Boston: Beacon Press, 1968. A powerful analysis of the failures of liberalism, from the perspective of philosophical content.

5

Black Liberation

The status of the Negro in the United States was one of the most critical areas of conflict in the 1960s and continues to be during the 1970s. Often neglected behind news coverage of sit-ins and riots, however, is the evolving political and economic ideology of black liberation. In the course of their struggle for freedom and equality, black thinkers, articulating profound criticisms of the American system, have attempted to present an alternative view of the good society. In this chapter, under the rubric of black liberation, we will describe the challenge to traditional American ideologies developed by contemporary black thinkers.

For a number of reasons, this is an extremely difficult task. First, there are intrinsic difficulties for the white person in attempting to analyze black thought. In *Soul on Ice,* Eldridge Cleaver eloquently describes the intense demythologizing experience he believes whites must undergo if they are to understand and accept what he calls "the black world's vision" of the United States.[1] It is necessary to suspend many unexamined attitudes and beliefs about the nature and processes of the American system and, in Malcolm X's phrase, "to look at America through the eyes of the victim." [2] Despite the

---

[1] Eldridge Cleaver, *Soul on Ice* (New York: Dell, 1968), pp. 77–79.

[2] Malcolm X, quoted in George Breitman, ed., *Malcolm X Speaks* (New York: Grove Press, 1965), p. 26.

difficulties, it is vital that we try to understand and interpret the black critique.

The second difficulty arises from the fact that the black critique is constantly evolving. The *Autobiography of Malcolm X,* which traces the activist stages and intellectual development of one of the most dynamic black leaders, is striking testimony to the capability of black thought to push beyond old formulations. Because the black thinker is often an activist as well as an ideologist, his work often reflects the changing lessons of his immediate field experience. For the same reasons, the work of black thinkers often has an unfinished quality. Many of its expressions come to us in the form of speeches rather than painstakingly developed written statements. The activist thinker also runs additional risks and may not be able to complete a system of thought. Both Martin Luther King and Malcolm X were assassinated at points in their lives when they seemed about to articulate new formulations.

A further difficulty arises from the fact that there are significant differences and disagreements within the black movement. These differences are most apparent on the level of tactics. For example, there is the well-publicized debate between the proponents of nonviolent direct action and those of aggressive self-defense, usually described as nonviolence vs. violence. It is important to realize that such differences exist at *all* levels of black thought. Disagreements over tactical matters devolve ultimately from variations in the fundamental view of the American system and the related question of the proper goals of the black movement. Thus, in this chapter, we must attempt to present both what is general and what is diverse in black thought.

To accomplish this, we will first describe black liberation ideology in a general manner, emphasizing themes that appear in some form in the work of all the prominent black leaders. That is, we try to abstract the unifying core of the "black world's vision" and to contrast this with the core of traditional American ideologies. Here the emphasis is on what unites black thinkers and differentiates them from liberal and other mainstream ideologists. In the second section, we shall focus on the major areas of disagreement among black thinkers; the emphasis there will be upon the complexity and diversity of black thought.

World View

Black thinkers begin from a basically critical, rather than approving, posture toward the American system. The depth and tone of black disapproval are visible in every leader's work and are an appropriate frame for our analysis. Martin Luther King, often thought of as a moderate, has written:

> When you have seen vicious mobs lynch your mothers and fathers at will and drown your sisters and brothers at whim; when you have seen hate-filled policemen curse, kick and even kill your black brothers and sisters; when you see the vast majority of your twenty million Negro brothers smothering in an airtight cage of poverty in the midst of an affluent society . . . when you are harried by day and haunted by night by the fact that you are a Negro, living constantly at tiptoe stance, never quite knowing what to expect next, and are plagued with inner fears and outer resentments; when you are forever fighting a degenerating sense of "nobodiness"— then you will understand why we find it difficult to wait.[3]

Malcolm X has written:

> Our people in this particular society live in a police state, a black man in America lives in a police state. He doesn't live in any democracy, he lives in a police state. That's what it is, that's what Harlem is. . . . Any occupied territory is a police state; and this is what Harlem is. Harlem is a police state; the police in Harlem, their presence is like occupation forces, like an occupying army.[4]

And Eldridge Cleaver:

> The boxing ring is the ultimate focus of masculinity in America, the two-fisted testing ground of manhood, and the heavyweight champion, as a symbol is the real Mr. America. In a culture that secretly subscribes to the piratical ethic of "every

---

[3] Martin Luther King, *Why We Can't Wait* (New York: New American Library, 1964), pp. 81–82.
[4] Malcolm X, *op. cit.,* p. 66.

man for himself"—the social Darwinism of "survival of the fittest" being far from dead, manifesting itself in our rat race political system of competing parties, in our dog-eat-dog economic system of profit and loss, and in our adversary system of justice wherein truth is secondary to the skill and connections of the advocate. The logical culmination of this ethic, on a person to person level, is that the weak are seen as the natural and just prey of the strong.[5]

As these examples suggest, the images of freedom, order, justice, and plenty that comprise conventional descriptions of American society are not to be found in black thought. Instead, the vision is one of prisons, suffering, brutality, starvation, and decay. A unifying theme running throughout black ideology is that the United States presents a social environment that is fundamentally dehumanizing for black people. From the outset, the traditional ideologies' image of the United States as the land in which human beings have been provided the maximum opportunity to fulfill their human potential has been reversed. Black thinkers ask their audiences to conceptualize a society that has failed in human terms, failed to provide the basic necessities of material comfort and security, and failed even more drastically to provide an opportunity for human fulfillment. With this general image in mind, let us turn to a consideration of three specific concepts used by black thinkers to describe and analyze this society.

(1) RACISM

The most basic characteristic of the United States society from the perspective of the black thinkers is that it is racist. It is a society that systematically assigns one ethnic group an inferior position in the social structure. Most traditional ideologists would also recognize racism, particularly in the past, as a regrettable flaw in the system. But they view it as a peripheral characteristic of the system and one well advanced toward elimination. Black thinkers differ in that for them, racism is a basic characteristic of American life, woven deep into both its past and its present. It is the fundamental

---

[5] Eldridge Cleaver, *op. cit.,* p. 84.

concept they employ for the description and analysis of the American social structure.

The major uses and meanings of the term racism as used by black thinkers have been well summarized by Stokely Carmichael and Charles Hamilton in their book *Black Power*.[6] They begin with a basic definition of racism as "the predication of decisions and policies on consideration of race for the purpose of *subordinating* a racial group and maintaining control over that group." [7] They then distinguish two forms of racism. The first is individual and overt. It consists of violent destructive acts by individuals against individuals, such as the bombing of a black church and killing of black children. It is easily identified and often condemned. It is this aspect of racism that whites are most sensitive to, and the fact that such acts of individual racism are relatively rare allows whites to assert that racism is declining.

The second form of racism is termed "institutional." It is found in the "operation of established and respected forces in the society." [8] This racism takes the form of support for societal procedures that keep black people underemployed and confined to ghettos, procedures that are not overtly racist but have racist effects. Carmichael and Hamilton point out that respectable individuals can consider themselves blameless because they are not sensitive to racism of this type. "*They* would never plant a bomb in a church; *they* would never stone a black family. But they continue to support political officials and institutions that would and do perpetuate institutionally racist policies. . . ." [9] Because institutional racism is structural rather than individual, its consequences can be both more devastating and more difficult to combat than individual racism. Carmichael and Hamilton consider the death of five hundred black babies a year in Birmingham, Alabama, a function of institutional racism. These deaths are caused by failure to provide blacks with proper food, shelter, and medical facilities. But since institutional racism is less dramatic than more overt forms, it is easily ignored and forgotten.

---

[6] Stokely Carmichael and Charles V. Hamilton, *Black Power: The Politics of Liberation in America* (New York: Vintage Books, 1967).

[7] *Ibid.,* p. 3.

[8] *Ibid.,* p. 4.

[9] *Ibid.,* p. 5.

Underlying and supporting individual and institutional racist acts are the racist attitudes that permeate the society. Carmichael and Hamilton describe the basic feeling among whites that they are better than blacks. This racist attitude has its root in the history of the slave economy, when the very humanity of slaves was questioned, and continues into the present in the form of the conviction of white group superiority.

Black thinkers are concerned with the numerous destructive consequences of individual and institutional racism upon blacks. The first, and most obvious, is the material deprivation that blacks suffer as a result of racism. Black leaders emphasize the fact that by any indicator of economic well being—employment, wages, housing, education, and mortality—blacks as a group are deprived relative to white Americans. This deprivation is the result not of the unwillingness of black people to work or lack of ability, but of the systematic economic discrimination to which they are subjected.

But black thinkers also emphasize the social and psychological consequences of racism. Denied all status and respect in the society, the black man questions his worth as a human being. Accepting the white-imposed negative vision of himself, he begins to despise, devalue, and even hate himself. This development both psychologically damages the individual black person and reinforces the negative attitude of the dominant white group.

(2) EXPLOITATION

Closely linked to this view of the American social system as racist is the image of it as exploitative. In applying the concept of exploitation to the United States, black thinkers have departed significantly from the traditional principles and assumptions of American capitalist ideology. Where traditional thinkers, for example, describe an economic system that has created unparalleled wealth and power, in contrast, black thinkers have focused upon the material deprivation that exists. Beginning with different images of the consequences of the capitalist economy, they stress the poverty, hunger, and misery that are often obscured by images of "the affluent society."

Perhaps more significant, however, is the distinctive description and explanation of the workings of the economic system, the actual processes of capitalist success, which are presented by black thinkers. Traditional thinkers describe a society in which free individuals compete and are rewarded on the basis of labor and merit. For the individual, upward mobility is theoretically unlimited. Black thinkers start with the fact of a slave economy in which human beings were treated as property and denied the fruits of their labor. Only through utilization and exploitation of this labor, they assert, was the United States able to lay the foundations of what is today its powerful economy. Malcolm X, speaking to a black audience, described the origins of American economic strength in this fashion:

> Our mothers and fathers invested sweat and blood. Three hundred and ten years we worked in this country without a dime in return—I mean without a dime in return. You let the white man walk around here talking about how rich this country is, but you never stop to think how it got rich so quick. It got rich because you made it rich.[10]

Even in the more moderate Martin Luther King we read: "Few people consider the fact that in addition to being enslaved for two centuries, the Negro was during all those years robbed of the wages of his toil." [11]

With this perspective on the historic development and contemporary workings of the economy as their basis, black thinkers challenge the justice of the present distribution of economic rewards in the society. From this challenge, at least in part, flow demands as diverse as the $10,000,000,000, "Freedom Budget" proposed by A. Philip Randolph and the Urban League and the Nation of Islam's demand for exclusive possession of six or seven southern states. From it, in addition, comes a demand for economic equality in fact rather than mere equality of opportunity, and the related demand for preferential treatment for blacks. On the question of preferential or compensatory treatment of blacks, Martin Luther King has written "It is impossible to create a formula for the future that does not take into account that our society has been doing something special against the Negro for hundreds of years. How then can he be ab-

---

[10] Malcolm X, *op. cit.*, p. 32.
[11] Martin Luther King, *op. cit.*, p. 137.

sorbed into the mainstream of American life if we do not do something special *for* him now, in order to balance the equation and equip him to compete on a just and equal basis?" [12] While King here preserves the image of mobility through competition, which is a basic precept of capitalist ideology, he also demands recognition that all individuals and groups have not been accorded the opportunity to compete on an equal basis and suggests that society must compensate the black man for withholding this right.

The black thinkers' demurrer from the basic assumption concerning the workings of the economic system and their assertion that its processes are exploitative threaten to open a Pandora's box which has usually remained closed in American ideologies' discussion of the economy: the issue of alternative forms of economic organization. Harold Cruse has suggested that "history has placed Negro leadership in the favorable position of not having to beg the question of free enterprise, for it is free enterprise that must prove itself.[13] Many, perhaps most, black thinkers continue to see the capitalist economy as viable in theory although in need of modification. Their position is much like that of reform liberals who assert that modification and reforms are necessary to eliminate the injustices sometimes wrought by the operation of the market but do not propose an elimination of the market itself. However, a minority of black thinkers have taken the black critique of the economy further. They have asserted that capitalism is intrinsically exploitative, and have begun to search for alternative modes of economic organization, both for the black community and for the United States as a whole. It is at this point that the consensus in the black economic critique breaks down. We will consider these differences in greater detail in the second section.

(3) MONOLITHIC PLURALISM OR WHITE POLITICAL DOMINANCE

Like the economic system, the political system is viewed differently by black thinkers than by traditional ideologists. As we have

---

[12] *Ibid.,* p. 134.
[13] Harold Cruse, *The Crisis of the Negro Intellectual* (New York: Morrow, 1967), p. 94.

seen, liberalism conceives of the political system as a pluralist democracy. All individuals are thought to have access to the basic democratic institutions such as political parties and the electoral process. Even more important, all major groups are represented in the bargaining and negotiation processes and therefore their interests are represented in government policy decisions. Power is viewed as diffused throughout the system rather than concentrated in a few individuals or a particular social class.

For black thinkers, the United States is an incomplete democracy at best. They view it as a system which has excluded a major group from participation in its political processes. Black ideologists argue that, historically, black people in the South were excluded by law from participation in the most basic democratic acts such as voting. When such laws were declared unconstitutional, informal norms sanctioned by economic power and terrorism were utilized. They point to the fact that as late as 1968, attempts by blacks to register to vote resulted in the murder of voter registration workers in southern communities. In the North, more subtle measures such as gerrymandering were and are used to achieve similar results. The consequence is that blacks continue to be excluded from decision-making power on both the local and national levels. The open processes of the pluralist society have remained closed to them. Carmichael and Hamilton have coined the phrase "monolithic pluralism" to describe such a system in which power, while diffused, is denied to one group, in this case a racial minority.[14]

A minority of black thinkers have gone farther in their critique of the American political processes and questioned the validity of the pluralist model entirely. They pose, instead, a ruling class model in which power is concentrated in a small group which makes decisions primarily in its own interests. The United States thus operates as a democracy neither for blacks nor for the majority of whites. This viewpoint, while probably not widely shared within the black liberation movement, has important theoretical implications which will be explored in the second section.

Let us pause at this point to summarize the major elements of

---

[14] Carmichael and Hamilton, *op. cit.*, p. 7.

the black thinkers' world view considered thus far. We have described what we take to be the basic core of the black world's vision, the concepts of racism, exploitation, and incomplete democracy or monolithic pluralism. These images contrast sharply with the picture of a free, egalitarian and open society pictured by traditional ideologies.

We have further noted that although there is consensus among black thinkers on these general themes, they draw different implications from them. For instance, not all black thinkers conclude that capitalism is intrinsically exploitative from their observation concerning its historical operation with regard to blacks; and only a minority of black thinkers abandon completely the image of the United States as a pluralist democracy. Thus, while black thinkers share common concepts and images of the American system, there are degrees of disenchantment within the general framework of disapproval.

There is an additional important difference to be noted concerning the breadth of application of these concepts. Some black thinkers have begun to apply the concepts of racism, exploitation, and white political domination not only to the domestic processes of the United States but also to its relationships with other countries, particularly those of the Third World. Rather than viewing international relations in terms of a conflict between the free world, led by the United States and the encroaching Communist powers, they see it primarily as a struggle between white and colored peoples. The Western white nations led by the United States are seen as the exploiters and colonizers of black, brown, and red peoples on a worldwide scale. For a century, this exploitation has been a fundamental aspect of U.S. foreign policy. In the decades of the fifties and sixties, the Third World peoples have struggled, often successfully, to regain their political and economic freedom. Black thinkers who subscribe to this international perspective make a connection between the struggle of blacks in the United States and the struggling Third World peoples. They consider the Third World, particularly the African nations, as actual or potential allies. We will consider further the implication of this international perspective in the second section.

Values and Goals

The general values and goals of black thinkers appear to be the familiar ones expressed in mainstream American political ideology. Probably no black thinker has stated them as frequently as has Martin Luther King. For example:

> There will be neither rest nor tranquility in America until the Negro is granted his citizenship rights. The whirl-winds of revolt will continue to shake the foundations of our nation until the bright day of justice emerges.[15]

But one might as easily quote Malcolm X:

> All of our people have the same goals, the same objective. That objective is freedom, justice, equality, all of us want recognition and respect as human beings.[16]

Thus, in almost identical language, different black thinkers assert the desire for freedom, justice and equality. A universal goal specified by black leaders is to create a society in which each black person can respect himself and his people.

But despite apparent similarity, black thinkers typically see the traditional values and goals as different from or even an obstacle to their own. The mildest critique of prevalent U.S. values and goals offered by black ideology is one which questions the extent to which the articulated values and goals are implemented in the present social order. Traditional thinkers see the society as actually operating on the broad principles of freedom, justice and equality. Black thinkers see instead a society that hides oppression in this rhetoric. How, they ask, can a social system claim to promote equality when it denies equal access to job opportunities? How can it speak of a commitment to justice when black citizens seeking to exercise their right

---

[15] Martin Luther King, quoted in David L. Lewis, *King: A Critical Biography* (New York: Praeger, 1970), p. 228.
[16] Malcolm X, *op. cit.*, p. 51.

to vote are brutalized? The American social system fails to live up to its own most frequently articulated standards. Thus, for some black thinkers, a major goal of the black liberation movement is to move the American social system toward an implementation of those values and goals upon which it is supposedly founded.

A second common critique of traditional values and goals is one which questions the nature of the hierarchical arrangement of values found in liberalism and capitalism. Here, black thinkers go beyond issuing a challenge to implement the traditional values and raise some questions about their validity and about the real priorities that usually accompany them. Because their pride and dignity have been ravaged by racism and discrimination, black thinkers are sensitive to the extreme difficulty of building a social structure in which human values are truly served. They see a society that emphasizes property rights to the extent that the American system does as particularly likely to sacrifice human values. American society is seen as improperly stressing materialistic values and goals and placing humanistic values second in order of priority. Black thinkers place emphasis upon the conflict already noted between the right to acquire property and the right to equality and liberty embedded in the U.S. Constitution. They see an unacknowledged conflict between the two values which, in practice, is resolved in favor of property rights. For the black thinkers who make this analysis, a major goal of the black liberation movement is the reorientation of the American system to an emphasis upon the equality strand of the value system.

However, some black thinkers deny that such a reorientation is possible because they deny that there really is such a value conflict in American society. These thinkers assert that American society is almost exclusively motivated and structured in terms of property values. They argue that it is overly generous for black thinkers to speak in terms of such a conflict because it vastly overemphasizes the extent to which a humanistic dimension is present at all in the American value system. Carmichael and Hamilton have written of middle class America that it is, as a whole, "without a viable conscience as regards humanity. The values of the middle class permit the perpetuation of the ravages of the black community. The values of that class are based upon material aggrandizement, not the expansion of humanity." [17]

---

[17] Carmichael and Hamilton, *op. cit.,* p. 40.

For black thinkers of Carmichael and Hamilton's persuasion, the values and goals of liberalism and capitalism are intrinsically flawed rather than merely inadequately implemented or improperly emphasized. The stress these values place upon individualism, competitiveness and conflict is seen as following from a view of man that is fundamentally incorrect. This incorrect vision is the basis for a social system that in its emphasis upon material accumulation prevents men, both black and white, from developing as full human beings. As these black thinkers analyze American society, the race problem in the United States does not result from a failure to implement American values but is a logical and predictable extension of those values.

It follows from this analysis that a fundamental task of the black liberation movement is articulation of an alternative set of values and goals that can serve as the basis for a society which is truly humanist in its orientation. James Baldwin expressed the feelings of many black thinkers: "White people cannot, in the generality, be taken as models of how to live. Rather the white man is himself in sore need of new standards, which will release him from his confusion and place him once again in fruitful communion with the depths of his own being." [18]

Different sources of these alternative standards have been suggested. The young organizers of SNCC saw the poor black people of the South as possessing a beautiful and morally superior life style. Others have pointed to the distinctive culture of the northern black ghetto. Finally, there are those, like Carmichael, who see the Third World, and especially Africa, as the source of the appropriate new model. Although the suggested sources differ, common themes are found in the partial formulations of alternative values that black thinkers have attempted. There is a universal rejection of the cult of individualism and the cult of materialism which are considered basic tenets of American and white western value systems. It is asserted that wherever black culture is found, it is based upon the cooperative, rather than the competitive, aspects of human nature. The group is characteristically seen as having value—value that complements, but does not deny, the development and freedom of the individual. The communal and egalitarian organization of the African tribe is often

---

[18] James Baldwin, *The Fire Next Time* (New York: Dial Press, 1963), pp. 110–111.

cited as an example of a social structure based upon a superior conception of human nature.

While black liberation leaders may not be in agreement on the characteristics of black culture and values outlined above, the mere fact that a portion of the movement places emphasis upon articulation of new values indicates an important departure in American ideologies. White Anglo-Saxon values and goals have been relegated by these thinkers to the status of one of many possible value systems, one which is specific to the white western world—and one which (present performance suggests) is inadequate and often destructive. In addition, a new right, or a new understanding of the right to freedom and equality, has been asserted, that of the right of self definition for a group. Black thinkers argue that the right to reject the dominant values, goals and norms of white society and to create new ones that will accord with the cultural and historical experience of black people is the most important right that can be established by the black liberation movement. Black thinkers who subscribe to this view are separated by a considerable distance from those who see the implementation of traditional American values as the critical task of the movement. This brings us to consideration of one of the most important issues dividing black leaders, the issue of integration vs. some form of nationalism.

Substantial agreement among black thinkers as to the goals of the liberation movement on a general level begins to break when more proximate goals are considered, the most dramatic and important example being the debate between the integrationist and the nationalist. (The intricacies of this debate will be the principal topic of the second section, and we merely suggest its outline here.) Integration as a goal of the black liberation movement means that the movement is oriented toward assuring that black people participate fully and equally in the American social system. This subideology emphasizes the essential similarity and equality of blacks and whites and is more concerned with the implementation of what it takes to be traditional American values than with the articulation of new ones. Nationalism rejects the blending of blacks and whites into one society. It emphasizes the historical and cultural distinctiveness of blacks and advocates the creation of a separate black nation or community in which blacks live in terms of their own values.

The debate between the integrationists and nationalists is not a new development. It has run throughout the work of black thinkers since the Civil War. However, in the 1950s and early 1960s integration was the universal goal of the black organizations that received press coverage, such as the NAACP. This situation appeared to be suddenly and radically transformed with the media discovery of the Nation of Islam which preached a separatist ideology and by the subsequent advocacy of SNCC and CORE of the "black power" slogan. The latter event in particular touched off bitter debate among black liberation leaders concerning the proper goals of the liberation movement. This debate is rooted in the differences in world view and understanding of values which, as we have just seen, permeate the black movement.

Social Change and Tactics

The ideology of black liberation is obviously concerned with extensive change in the American social system. For even the most moderate black leader, the disparity between the reality of life for black people in the United States and the values which they seek to implement and the goals to which they aspire, is very great. The elimination of racism and the various forms of economic and social discrimination woven into American society is seen as a task that requires intense commitment and the mobilization of societal resources on an unprecedented scale.

Black thinkers often describe the scope and pace of the social change that they demand as revolutionary. Leaders as diverse as Malcolm X and Martin Luther King refer to the black movement as a revolutionary movement. As we have seen, black thinkers do articulate sweeping criticisms of the present social system. It remains to be seen, however, which of them if any really fit our definition of revolutionary ideology. We will consider this question further when we deal with variations in black thinking. Here we need only note that there is a consensus among black leaders that, in some sense, revolutionary change is a necessity in the United States.

The area of social change and tactics is one like that of goals, in which the differences among black thinkers are dramatic. The disagreement among black leaders over the question of violent vs. nonviolent tactics and the proper relationship of whites in the black movement has received a great deal of public attention. However, when the general approach to social change of the black thinker is contrasted with the views on methods of social change of the more traditional ideologists, it is clear that there are unifying themes in black ideology.

Black thinkers, in general, are far less convinced than traditional American thinkers of the efficacy of following established procedures. They begin from the position that the traditional methods of social change through the electoral process or legal channels have broken down in relation to blacks. They see few indications that American society is equipped to handle a problem of social change of the magnitude of racism in the peaceful and semi-mechanical manner pictured by traditional ideologists. Black thinkers interpret their 300 year history in the United States as denying the liberal and capitalist assumptions that American society is somehow self-correcting. That is, that social injustices are slowly but surely eradicated and that no reasonable demand goes unfilled. It is their contention that (for blacks) conditions have *not* improved, reasonable demands have been denied and, in fact, things do not get better. They get worse. Instead of seeing a continuous line of improvement from the Emancipation Proclamation to the present, they see a continuing series of broken promises. From their perspective, the genius of American politics has not been the ability to change when necessary, but the ability to preserve the status quo while presenting the illusion of change.

While there are major black spokesmen who still view the traditional procedures, particularly the courts, as major instruments of social change, the focus of emphasis appears to have shifted decisively to collective methods. Bayard Rustin has suggested that Martin Luther King's Birmingham campaign represented the victory of the concept of collective struggle over individual mobility as the road to black freedom.[19] While formerly the emphasis was on breaking down legal barriers and the winning of such individual tokens as the admission of one black student to a southern university, the emphasis has changed to the mobilization of *group* economic, political, and at times physical power. While this conception of the proper

---

[19] Bayard Rustin, "From Protest to Politics: The Future of the Civil Rights Movement," *Commentary*, Feb. 1965, p. 25.

instrument of change is superficially similar to the pluralist conception, most black thinkers place more emphasis upon the conflict and power dimensions of the group struggle than is found in the traditional liberal version.

The black liberation image of change differs also in that a majority of its adherents take it as established that under certain conditions, extralegal methods will be used. Martin Luther King was viewed as an extremist when he suggested in 1966 that civil law is at times superceded by a higher moral law and led his followers on illegal marches and sit-ins. The direct action approach is now a common tactic and is considered controversial only when accompanied by deliberate acts of violence or property destruction. This position is clearly in stark contrast to the liberal emphasis upon following established procedures and preserving the sanctity of the law.

At this point the tactical agreement between black thinkers begins to break down. In addition to the issue of violence vs. non-violence, they disagree about the proper role of whites in the black liberation movement. Integrationists are committed to a strategy of coalition with white groups, such as labor and liberal reformers. They would direct the energy of the mobilized black masses to restructuring the present party system to increase the responsiveness of the federal government. Nationalist leaders are more likely to mobilize at the community level and to form all-black third-party movements. It is time to consider all of these differences in more detail.

Variations in Black Ideology

This section will elaborate the differences among black thinkers —their varying attitudes toward capitalism, the relationship of their struggle to Third World liberation movements, the integration-nationalism argument, and their claims to types and processes of change that may be properly understood as revolutionary. Our discussion will be organized around the disagreements over goals and tactics, which we have already noted, because this reflects most faithfully the way in which black thinkers themselves experience their differences. In the section on goals, we will examine four different types. In regard to tactics, we shall concentrate on the issues of coalition versus independent black organization and violent versus nonviolent methods.

Contending Goals: Four Formulations

INTEGRATION

Proponents of integration, the most familiar of black goals, hold that black freedom and equality can be achieved only by full admission of the Negro into the mainstream of American life. Forced segregation of blacks into separate institutions is viewed as the major obstacle to progress, and the goal of integrationists is the destruction of each and every barrier that separates whites and blacks.

At various times, different institutions have been the focus of attack. All integrationists point to the 1954 Supreme Court decision ordering the integration of the schools as a major landmark in the black liberation movement. The dramatic sit-in movements in the early 1960s had as their object the integration of dime store lunch counters. But realization that economic handicaps prevented full enjoyment of the new legal rights soon followed. Many blacks could not afford to eat in integrated restaurants and use other public accommodations integrated by the Civil Rights Act of 1964, for example. Nor were they able to compete fairly for jobs without adequate training. Integrationist leaders have therefore come to focus increasingly on the problem of jobs, education, and housing, seeking to open up unions, universities, and white-collar opportunities. Bayard Rustin has suggested that the focus has shifted from relatively peripheral institutions to those that are basic to the social and economic order.[20] Despite the shift in the types of institution that are the specific targets, the integrationist goal remains the same: black progress through the opening of white institutions to blacks.

The integrationist perspective emphasizes the essentially *American* character of the struggle for black liberation. Martin Luther King has written, "Abused and scorned though we may be, our

---

[20] *Ibid.*

destiny is tied up with America's destiny." [21] Integrationists take the Declaration of Independence as their model and see the black movement as forcing the United States toward the realization of the values and goals stated in that document. The Third World and Africa enter into integrationist thinking only very peripherally. The development of free African nations is seen as an inspiration for blacks in the United States but concrete connections between the black struggle in the U.S. and the Third World are not made. Nor is the United States seen as the oppressor of the African nations. Martin Luther King, for example, was more likely to make analogies between the black movement and the American Revolution than between the black movement and African revolutions.

While the integrationist thinkers share the goal of creating black pride and dignity, they do not relate them to the distinctiveness of Afro-American culture as other black thinkers do. Martin Luther King saw blacks as exercising their right to self-definition through participation in nonviolent direct action. Through such participation, the black man rejects the American eye-for-an-eye ethos, and by creating his own means of changing society, generates self-respect and wins the respect of others. It is through the fulfillment of traditional Christian values that the black man frees himself. Bayard Rustin, in a direct attack upon the nationalist tendency to advocate pride through black distinctiveness, has written that "pride, confidence, and new identity cannot be won by glorifying blackness or attacking whites; they can only come from meaningful action, . . . from good jobs, and from real victories." [22] Thus, while the integrationists share the concern with black self-identity that is found throughout the black liberation movement, they see its source in the American context and its achievement as coming through typically American modes of action.

Integrationist leaders see the American system as at least moderately responsive to black demands for change. Martin Luther King considered the Birmingham mass action a success, pointing to the token integration of formerly segregated facilities and the promises of

---

[21] Martin Luther King, *Why We Can't Wait*, p. 93.
[22] Bayard Rustin, " 'Black Power' and Coalition Politics," *Commentary*, Sept. 1966, p. 39.

the white business sector to begin to open jobs to blacks. The passage of the Civil Rights Act of 1964 and the Voting Rights Act of 1965 are often cited as proof of the ability of black pressure to elicit change. Although integrationist leaders are dissatisfied with the *rate* of change, they do argue that there is movement in the desired direction.

This is not to say that the integrationist leaders are uncritical of the present social structure of the United States. Leaders such as Whitney Young, Bayard Rustin and Martin Luther King share the view of American society as racist and exploitative and therefore in need of basic change. Martin Luther King presented the civil rights movement as potentially accomplishing the moral rejuvenation of the United States. He wrote,

> The civil rights movement will have contributed infinitely more to the nation than the eradication of racial injustice. It will have enlarged the concept of brotherhood to a vision of total interrelatedness.[23]

King is concerned with change on a cultural and moral level. American society, in rejecting segregation and accepting and promoting integration, corrects the perversion of its values and turns toward the positive American values. His formulation is a good example of a black leader viewing American values as essentially sound but in need of implementation and reemphasis.

Bayard Rustin, taking a more pragmatic approach to the question of societal reorientation, has suggested that black demands cannot be objectively satisfied within the framework of existing political and economic relations and that the black liberation movement will ultimately lead to a "refashioning of the political economy."[24] Rustin argues that the insistence of the black movement that emphasis be placed upon equality of condition rather than equality of opportunity will accelerate the existing tendency toward the expansion of the public sector and result in substantial social change. Despite these arguments, the complaint of Harold Cruse that "Negro leadership is not really fighting *against* the system, but

---

[23] Martin Luther King, *Why We Can't Wait*, p. 152.
[24] Rustin, "From Protest to Politics," p. 25.

against *being left out of* it." [25] is more applicable to the integrationist perspective than any other subideology within the black liberation movement. The final vision of Rustin and many other integrationists appears to be the creation of an inclusive welfare state within the capitalist framework. Theirs is a vision of change similar to that of the reform liberal, rather than the kind of call for the total reordering of the system that distinguishes revolutionary goals. As the vision of integration begins to fade amidst the hard realities of the 1970s, of course, these leaders may escalate their goals and call for far more sweeping changes.

SEPARATISM

The ideology of Elijah Muhammad's Nation of Islam (Black Muslims) presents a dramatic contrast to the integrationist perspective.[26] This ideology completely rejects any solution for the black man within the context of the American social system. Muhammad's doctrine advocates complete withdrawal of the black man from the governmental and territorial jurisdiction of the United States. It demands that the United States relinquish several southern states, out of which an independent and separate black state is to be established. The ultimate goal of its adherents, then, is separatism in its purest (geographical) form.

As a more proximate goal, voluntary separation of blacks into the black ghetto or community is advocated. There, through a program of self-help, the black man will prepare himself spiritually and economically for the coming complete separation from white society. Unlike the integrationist perspective, which directs its energies to the opening of the institutions of white society, the Nation of Islam focuses upon developing and strengthening the existing black community.

An involved and sweeping religious creed is the underlying rationale for both the ultimate and proximate goal. Elijah Muham-

---

[25] Cruse, *op. cit.,* p. 371.
[26] The description of the ideology of the Nation and Islam that follows is drawn from Malcolm X, *The Autobiography of Malcolm X* (New York: Grove Press, 1964); Louis Lomax, *When the Word Is Given* (New York: Signet, 1964), especially pp. 169–180; E. Essien Udon, *Black Nationalism: A Search for Identity in America* (Chicago: University of Chicago Press, 1967).

mad teaches that humanity is divided on a worldwide basis into the Black Nation and the white race. There is continual conflict between the two. The original man created by Allah or God was black and the white race was grafted from the black. The inferior and evil white race fought and later enslaved the black race. Recent history has witnessed the struggle of the Black Nation to free itself from white enslavement. American Negroes, collectively constituting the Nation of Islam, occupy a special position in that they have been chosen by Allah to redeem the whole black nation from evil before the coming Apocalypse in which the white race and a portion of the black nation will be destroyed by the wrath of Allah. Specifically, they must lead the American Negro to the realization that his true spiritual and temporal home lies with Islam and with its center in the Arab world and Mecca.

Although much of the ideology of the Nation of Islam is framed in religious mystical language, many of the themes that run throughout more secular black thinking are clearly present. The speeches of Elijah Muhammad and, even more, those of Malcolm X (during his Muslim period) contain the most sweeping condemnation of the United States to be found in black writing. The white man's treatment of the black man, historically and in the present, is offered as proof that the white race is evil, cannot be redeemed, and has earned the wrath of Allah. Although vehemently opposed to integration themselves, the Black Muslims point to the white man's continual refusal to allow it as proof of his evil nature. Again and again, the moral degeneracy of the white man is emphasized and America is termed the modern Babylon. Their rejection of integration is seen as a refusal to integrate with evil.

The Nation of Islam strongly emphasizes the essential dignity and worth of the black man. Two strands of the ideology reinforce this theme. In many of Elijah Muhammad's speeches, the fact that God is a man and black is emphasized. The black man is presented as deriving his worth from the fact that he is the original man made in the model of Allah. The explicitly stated corollary is that the inferior white man is to be equated with the devil.

The second theme, often stated by Malcolm X, is less overtly religious and mystical. Malcolm emphasized the cultural identity of American blacks with Arabian and African cultures. Malcolm told his audiences that they descended from civilizations that were rich and flourishing when the white Europeans still inhabited caves. Blacks were stolen from their "culture of silks and satins" and enslaved in the United States. The Nation of Islam invites black people to renounce their slave names, their Christianity, and their American identity, and regain their true identity in Islam.

The Nation of Islam presents a strong version of the internationalism that runs throughout black thinking. As already noted, their eschatology presents the whole world as divided into combatant blacks and whites. The Nation of Islam asserts that blacks must identify with Arabian civilization. The trips of both Elijah Muhammad and Malcolm X to Mecca emphasized the cultural roots of blacks in Muslim lands. In Black Muslim schools, black children are taught to speak Arabic and Muslim religious rituals are performed in the Black Muslim home. The demand for southern states is seen as an expedient, albeit one completely justified by white exploitation of blacks, rather than as acknowledging any black identification with the United States.

Despite this sweeping condemnation and the character of its demands, it is difficult to classify the Nation of Islam as a revolutionary ideology except in a very special sense. The eschatology certainly envisions drastic change—in fact, the destruction of the white world. But Elijah Muhammad appears to have no specific program for either forcing separation or destroying white civilization. The Black Muslims are withdrawn from politics at any pragmatic or practical level. The apocalypse is awaited fatalistically. It appears that it was this passivity that was at least partially responsible for the split between Elijah Muhammad and Malcolm X. We will consider Malcolm's more secular goal formulations for the black liberation movement shortly.

BLACK POWER

The slogan "black power" is often equated with a shift in the black liberation movement from nonviolence to violence. This is a very superficial characterization, and in any event, the real significance of this development may lie in its reflection of the attempt to formulate new goals within the framework of nationalism. The ideology of black power embraces many of the themes of the Nation of Islam, but expresses them in a secular and political, rather than religious, manner. In addition, black power advocates draw the thinking of Third World revolutionary writers such as Franz Fanon into the black liberation movement, applying their concepts to the relations of blacks and whites in the United States. In describing black power thinking, we will rely principally on two sources: the speeches of Malcolm X after his break with the Nation of Islam, and the more extended statement of Stokely Carmichael and Charles Hamilton in their *Black Power*.

Like the Nation of Islam, black power thinkers emphasize the cultural distinctiveness and need for independence of black people and reject integration as a degrading solution. They recommend, however, not complete territorial independence from the United States, but development of an independent black community within its present boundaries. They call for blacks to take control of the political, economic, and social institutions of their communities. As Carmichael and Hamilton put it, "The goal of black self-determination and black self-identity—black power—is full participation in the decision-making processes affecting the lives of black people." [27]

This goal, a kind of modified separatism, is based upon an analogy with the colonial situation of other nonwhite peoples of the world. Blacks in the United States are seen as the colonial subjects of the white rulers; they are not an integral part of the United States but constitute a separate nation within a nation. Like other oppressed peoples, they must throw off the oppressor, reject their colonial status, and assert their identity as a nation of free and independent people. Integration is not a possible solution, for it would destroy, rather than recreate, the black nation.

Carmichael and Hamilton detail three characteristics of the black-white relationship in the United States that (combined) define the colonial situation. First is the political powerlessness of American blacks. The black man, they assert, has always had his political decisions made by whites. Through the manipulation of political boundaries, indirect rule, and terrorism, he has been denied political power systematically. Despite the fact that in many geographic areas blacks constitute a majority of the population, they possess almost no political power. Second, like a colonial subject, the black man has been economically exploited. As a laborer, he is assigned to the menial jobs and compensated at a minimal level. The meager

---

[27] Carmichael and Hamilton, *op. cit.,* p. 47.

housing and business resources of the ghetto community are owned by whites and operated for profit. Like all colonies, the black ghetto exists for the sole purpose of enriching the colonizer.

Finally, the black man in America resembles the oppressed colonial because he is assigned a socially inferior status. The colonial social structure acts to convince the native colonial of his inferiority. Values and traditions are derided and basic social structures such as the family or tribe are destroyed. Denied respect since they were brought to the United States as slaves, black people doubt their worth as human beings. The mark of a colonial subject is that he has succumbed to myths of his own inferiority and been led by its acceptance to self-hatred.

Closely related to the black power analysis of the race problem in colonial terms is the tendency to place the problem in an international context. The struggle of blacks in the United States is equated with Third World (and particularly African) struggles to free themselves from white oppression by the West. Malcolm X expressed this connection to a black audience as follows:

> You can't understand what is going on in Mississippi if you don't understand what is going on in the Congo and you can't really be interested in what is going on in Mississippi if you don't understand what is going on in the Congo. They're both the same.[28]

This strong internationalist perspective of the black power ideology has a number of significant implications. First, it leads black thinkers to a particularly bitter condemnation of the United States since this country is seen not only as the oppressor of American blacks, but as the exploiter of the colored peoples of the world. At the same time, it offers black thinkers a vision of their people not as a hopelessly outnumbered minority, but as at least potential members of a worldwide majority, a majority which every day grows more restless. Finally, it provides American blacks with concrete models of other economic, political and cultural forms.

The colonial analogy made by the black power thinkers serves to integrate many of the general views of other black leaders. White racism, exploitation, and failures of democracy may be seen as

---

[28] Malcolm X, *Malcolm X Speaks,* p. 125.

related phenomena, adding up to a relationship between blacks and whites that can only be described comprehensively as colonial. As in the Third World countries, the existence of a colonial situation in the United States is seen as implying and justifying a revolutionary situation. Black power ideology asserts that like other colonized subjects, the black man in the United States can alter his status only if he self-consciously asserts his own value and frees himself through the creation of group political and economic power. Carmichael and Hamilton point out that American blacks, although representing a small proportion overall of the population, constitute majorities in a number of southern counties and in some northern cities. Further, the population trend is toward increasing concentration in the northern cities. It is therefore realistic for blacks to unite and take control of local structures such as city councils, schools, and economic institutions. They can create enclaves within the United States in which they are free to define themselves culturally and create political, social, and economic institutions of their own design. Thus, their goal is not, like integrationists', to eliminate the ghetto, but to transform it into an independent community that will operate under a set of values formulated to fill the needs of the black community and necessarily different from those of the majority white society.

Black power ideology places particular stress upon the cultural and social dimensions of oppression. Carmichael and Hamilton assert that it is essential for blacks to reclaim their history and identity. The struggle in America is conceived less in material terms than in terms of the struggle for the right of self-definition, a struggle "to create our own terms through which to define ourselves and our relationship to the society, and to have these terms recognized." [29] Throughout their works and those of other black power advocates, there are scattered references to the different forms that the black community would take. As we have seen, on a very general level, it is usually presented as a community that will be organized around a true concept of humanity and brotherhood rather than around a competitive struggle for material goods. "Reorientation," Carmichael and Hamilton write, "means an emphasis on the dignity of man, not on the sanctity of property." [30] More specifically, they call for collective

---

[29] Carmichael and Hamilton, *op. cit.*, p. 35.
[30] *Ibid.*, p. 41.

economic institutions and a return to communal rather than private forms of property relationships. Late in his career, Malcolm X specifically suggested that some form of socialism was the proper goal of the black liberation movement.

The black power movement is clearly an example of the tendency in black liberation thinking to reject the legitimacy of American values. It does not, however, provide a full articulation and description of alternate values and institutions. For this reason (and a number of others) we can only tentatively classify black power as seeking a degree of change properly understood as revolutionary. Despite black power's vehement denunciations of the United States in both domestic and foreign policy terms, the ultimate goals of black power ideology are ambiguous and/or contradictory. Carmichael and Hamilton, for example, make statements concerning the basic reorientation of the American system that encourage their classification as revolutionaries. But, in concrete terms, their goal appears to be the transformation of the ghetto rather than society as a whole. They speak of blacks receiving a proportionate share of societal power but not of a total change in power distribution. Finally, their failure to clearly specify the values and goals in terms of which the ghetto is to be transformed has allowed a number of alternate definitions of "black power" to develop. Among them is the very *non*-revolutionary concept of black capitalism or the creation of a parallel capitalism in the ghetto. The limited nature of these prescriptions for changes appears to be based upon more than a pragmatic calculation of what is possible. It seems to grow also out of the character of black power's analysis of the American system —a view which sees the system as brutal and dehumanizing in relation to blacks but is unconcerned with its effect on whites. Whites, with the possible exception of poor whites, are assumed by Carmichael and Hamilton to have power and to escape exploitation. It therefore becomes difficult to assert a need for revolution on a nationwide basis in a country where a majority of the population is admittedly not oppressed. These assumptions appear to exist side by side with a tendency to denounce both capitalism and pluralism in more general terms. But it is the former, more limited, conception on which concrete goal prescriptions seem to be based.

It is perhaps the ambiguity of the black power position combined with what many black thinkers perceive to be growing intransigence and racism among whites that has led one of black power's major spokesmen, Stokely Carmichael, to endorse a new position, revolutionary Pan-Africanism. The essence of this position is the establishment of a land base in Africa to which American blacks can return and join African and other Third World countries in their struggle against U.S. imperialism and capitalism. This perspective ultimately involves revolution on a world scale, with the United States as the principal target, but the timetable is a long one. Carmichael sees this as a natural development of black power and the black struggle generally.

> I think that, in terms of reality and history and my own ideology, all of the movement that we have been building up in terms of black nationalism, from the sit-ins to "black power" runs straight to Pan-Africanism. . . . We need a land base. . . . In the final analysis, all revolutions are based on land.[31]

REVOLUTIONARY NATIONALISM

The Black Panther Party, led by Huey P. Newton and Bobby Seale, represents a distinctive subideology of the black liberation movement which terms itself revolutionary nationalism. The ideology of this group, formed in Oakland, California in 1966, has carried the internationalist perspective and colonial analogy of black thinking to an unambiguously revolutionary conclusion. Like the black power advocates, the Black Panthers specify the goal of self-determination for the black community but place it within the context of a nationwide socialist revolution that will totally transform the economic and political systems. They argue that freedom, justice and self-determination for blacks are possible only when the capitalist system is replaced by a socialist one. Panther ideology reaches this conclusion from an analysis of the U.S. system that employs both the class terminology of Marxism and the colonial terminology of black liberation. As in the black power analysis, racism, exploitation, and

---

[31] Stokely Carmichael, "Pan-Africanism—Land and Power," *The Black Scholar,* November 1969, p. 39.

powerlessness are seen as intimately linked, but in Panther ideology, capitalism is explicitly identified as the cause of the other ills.

Black Panther spokesmen argue that racism and capitalism are linked, both historically and at present. The capitalist system created and maintains racism in order to continue to rationalize economic exploitation. One Panther spokesman expresses it thus:

> We understand we have two evils to fight—capitalism and racism. We rightly view one as "cause" (capitalism) and the other as "effect" (racism). The Black Panther Party knows that racism has always existed in lower forms, but that capitalism has institutionalized, commercialized, and massproduced racism to such a high degree that it is sometimes thought of as a separate entity.[32]

While not denying the reality of racism as a psychological and structural characteristic of the American system, Panther ideology asserts that it can be eliminated only if capitalism is eliminated.

In addition to these links between capitalism and racism, the Panthers see the capitalist system as intrinsically exploitative and oppressive, because it is motivated by a production for profit rather than production for human use. In such a system, the masses of people become tools. Denied the opportunity to participate in decisions concerning production, they are, in fact, slaves.

This analysis of capitalism as intrinsically oppressive leads the Black Panthers to break, on one level at least, with the black liberation vision of black people as uniquely oppressed. "We realize," Huey Newton writes, "that not only are blacks kept in a slave condition, all persons in this country are essentially in that condition. In order for us to become free, all citizens will have to be free." [33] Therefore, freedom of the majority of members of the society, both black and white, becomes the goal of black liberation. To express this, the Black Panther Party has replaced the slogan "Black Power" with the expression "All Power to the People," indicating that a total redistribution of power is necessary. The image of a white, open

---

[32] Sylvester Bell, "Who's on the People's Side," *The Black Panther,* August 30, 1969, p. 9.

[33] Huey P. Newton, in *The Black Panther,* August 23, 1969.

democratic society from which blacks are excluded, which runs throughout much of black thinking, is decisively abandoned by the Panthers in favor of a ruling class image. The capitalist businessmen, the owners of the means of production, are seen as politically dominating blacks and whites alike. The majority of blacks and whites are equally excluded from real power, although they may differ in the degree of material deprivation and overt oppression to which they are subject. Eldridge Cleaver writes, "The black and white communities are controlled by the same ruling class. Towards black people, this ruling class uses racism as a tool of oppression, turning this oppression into a National Question. In the white community oppression is a Class Question, provoking the response of Class Struggle." [34]

Although the Black Panthers insist upon the importance of defining the goals of the black liberation movement in national revolutionary terms, they continue to emphasize the view of the black community as a colony. It is in the black community that capitalist oppression is seen as most overt and, as the quotation above from Eldridge Cleaver indicates, the processes of oppression are distinctive in that they are based on racism. The Panthers see the black community as a nation within a nation and have expressed the colonial analogy in one of its most militant forms. They focus not only upon economic exploitation and political powerlessness, but also upon the overt and brutal physical oppression to which black people are subjected. Panther spokesmen have particularly emphasized the behavior of city police departments. Like Malcolm X, they regard the police as an occupying army operating to assure the quiescence and subservience of the colonized people through brutality and terror. The early activities of the Black Panther Party included the formation of armed black patrols to protect ghetto residents from police harassment. Although this practice has been discontinued, the prevention of police brutality remains a focus of Party activity.

Black Panther spokesmen have added to the demands of many black leaders for control of community institutions the demand that police departments be subject to the control of the community. They have also challenged the working of the entire legal system, sug-

---

[34] Eldridge Cleaver, "On Meeting the Needs of the People," *The Black Panther,* Aug. 16, 1969, p. 4.

gesting that it operates as an oppressive mechanism in the interests of the ruling class and that many black leaders accused of "crimes" are thus in reality political prisoners. In effect, while stating the long-range goal of total revolution, they specify decentralization and community control as more proximate goals in terms similar to those of the black power advocate. But they are precise and explicit about the form such community control should take, and work in concrete ways to create what they consider revolutionary social structures in the ghetto communities they seek to serve. Their commitment to socialism makes them particularly contemptuous of attempts to create "black capitalism" or other types of parallel capitalism in the ghetto. The Panthers assert that a black man in a capitalist relationship to another black man is just as much a slave as if he were in the same relationship with whites. They reject capitalism for blacks not because it is foreign to African culture, but because it is not revolutionary. They see the value and distinctiveness of ghetto culture in the fact that it *is* a revolutionary culture.

Similar considerations guide the Black Panther brand of internationalism. Party ideology contains fervent statements of the commitment to the liberation of Third World peoples and the identity of the American struggle with that of the Third World. But the Panthers go on to insist that the international struggle must be conceptualized not in terms of whites against blacks, but as capitalist imperialism against revolutionary socialism. They point out that oppression of colored peoples by other colored peoples is a reality in the Third World. The example of Haiti is frequently cited as a situation in which blacks replaced whites in power but in which the oppressive social system remained unchanged. Thus, on both the national and international level, the Panthers emphasize that a change in the color of the ruling class does not amount to a restructuring of the society. Only a change in the basic economic and political system can create the basis for a new society.

Tactical Differences

Our discussion of the variations in goal formulations of black thinkers establishes the context within which tactical differences should be understood. Both major tactical disagreements, the argument concerning the proper relationship of whites to the black movement, and the question of violence vs. nonviolence generally follow the integrationist-nationalist split. For integrationist thinkers, with their lesser concern with the need for independent cultural definition and their less extreme view of necessary social change, viable coalitions between blacks and moderate whites, and nonviolent tactics, seem both necessary and fruitful. For the nationalists, with their emphasis upon cultural differences and belief in the need for more fundamental social change, coalitions are suspect and violent methods justified and necessary. We will consider each of the disputed areas in turn.

RELATIONSHIP WITH WHITES

A number of black organizations have always refused membership to white individuals and declined to cooperate with white groups. The Black Muslims are an obvious example, and the rationale for this policy requires little elaboration if we recall the role accorded whites in their general world view. Until recently, however, the common form of organization for the best known of the black liberation groups has been interracial, and they have pursued a deliberate policy of coalition with liberal and left liberal groups such as labor unions, and in general worked within the structure of the Democratic Party. However, in 1966, SNCC adopted the black power position already examined, expelled its white members, and turned toward the organization of independent black political groups. In 1964, Malcolm X had announced his break with the Nation of Islam and formed the all black Organization of Afro-American Unity. The NAACP and other integrationist groups continued to maintain white membership and to pursue the traditional coalition policies—and debate over the propriety and efficacy of different oganizational forms was on.

In *Black Power,* Carmichael and Hamilton have summarized most of the major arguments made for rejection of the traditional coalition policy. Their major contention is that there is a lack of identity of interests between the goals of blacks and most whites. Traditional coalitions, they argue, were based upon the assumption that what is good for white America is automatically good for black people. But this is an erroneous assumption because whites, in general, are opposed to the fundamental reorganization of the society which the black liberation movement has as its goal. Because it is in their interest, whites are consciously or unconsciously dedicated to the preservation of the prevailing norms and institutions. Further, it is difficult for whites to conceive of a society in which white Anglo-Saxon norms do not prevail. In contrast, the need of black people for self-definition challenges the preservation of these very norms and institutions and requires basic change in the society.

Carmichael and Hamilton argue that, even judged by their own standards, supporters of the traditional coalition policy should admit their lack of achievement. They can point only to tokens as the accomplishment of the policy they have pursued. The material conditions of the black masses have either remained unchanged or actually declined in recent years. In addition, the coalition policy has been positively destructive to black pride and dignity because it reinforced the prevalent image of black inability to progress without white leadership.

Black thinkers with an integrationist perspective have responded to this analysis with a number of charges and queries of their own. They reject the contention that coalition policies, in the past, have had little effect and suggest that the stronger, more militant coalitions of the present can be even more successful if the black liberation movement unites around them. They suggest that there is, in fact, an identity of interest between blacks and whites. They emphasize that material deprivation is shared by whites, who are thereby led to support considerable change in the society. Most emphasized, however, is their view that there is in reality no alternative to coalition politics. Black power advocates and other nationalists see the concentration of blacks in southern counties and northern cities as an untapped source of strength. Supporters of coalition politics see this strength as more illusory than real. They point out that on a national basis, blacks constitute a small minority of the population and need allies to move the federal government, since it is here, and not on the local level, that the critical decisions are made. They contend that alliances with Third World countries are unacceptable to the masses of blacks and impractical in any case, since the Third World countries are struggling for their own survival and are in no position to aid the American black liberation movement. Thus, proponents of the contending views reach an impasse over questions of both fact and ideology.

Often overlooked in the debate is the fact that Carmichael and Hamilton and other nationalist leaders have not rejected coalition politics per se, but have merely rejected the form that coalition politics has traditionally taken. In *Black Power*, the authors analyzed the reasons for failure of the traditional coalition politics and specified the criteria for viable coalitions. A minimum condition was that coalitions were possible only with white groups that were committed to the total restructuring of the society. In fact, some of the more militant black liberation groups have made alliances with white radical groups. For instance, in 1968 the Black Panther Party formed a coalition with the predominantly white Peace and Freedom Party to run candidates in the 1968 presidential elections.

VIOLENCE VS. NONVIOLENCE

Like the dispute over coalition politics, the debate over violent vs. nonviolent tactics has generally followed the split between integrationist and nationalist perspectives. The major spokesman for the nonviolent position has been Martin Luther King, who has attempted to apply Ghandian principles of passive resistance to the black liberation struggle in the United States. Opposing him are leaders like Malcolm X, Stokely Carmichael, and the Black Panther Party who insist that violence under some circumstances, particularly those of self defense, is necessary and justified.

At the core of the case for nonviolence is a moral and ethical argument. Martin Luther King has expressed a moral standard in the following words: "Over the past few years I have consistently preached that nonviolence demands that we must be as pure as the ends we seek. I have tried to make it clear that it is wrong to use immoral means to attain moral ends." [35] Violent tactics, King argues, defeat the purposes of the black movement by reducing the freedom fighter to the level of the oppressor. By utilizing violent means, the black man might gain a few concessions, but he would not attain the pride and dignity that results from passive resistance.

---

[35] Martin Luther King, *Why We Can't Wait*, pp. 93–94.

The method of nonviolence is expected to lead to the moral rejuvenation of the black man and the reformation of white society. Passive resistance methods, King argued, are effective because they dramatize for whites the existence of injustice and brutality. It is argued that violence and injustice, once observed, will be rejected and remedied. King, describing the Birmingham marches, wrote, "The brutality with which officials could have quelled the black individual became impotent when it could not be pursued by stealth and remain unobserved." [36]

King also used more pragmatic arguments to argue the case for nonviolent direct action methods. He pointed out that, when combined with economic boycotts as they were in Birmingham, they add economic power to the moral challenges raised by the other methods. Finally, and most pragmatic of all, he argued that violent attempts to produce social change are doomed to failure. The fate of the American Indian indicates the likely outcome of militant attempts to force social change. In any violent confrontation between blacks and whites, blacks, vastly outnumbered and possessing few technological resources, would surely be defeated.

More militant black leaders take exception to every point in the argument for passive resistance and nonviolent direct action. First, they reject the premise that self-defense is morally impermissible. They argue that it is the moral right and duty of a man to defend himself when attacked. This is particularly true, they argue, in a society such as the United States where the brutalization of black people is commonplace and even the federal government has proven incapable or unwilling to protect them. Black dignity and pride are created not by turning the other cheek, but by the ability to command respect through strength. Malcolm X suggests that nonviolence is only justified where the oppressor himself is nonviolent. In his words "you should never be nonviolent unless you run into some nonviolence. I'm nonviolent with those who are nonviolent with me." [37] In addition, many black leaders argue that it is inconceivable that white America, which has itself perpetrated so much violence and brutality on black people in America and in the Third World, would be at all capable of feeling guilt for its acts. Leaders of

---

[36] *Ibid.*, p. 37.
[37] Malcolm X, *op. cit.*, p. 34.

white America are seen as hypocritically insisting that blacks limit themselves to nonviolent means of winning freedom while waging and justifying a violent war in Vietnam in terms of the necessity of defending freedom. To quote Malcolm X again,

> If violence is wrong in America, violence is wrong abroad. If it is wrong to be violent defending black women and black children and black babies and black men, then it is wrong for America to draft us and make us violent abroad in defense of her. And if it is right for America to draft us, and teach us how to be violent in defense of her, then it is right for you and me to do whatever is necessary to defend our own people right here in this country.[38]

Many black thinkers contend that the only time white America rejects violence is when blacks begin to organize themselves for self-defense. Any act by blacks to defend themselves is perceived by whites as a positive act of violence. However, at the same time, they are incapable of condemning their treatment of the American Indians, which stopped little short of genocide, or their treatment of American blacks and Third World peoples, which tends in that direction.

Finally, to the pragmatic argument that defeat is inevitable, they respond that there is little for blacks to lose in any case. The present situation of blacks is so intolerable that an honorable death in battle is preferable. Beyond this, they argue, violent means will not necessarily be defeated despite the obvious military advantages of white society. Black thinkers with an international perspective once again point to the Third World non-white majorities as a potential source of aid. More concretely, they suggest that the techniques of guerrilla warfare used in Cuba and in Vietnam have permitted revolutionary groups to defeat numerically greater and technologically more sophisticated enemies. The principles of guerrilla warfare could be applied to the black liberation struggle in America with similar results.

Despite the militant tone of some of these arguments, many black spokesmen often thought of as proponents of violence have done no more than advocate organized self-defense. That is, they

---

[38] *Ibid.*, p. 8.

have defended the right of American blacks to prepare to defend themselves when attacked. Their arguments often appear extreme because the groups that they are prepared to defend themselves against are often ones to which the white society accords legitimacy, such as the police. As we have seen, many black leaders view the police as instruments of brutality and oppression in the ghetto, and therefore advocate organization of people to provide protection from them.

At some point, the argument for organized self-defense does shade over into a justification of positive acts of violence. Malcolm X, in one of his more militant statements, coined the phrase "freedom by whatever means necessary," a slogan which has been adopted by a number of black liberation groups. Leaders of this persuasion have argued that freedom is a goal for which men have traditionally died and killed, that revolutionary violence is sanctioned even by the American Declaration of Independence, and that there is no reason to hold black men to any other standard. They are convinced that the condition of blacks in the United States is one that justifies revolutionary violence.

Despite this assertion of the justification for positive violence, there is still a tendency for even the most militant black leaders to view it as a last resort. They argue that the final choice of the means of social change remains with white society. If basic changes could be accomplished through peaceful means, there would be no necessity for violence. But black militants argue that white America has continually proved itself incapable of peaceful change. The inevitable result therefore will be violent revolutionary change.

Annotated Bibliography

Carmichael, Stokely and Charles V. Hamilton. *Black Power: The Politics of Liberation in America.* New York: Vintage Books, 1967. The most detailed exposition of the black power position.

Cleaver, Eldridge. *Soul On Ice.* New York: Dell Publishing Co., 1968. A major cultural critique of the United States, from the perspective of prison and emerging political activism.

Cruse, Harold. *The Crisis of the Negro Intellectual.* New York: William Morrow, 1967. A somewhat difficult but rewarding work tracing the historical development of various strands of black ideology.

King, Martin Luther. *Why We Can't Wait*. New York: New American Library, 1964. Perhaps the best of the many works by the leading exponent of integration and nonviolence.

Newton, Huey P. *The Genius of Huey P. Newton*. Berkeley, Cal.: Black Panther Party, 1970. A collection of the major statements of Black Panther ideology by the Party's Minister of Defense.

Rustin, Bayard. "From Protest to Politics: The Future of the Civil Rights Movement" *Commentary,* Feb. 1965. A brief but classic statement of the integrationist, coalition-seeking, traditional politics approach to black liberation.

Seale, Bobby G. *Seize the Time*. New York: Random House, 1970. A description of Black Panther Party history and ideology by the Party's Chairman.

X, Malcolm. *Malcolm X Speaks,* George Breitman, ed. New York: Grove Press, 1965. The collected speeches convey the tone and substance of Malcolm's attempt to reformulate black ideology after his break with the Nation of Islam; a precursor of both black power and revolutionary nationalism.

X, Malcolm. *The Autobiography of Malcolm X*. New York: Grove Press, 1964. A major critique of American society from the perspective of prison, and the Nation of Islam; traces Malcolm's own development as he moved to a more political and revolutionary stance.

Zinn, Howard. *SNCC: The New Abolitionists*. Boston: Beacon Press, 1964. A description of the activities of the Student Nonviolent Coordinating Committee and the early Southern phase of the civil rights movement.

6

The New Left

The new left, it is often noted, is not any one thing. It covers a spectrum from reform liberalism to the hippie or "Yippie" perspective in which the individual's commitment to a radical new life style often precludes what is traditionally thought of as political action.[1] The new left is closely linked to a cultural movement within the society, and many of its youthful members have abandoned familiar middle-class life styles. Thus, it is not necessarily wrong to include even a teen-age runaway who takes to drugs within the range of a definition of the new left. Our concern with political ideology as such, however, results in a presentation that ignores some of the elan and flavor of the new left as a youth movement. The emergence of value changes within this "counter-culture" is quite significant politically, at least potentially, but we shall deal exclusively with the more fully articulated political ideology that is related to this movement.

Even as a political ideology, the new left consists of many diverse strands. But all share some distinctive features. To begin with, the new left is clearly, sometimes drastically, distinguishable from reform liberalism. It addresses many of the same problems: poverty in the midst of affluence, racism, and unjust and brutal wars. But it offers a much more sweeping critique of the social system that

---

[1] But at least some leaders of these amorphous groups recognize the long-term political significance of the value change they advocate. See, for example, Abbie Hoffman, *Revolution for the Hell of It* (New York: Dial Press, 1968) or Jerry Rubin, *Do It!* (New York: Simon and Schuster, 1970).

produced such problems, and at a much more fundamental level. In a sense, the new left begins from the more extreme positions taken (or, in some cases, from undeveloped points made) by reform liberals and develops them into indictments of basic features of the American system. Its major themes are materialism, rigid hierarchy, and bureaucratic unresponsiveness. Sympathetic commentators Cohen and Hale put the matter very neatly:

> What, beyond economic, political, and racial inequality is wrong with this country? The New Left's answer is that there is plenty more wrong, that the standard American way of life is incompatible with a decent human existence.[2]

Because their analysis of causation is structural and institutional, new left thinkers call for sweeping changes and restructuring of the system itself—instead of placing the blame for current conditions upon misguided or evil individuals. Unlike the reform liberal, they accept neither the desirability nor the inevitability of the current capitalist economy, although very few directly embrace a socialist alternative. Nor do they consider it necessary, desirable, or profitable to work for change within the existing framework; they endorse and promote extralegal and sometimes violent alternatives as the only means with a real chance of success under the circumstances.

Clearly then, in some ways, the ideology of the new left resembles the ideology of some of the more militant representatives of black liberation. Like black liberation thinkers, new left adherents criticize the American social system, not just in terms of hypocrisy, unsolved problems, or exclusions, but also in terms of its constant effects upon those who are within it, effects which they consider to be dehumanizing. There are, however, important differences in perspective and emphasis. Perhaps the most basic of these is that, as we have seen, blacks view American society from without, with the eyes of the excluded—even of victims. The thinkers of the new left, predominantly white and middle class, view it from within, with the eyes of full participants, and find it lacking.

Mechanistic images about American society abound in new left

---

[2] Mitchell Cohen and Dennis Hale, "Introduction," in Mitchell Cohen and Dennis Hale, eds., *The New Student Left* (Boston: Beacon Press, 1966), p. xxvi.

writing. The terms Leviathan, colossus, and mass society are most often applied to it. In simplest terms, the new left views American society as a huge, brutal and irrational machine that runs in terms of efficiency and profitability—divorced from human purposes. The size and the overdeveloped, undercontrolled technology of the society make inhuman acts not only possible but routine. It is a society in which human suffering abounds but responsibility for such suffering is diffused and unperceived. Carl Ogelsby captured much of this imagery in an address to an antiwar gathering in Washington:

> We say . . . that good men can be divorced from their compassion by the institutional system that inhibits us all. Generation in and out, we are put to use. People become instruments. Generals do not hear the screams of the bombed, sugar executives do not see the misery of the canecutter, for to do so is to be that much *less* the general, that much *less* the executive.[3]

Much of the thinking of the new left is devoted to the description and explanation of a society in which people have become instruments and to the articulation of an alternative view of society and of man.

Before turning directly to a detailed analysis of the new left, we will describe the work of two academic writers who have strongly influenced (and been influenced by) new left thinking: philosopher Herbert Marcuse and sociologist C. Wright Mills. Although often moralistic in both its origin and expression, and grounded on direct experience in society, new left analysis also has roots in scholarly and academic sources. It is particularly related to a growing body of philosophic and sociological literature that examines the organization of contemporary western society in its highly industrialized and bureaucratized state and holds it to be pathological. From these sources, we have chosen the work of Marcuse and Mills as both significant and illustrative. Other authors of nearly equal importance (e.g., Paul Goodman, Norman O. Brown) might also have been selected, but Marcuse and Mills have come to be seen as more directly symbolic of the new left's academic roots; perhaps they also

---

[3] Carl Ogelsby, "Trapped in a System," in Massimo Teodori, ed., *The New Left: A Documentary History* (Indianapolis: Bobbs-Merrill, 1969), p. 186.

contribute more directly to understanding of some of its basic principles.

Precursors of the New Left:
Herbert Marcuse and C. Wright Mills

HERBERT MARCUSE

Herbert Marcuse's critique of American society is subsumed under a more general analysis of the present historical epoch. Basically, Marcuse sees the contemporary era as dominated by highly industrialized, bureaucratized societies in which human nature is twisted and destroyed by the structures it encounters. He sees the United States, with its capitalist ethos, as the leading example of the prevailing mode, but considers his analysis almost equally applicable to socialist nations such as the Soviet Union. Marcuse is concerned with the general quality of man's life and spirit, and he sees advanced technological society as presently organized as destructive. Man is shaped by the needs of the technology he has created, instead of the reverse.

In Marcuse's analysis, the present destruction of human life has an ironic quality since, for the first time in man's history, he possesses the opportunity to fulfill himself in completely new dimensions. The technological base has been established and developed to the point where the legitimate material aspirations of all men could be satisfied, the battle with scarcity and deprivation ended, and a free and full life established. Marcuse points out that the present level of technology could support a greatly reduced work-week, progressively liberating time for leisure and creative living. On this basis, there is the potential for a complete qualitative change in life, amounting to a change in human nature itself. For the first time in history, Marcuse believes, man is free to develop in a truly human way.

This formulation of the gap between potentiality and actuality in American society rests upon Marcuse's understanding of the psychological and social nature of man. Human beings have historically been violent and competitive, lacking attitudes of human solidarity and cooperativeness. But this is a quality induced by the necessity for the struggle for survival, rather than being intrinsic to the nature of man. The struggle against scarcity having ended, the truly human qualities in man are free to emerge. Marcuse only hints at the form which such a liberated life would take since it cannot truly be known by the unfree man in present society. In one passage where he does attempt a positive formulation, he writes:

> The Form of Freedom is not merely self-determination and self-realization, but rather the determination and realization of goals which enhance, protect and unite life on earth. And this autonomy would find expression not only in the mode of production and productive relations but also in the individual relations among men, in their language and in their silence, and their gestures and their looks, in their sensitivity, in their love and hate. The beautiful would be an essential quality of their freedom.[4]

This sense of the discrepancy between the potential and the actual, not only in a material but also in a psychological or spiritual sense, is also found, as we shall see, in a variety of forms among new left thinkers.

The fact that society and man fail to transform themselves is explained by Marcuse in terms of a number of factors. Most basic is the desire of a vaguely defined ruling group to maintain power and thus necessarily the established social relations. Although coercion and violence are used by the establishment, their primary method is cultural manipulation. The media of communication and other cultural apparatus are used to instill the materialist and competitive values that keep men slaves. In industrial society, man is constantly bombarded with messages concerning commodities and gadgets connected to accumulative and violent life styles. The media also manipulate political judgments, presenting alternatives such as socialism as beyond the pale. The accumulative effect of training and media manipulation is so great that it not only affects attitudes, but structures

---

[4] Herbert Marcuse, *An Essay on Liberation* (Boston: Beacon Press, 1968), p. 46.

the physical needs of men. "The people recognize themselves in their commodities, they find their soul in their automobile, hi-fi set, split-level home, kitchen equipment." [5] Man has been transformed into "one dimensional man" in whom "the inner dimension of the mind in which opposition to the status quo can take root is whittled down," in whom the power of critical thinking is absent.[6]

Thus, for Marcuse, the full realization of a bureaucratic welfare state, or even a socialist society in which one receives goods according to his needs, is insufficient as a goal because needs themselves are the (suspect) product of manipulation. The problem of social change is monumental because the repressive mechanisms of society have so thoroughly distorted human nature. As we shall see, new left thinking parallels much of Marcuse's thought without accepting these pessimistic conclusions regarding change.

C. WRIGHT MILLS

C. Wright Mills presents a view of society that, in general, is similar to that of Marcuse. His work, however, focuses more specifically and in more detail upon social institutions and is more explicitly political. This is particularly true of his analysis of the power elite and the middle and working classes, which we will consider in some detail.

Mills saw the United States in the process of transformation into what he termed a "mass society," one in which masses of individuals are manipulated by remote rulers and lose any potential for democratic direction of important societal institutions. The underlying tendency is toward bureaucratization and centralization of all institutions and a related trend toward stark disparity between the few powerful and the great mass of the powerless. Mills explicitly criticized the liberal notion of a pluralistic political and social structure in which competing groups exercise power. He argued that the United States was, in fact, governed by a power elite composed of corporate leaders, political leaders, and military men or "war lords." He asserts that the traditional pluralist institutions, such as voluntary

---

[5] Herbert Marcuse, *One Dimensional Man* (Boston: Beacon Press, 1969), p. 9.

[6] *Ibid.*, p. 10.

associations or political parties, are hollow shells capable of no meaningful exercise of power on the national level.

Mills identified two trends of great importance. The first centralization and bureaucratization of the political, business and military institutions, we have already mentioned. The second trend is the increasing interdependence and interpenetration of these institutions. "There is no longer," he writes, "on the one hand, an economy, and, on the other, a political order, containing a military establishment unimportant to politics, and to moneymaking. There is a political economy numerously linked with military order and decision." [7] This centralization and interlocking, combined with technological development, created power of an unprecedented nature in the hands of a small circle of men, whom he termed "the power elite." [8]

Mills criticized not only the centralized and exclusive nature of the structure of power, but also the substance of the policies pursued or allowed to emerge by the power elite. He was primarily critical of the power elite-constructed policy of "cold war," feeling that against all rationality and common sense, foreign policy decision-makers pursued policies that increased the chances of a deadly world war. The permanent threat of the cold war period created a situation in which political and economic judgments were made with reference to a military definition of reality. The domestic consequence was the creation of a permanent war establishment. In Mills' view, the power elite was motivated in these decisions by both economic and ideological considerations fearing the loss of U.S. capitalism's position as the primary world power from both perspectives.

Mills also criticized the power elite for its failure to properly control and guide technological development. Rather than becoming an instrument of man's advancement, development becomes a social fetish devoted to frivolous or harmful ends. Technological gadgets accumulate, but produce a decline rather than an improvement in the quality of human life. This results, in part, from the need of the power elite to use technology as an instrument of manip-

---

[7] C. Wright Mills, as quoted in Irving L. Horowitz, ed., *Power, Politics and People: The Collected Essays of C. Wright Mills* (New York: Ballantine Books, 1965), p. 27.

[8] Mills' description of the power elite referred specifically to national power. He felt that the pluralistic model of multiple groups was a more realistic description of what he termed the middle ranges of power.

ulation and control. In Mills' view, the rulers of the United States were not only powerful but also commensurately irresponsible.

Mills' analysis of other strata of society extended and supported his thesis of the power elite. The middle class which Mills identified as critical to the political power descriptions of liberal theorists was, in his view, increasingly impotent with regard to national decision-making. He pointed out that farmers and small businessmen, who were historically possessors of power, had declined drastically in numbers. The new middle class of white-collar workers and professionals, including the professional and technical workers who Galbraith and others make much of, had failed to develop their power potential. Mills acknowledged the growing importance of expertise and technical skill in U.S. society, but felt that power emerged from conscious exercise and political organization rather than automatically accruing to functional importance. He found no such consciousness among the disorganized, disoriented, and ideologically subservient professional classes.

Mills saw the working class as similarly reduced to powerlessness. As a class, it was declining as a proportion of the population —replaced by the growing importance of the white-collar employee. Unions that were once potential sharers of power have sunk to the middle ranges and, subject to the same tendencies as other institutions, have become bureaucracies that contain, rather than press, the demands of the workers. Thus, both the middle class and the working class are part of the mass. Denied any participation in meaningful decision-making, they devote themselves to material acquisition and the pursuit of status.

Like Marcuse, Mills identified the media of communication as important instruments of mass subservience. Controlled by the elite, the media confuse and trivialize issues. Other nominally independent institutions, such as the churches and particularly the universities, are equally culpable. Thus, the institutions of pluralism are not working, and the power elite is effectively unchallenged in its management of the masses.

Mills, like Marcuse, viewed the problem of social change pessimistically, seeing little if any chance of breaking into the cycle of rule and manipulation. Both Marcuse and Mills concentrated on explication of the scope and nature of problems, and of the depth of their roots in the fundamental values and institutions of American society. In places, both appear to have assumed that some individuals would be able to free first themselves, and then others, but neither described the process. This is where the new left takes over, both expanding and refining their analysis and developing the prescriptions for change.

The World View of the New Left

Much of new left analysis is developed in the context of critiques of particular societal institutions or practices, and little in abstract theorizing. We shall examine some of these issue-oriented critiques in a special section. There are, however, a number of general beliefs about American society that are broadly shared. We shall explore three central themes: technocracy and materialism, bureaucracy and unresponsiveness, and alienation. The Port Huron Statement (the founding document of S.D.S., named for the Michigan town in which the convention of 1962 was held) is a seminal document that may serve as a principal source. Although dated with regard to emphasis and some specifics, it is an excellent summary of the new left world view.

TECHNOCRACY AND MATERIALISM

Perhaps the most pervasive concern of new left thinkers is the heavily technological and industrialized character of the United States. New left ideology does not celebrate or even accept the inevitability of industrialization as do the dominant ideologies. Technology is seen, at best, as a mixed blessing carrying with it the potential for both the enhancement or the destruction of human life. Machines that can create leisure are alternately sources of unemployment or destructive weaponry. New left writing is somewhat ambivalent as to whether technology per se or the uses to which it has been put are the core of the problem. The latter position is probably endorsed by most. Technology is susceptible to abuse and, in the opinion of new left thinkers, has been cruelly abused in capitalist American society.

The Port Huron Statement points to the creation of a permanent war economy, frivolous materialism, and superconsumption as perversions of technological promise. In the United States, it claims, technological skill and industrial fruits are channeled into wasteful production rather than into the solution of pressing human problems such as poverty and discrimination. In American society, "the potentiality for abundance" becomes "a curse and a cruel irony." [9] This irrational establishment of priorities is attributed to the existence of the "military-industrial complex," which is in turn related to another major theme of the new left—the decline of democracy caused by bureaucratization and centralization of power.

BUREAUCRACY AND UNRESPONSIVENESS

In opposition to liberal notions of an open, flexible, and competitive society, the new left offers the image of a bureaucratized and increasingly stagnant society. For new left thinkers, bureaucracy is equated not with productivity, efficiency and rationality, but with irrationality, waste, and the destruction of human potential.

With regard to the political system, new left thinkers reject the democratic model accepted by liberals and reform liberals. The Port Huron Statement characterized the major national political institutions as antiquated, calcified and fossilized. The major political parties, assumed by the dominant ideologies to outline differences and organize conflict, were characterized as homogenous and lacking in issue orientation. Congress was seen as reduced to meaninglessness by virtue of the domination of the conservative committee system. Institutions that are capable of action, such as the executive, were seen as dominated by business and military interests.

This characterization of stagnancy and unresponsiveness was based both on academic analysis and first-hand new left experience in attempting to produce change. Throughout the sixties, the left activists tested the responsiveness of the political system in a variety of ways and always with the same result. The lack of federal government aid for civil rights workers in the South and failure to seat the Mississippi Freedom Democratic Party Delegation at the 1964

---

[9] Students for a Democratic Society, *The Port Huron Statement* (Chicago: SDS, 1966), p. 20.

Democratic Convention exposed the reality as opposed to the rhetoric of the government's position on racism. Experiences in the northern urban ghettoes, both black and white, with urban renewal, welfare, and other issues indicated the intransigence and destructiveness of both national and local bureaucracies. Finally, Eugene McCarthy's 1968 presidential campaign and its outcome confirmed for the new left the inability of the political system to tolerate even the mildest of reformist modification.

Thus, for the left, both academic analysis and personal experience confirm the imagery of unresponsiveness and irresponsibility of the political institutions. They exist to insulate men who are in powerful positions from the mass public and to provide a confusing facade of democratic processes. The result is a politics of confusion, structurally induced, in which the individual citizen abdicates political responsibility in the face of apparently overwhelming complexity.

The power potential of the economic institutions is seen as equally inaccessible and irresponsible. The wealth of the country is concentrated, rather than diffused. Large corporations, monopolies and conglomerates dominate the economy and prevent the competition that is supposed to result in diversity and consumer welfare. Economic decisions have dramatic impact upon society as a whole, in every area from domestic welfare to foreign affairs, but there is neither responsiveness nor public control of its functioning. Contrary to the beliefs of reform liberals like Galbraith, the new left thinkers assert that profitability rather than humanistic values remains the criterion of decision-making in the economy. One result is a nation where poverty and misery, planned obsolescence, and a welfare state that is more rhetoric than reality exist despite abundance. Another is a system that is unable to deal with pressing economic problems, such as automation, that promise to cause increasing difficulty and misery in the future unless faced from a humanistic perspective.

These notions of the bureaucratization and unresponsiveness of political and economic institutions come together for the new left in the concept of the military-industrial complex. In terms reminiscent of C. Wright Mills, the Port Huron Statement refers to "the powerful congruence of interest and structure among military and business elites which affects so much of our development and destiny." [10] According to new left thinkers, elites in these two fields combine to create and foster the war economy described earlier. From positions of power, they direct societal resources to create a domestic warfare state and a foreign policy that is adventuristic and imperialistic. These decisions are made not on the basis of necessity or for the public good, but, as noted before, on the basis of what is beneficial for private enterprise—particularly, what is profitable for the giant corporations. The new left asserts that much of defense spending is motivated by orientation to profit rather than reaction to threats of external aggression from Russia or China. They point to the work of revisionist historians which indicates that the cold war was the result of the aggressiveness of the United States rather than the intransigence of the Soviet Union. We will consider this theme of new left argument in more detail when we turn to the specific issue of Vietnam as treated by the left.

ALIENATION

The new left's analysis of the distribution of meaningful power and control compels the conclusion that alienation and deprivation exists at all levels of American society. Blacks and poor whites suffer most because they are subject to economic deprivation and political powerlessness. But the relatively affluent worker and the middle class are also deprived, since they are equally isolated from the decisions that affect their lives. This powerlessness is most obvious with regard to the most critical of all decisions, to make war, and other closely related decisions such as the relative levels of government spending for defense as opposed to welfare.

But this powerlessness also affects the individuals' lives in other less obvious ways. In their employment, men are lost in massive hierarchical institutions in which they function as easily replaced cogs. The blue-collar worker takes part in a mechanized production process that he does not understand and is unable to control. The working conditions of the middle-class individual are somewhat more pleasant but almost equally mechanical. In addition, all are subjected to the constant barrage of media propaganda that shapes

---

[10] *Ibid.,* p. 17.

their activities and desires even (or particularly) in connection with their leisure time.

This aspect of the new left's world view—deprivation of the affluent—is based upon the perception of the gap between the actual and the potential in human development that Marcuse noted. It means that the new left thinker conceives of himself as not concerned solely with the need for freedom of less fortunate individuals such as the poor, but as concerned with his own freedom, which is equally threatened by the American social system. This vital theme of the new left is expressed incisively by Greg Calvert in the course of distinguishing the radical and the liberal:

> The liberal reformist is always engaged in fighting "someone else's battles."
> He does not sense himself to be unfree.
> Radical or revolutionary consciousness perceives contradictions in a totally different fashion. The gap is not between oneself and the underprivileged but is the gap between "what one could be" and the existing conditions for self realization. It is the perception of oneself as unfree, as oppressed—and finally it is the discovery of oneself as *one of the oppressed* who must unite to transform the objective conditions of their existence in order to resolve the contradictions between potentiality and actuality.[11]

The Values and Goals of the New Left

The Port Huron Statement indicates the nature and general direction of new left values: "We regard *men* as infinitely precious and possessed of unfulfilled capacities." For all new left thinkers, the emphasis is upon the essentially good, capable and cooperative nature of man. New left thinkers see themselves as consciously setting this view of human nature against a dominant one which emphasized the limitations of man and therefore his need to be controlled and manipulated—to be reduced, in the terminology of the

---

[11] Gregory Calvert, "In White America: Radical Consciousness and Social Change," in Teodori, ed., *op. cit.*, pp. 414–415.

Port Huron Statement, "to the status of things" [12]—for the sake of efficiency and the smooth functioning of the society. The value premises of new left ideology and its concept of human nature replace elitist conceptions of human development and progress with an affirmation of the innate capabilities of all men. In the words of Tom Hayden, "Above all, I reject the claim that only a privileged few can be independent, the view that creativity is necessarily the function of culture-preserving elites. I believe that independence can be a fact about ordinary people. [13]

In the new left scheme, property all but ceases to exist as a value. Certain material necessities are seen as the basis of an independent life, but emphasis is on the human qualities of freedom, creativity and spontaneity that reasonable material security can foster. The value which liberal thinkers place upon the accumulation of property and competition is seen not as a source of progress, but as one cause of the alienation of men from their true humanity.

Similarly, the value liberals place on technological and industrial progress is subordinated to human values. As we have already noted, new left thinkers place little value per se upon technology and believe that when misapplied, the costs of technological progress outweigh the benefits. In the words of the Port Huron Statement, "The personal capacity to cope with life has been reduced everywhere by the introduction of technology that only minorities of men (barely) understand." [14] The writers go on to suggest the need to control, and even to reverse in some cases, the trend toward increased mechanization and bureaucratization. Decentralization is offered as an important means by which institutions can be reduced to manageable size and man can recapture the sense of mastery over his environment. The Port Huron document asserts further that "The transfer of certain mechanized tasks back into manual form, allowing men to make whole, not partial, products, is not unimaginable." [15] The argument made by the new left is not in behalf of a complete return to the virtues of an agrarian society. It is simply that in pur-

---

[12] S.D.S., *op. cit.,* p. 6.
[13] Tom Hayden, "Student Social Action: From Liberation to Community," in Cohen and Hale, eds., *op. cit.,* p. 293.
[14] S.D.S., *op. cit.,* p. 50.
[15] *Ibid.*

suing technological innovation the criteria of human needs and preferences must always be applied. These somewhat negative goals, emphasizing the need to reverse trends and break down institutions, are related to a major positive goal of the new left—the desire to create a community.

COMMUNITY

By community, the new left means the creation of a society in which the principles of organization are no longer competition and struggle but cooperation and brotherhood. "Human brotherhood," the Port Huron Statement asserts, "must be willed . . . as the most appropriate form of social relation." [16] A truly human society will be created only "when a love of man overcomes the idolatrous worship of things. . . ." [17] Society, then, must be organized not primarily to foster technological and material progress but to foster the development of human independence and freedom. Individual freedom is conceptualized as complementary rather than contradictory to the concept of community since it is believed that freedom is expressed in solidarity with other men rather than in competition with them.

For new left thinkers, the goal of community is seen not as a distant Utopia growing out of abstract notions, but as something that can be created and experienced in the present. Writing of his experiences in the Free Speech movement in Berkeley, Gerald Rosenfield expresses this aspiration eloquently:

> What this experience gave us, and what their experience in the civil rights movement gave students who committed themselves to it, was the knowledge that a community is possible, that the basis for a viable society is not the protection of each man from his neighbor, who without restraint would be his enemy and destroy him for his own ends, but rather a shared humanity and material need for each other.[18]

---

[16] *Ibid.,* p. 7.

[17] *Ibid.*

[18] Gerald Rosenfield, "Generational Revolt and the Free Speech Movement," in Paul Jacobs and Saul Landau, eds., *The New Radicals* (New York: Vintage Books, 1966), p. 214.

The campus and community organizing experiences also convinced many of the new left thinkers that a second goal, participatory democracy, was both desirable and possible.

PARTICIPATORY DEMOCRACY

The basic meaning of the term participatory democracy is the return of the institutions of society to the control of the people. The bureaucratization and centralization of institutions that prevent masses of people from exercising power and allow elites to monopolize decision-making must be eliminated. Real substantive democracy must replace the formal rhetorical democracy that prevails in American society.

The new left's goal of participatory democracy has several implications for political institutions. As we have noted, the new left rejects the pluralistic image as descriptive of the present political system. (Certain portions of the Port Huron Statement and other early writings of the new left do seem to argue for a revitalized pluralism. But this description of the meaning of participatory democracy seems to be the truer and more prevalent one.) Further, it seems doubtful that the new left thinkers would find pluralism acceptable even if they saw it as an accurate description of reality. The new left's emphasis on the need for solidarity and brotherhood in the relationships among men contrast with the emphasis on bargaining, compromise and accommodated conflict that are components of pluralist politics. The new left notion of participatory democracy emphasizes the things that unite men rather than the differences among them. It appears to be conceptualized as a process in which face to face discussions in small groups produce consensus on issues and generate solutions to common problems.

Participatory democracy is not seen merely as a way for individuals to register their preferences and attain their desires, but as a process in which the lives of individuals are qualitatively transformed. Men move from alienation, isolation and powerlessness to participation, control and solidarity. "Politics," in the words of the Port Huron Statement, "has the function of bringing people out of isolation and into community, this being a necessary though not sufficient means of finding meaning in personal life." [19]

---

[19] S.D.S., *op. cit.*, p. 8.

Given this idea of its importance, the notion of participatory democracy applies not only to the institutions of the political system but extends to other societal institutions. In the words of Richard Flacks, "It means, too, the development of a concept of citizenship which extends beyond the conventional political sphere to all institutions of the society—the workplace, the school, the corporation, the neighborhoods, the welfare bureaucracies. The idea that men are citizens with respect to all exercise of authority, that each has responsibility for the actions of the institutions in which he is embedded." [20] Thus, not only political institutions, but all major societal institutions require restructuring to meet the criteria of participatory democracy. We will consider the implications of this for one institution of central concern to the new left, the university, in a later section; but they also apply to the organization of the economy.

The criteria of participatory democracy are the basis of the new left's rejection of the revisions of the economic system contemplated by liberals and reform liberals—completion of the welfare state. The welfare state is seen as deficient because it multiplies and complicates the problem of bureaucracy and centralization. In order to receive the social services that welfare bureaucracies provide, the individual seeking help must accept a definition and evaluation of himself applied by a middle-class professional. The operation is a "top-down" one in which the individual may receive some financial aid, but in which his essential condition of powerlessness remains unchanged. Again, Tom Hayden makes the point incisively:

> Our suspicion begins with the belief that welfare-state reforms, conducted within the private, selfish control of the economy, are ineffective because they are not conceived by the poor people they are designed for. Instead they mangle and manipulate the poor while relaxing most of the middle class into the comfortable sense that everything is being managed well.[21]

It is clear, then, that new left thinkers go beyond liberals and reform liberals in their vision of the necessary changes in the eco-

[20] Richard Flacks, "Is the Great Society Just a Barbeque?" in Teodori, ed., *op. cit.*, p. 195.
[21] Tom Hayden, "Up from Irrelevance," in Jacobs and Landau, eds., *op. cit.*, p. 271.

nomic system. However, the character of their more positive prescriptions in this area remain rather vague and general. In line with the commitments to participatory democracy and community, the Port Huron Statement declares the need to reverse the centralization of wealth and recapture the decision-making power it confers. The statement goes on to offer two basic principles for the economic sphere. First, "the economic experience is so personally decisive that the individual must share in its full determination," [22] and second, "the economy itself is of such social importance that its major resources and means of production should be open to democratic participation and subject to democratic social regulation." [23]

Statements like the preceding raise the question of the extent to which the goals of the new left can be described as socialist. This question becomes more pressing in view of the trend in the most contemporary new left literature to use terms such as "ownership of the means of production" and "monopoly capital," terms which clearly originate in the socialist traditions. There is also a tendency to emphasize the possibility of economic dislocations as the catalyst of revolution and, as we shall see, a new interest in the American working class as an actor in a revolutionary movement. The inference drawn by some commentators is that the new left is becoming increasingly socialist and therefore less original in its thinking.

To some extent, the problem depends upon one's definition of "socialist" and "new left." We believe, however, that a distinction can be made on the basis of the fact that the new left's approach to the economic system evolves from the emphasis on creating community and participatory democracy in all institutions, rather than more specifically Marxian analysis which identifies the economic institutions as uniquely important. In new left thinking, economic institutions are some among many that are in need of modification in the direction of decentralization and popular control.

Specific Issues and an Evolving Ideology

As already noted, much of new left ideology has developed and been articulated in the context of specific issue areas. In this

---

[22] S.D.S., *op. cit.,* p. 8.
[23] *Ibid.*

section, we will suggest how the general world view, values, and goals described above flow from specific issues confronted by the new left. We have chosen two of the many issues for their intrinsic importance and their suitability as illustrations. New left thinking regarding the university is illustrative of the new left analysis of a major societal institution. Foreign policy, with specific reference to the Vietnam war, is illustrative of new left treatment of a particular policy issue.

THE UNIVERSITY

The campus has been one of the major battlegrounds in the struggle of the activists of the new left. It has been the scene of protests, picketing, sit-ins, and even bombings. Students have made a wide range of demands upon administrations, running from abolition of the grading system to abolition of war research and ROTC. Many of these demands are related to broad societal issues, such as the war in Vietnam, but many stem from the specific new left analysis of the university as a societal institution.

New left thinkers make two related charges against universities. First, they are structural microcosms of the society, a society which, as we have already seen, they believe to be bureaucratized, authoritarian and manipulative. Second, in terms of the functions they perform for the larger society, they are no more than arms of the corporate economy and the defense establishment. New left thinkers argue that the university embodies all of the larger society's characteristics that they believe to be harmful to human development. Mario Savio expressed this feeling of identity at the beginning of the Free Speech movement in Berkeley in 1964:

> Last Summer I went to Mississippi to join the struggle there for civil rights. This fall I am engaged in another phase of the same struggle, this time in Berkeley. . . . The same rights are at stake in both places—the right to participate as citizens in democratic society and to due process of law. Further, it is a struggle against the same enemy.[24]

Although the specific issues raised in the context of the Berkeley confrontation were those of due process and free speech, the new

---

[24] Mario Savio, "An End to History," in Jacobs and Landau, eds., *op. cit.*, p. 230.

left thinkers conceptualized the free speech movement more generally as a struggle to democratize a depersonalized and unresponsive bureaucracy. The universities, it is argued, are run by bureaucrats for the purposes and convenience of bureaucrats without the participation of student citizens. As in the larger society, powerlessness is marked by participation in a meaningless charade of democracy, in this case by the existence of the ineffectual student government. In reality, the important decisions in a student's life are made by bureaucrats. Students are treated not as adults and citizens but as children, and the *in loco parentis* principle which (explicitly or implicitly) governs the relations between students and administration makes this clear. The authoritarian ethos carries over even into the classroom, into the relationship between teachers and student. Here, the mechanism is the use of exams and grades as a system of sanctions rather than as tools for teaching and learning.

As in the larger society, the environment is structured so that the human qualities of creativity and spontaneity are stifled. Competition rather than cooperation among individuals is fostered. The university offers a preconstructed mold into which students are expected to fit themselves. The substance of thinking and teaching in the university is also criticized by the new left. They claim that there is no real or unified attempt to deal with the specialization and compartmentalization of knowledge that accompanies the growth of an industrial society. Students are encouraged to regard big questions with moral dimensions as unanswerable and to submit themselves to technical expertise in limited areas because the problems they care about are too "complex" for their understanding. In short, they are taught to fit into, rather than to challenge, the prevailing structures.

The result of both these procedural and substantive deficiencies is much the same as in the larger society—alienation, apathy and retreat on the part of students. In the words of Tom Hayden:

> A sense of powerlessness evolves, powerlessness with regard
> to changing the state of affairs evoked by the ideology of
> "complexity." . . . To the student things seem to happen
> because of a mixture of graft and manipulation by an unseen
> them, the modern equivalent of "fate." [25]

---

[25] Tom Hayden, "Student Social Action," in Cohen and Hale, eds., *op. cit.,* p. 279.

A second effect of this type of education identified by Hayden is the relinquishment of concern and empathy for others. Value is placed not upon human development and happiness, but on orderliness and predictability.

New left thinkers also argue that this failure of the universities to produce individuals capable of dealing with the moral and human dimensions of their environment is not surprising in light of the functions that the university performs in the society as a whole—that of "knowledge factory" for the corporate liberal state. This brings us to the second major point in the new left critique of the university.

Far from being a neutral and independent institution capable of adopting a critical posture toward the society, the new left argues, the university performs servicing functions for the elite of the society. New left writers point to the fact that the boards of regents of the universities are composed of business leaders of the corporate liberal world and that government funds for defense and other war-related research are a major source of universities' money. Along all dimensions, the new left argues, universities are penetrated by business, government and military concerns. Their major activity is the transformation of students into young bureaucrats capable of efficiently running, but not of challenging, the major societal institutions.

This image of the university is not essentially different from that of Clark Kerr's, who coined the term "multiversity." The difference is that the thinkers of the new left, disapproving of the character of the society within which the university functions, see the interdependence not as a cause for celebration, but as a condition requiring change.

The new left activists have attempted to change the university in terms of both aspects of their critique. From a personal perspective, they wish to resist the channeling and manipulation of their lives. They are raising for the university the same demand that is raised with regard to other institutions in the society—that it restructure in terms of the criteria of participatory democracy. In the context of the university, this means raising issues such as the abolition of the grading system and the right of students to participate in the selection of teachers and in course and curriculum development. These, it is argued, are the critical decisions that take place in the university environment. They affect both the relationship of the student and the university and of the larger society and the university.

Ultimately, new left thinkers argue, the university must cease to perform its present functions for the (corrupt) society. Thus, in addition to raising questions about the relationship between student, teacher, and administration, they challenge the activities of the university in performing war-related research, in conducting ROTC classes, and in cooperating with the Selective Service System. Again in the words of Tom Hayden:

> They [students] did not want to be included in the decision-making circles of the military industrial complex that runs Columbia: *They want to be included only if their inclusion is a step toward transforming the university.* They want a new and independent university standing against the main-stream of American society, or they want no university at all.[26]

VIETNAM WAR AND FOREIGN POLICY

The opposition to the Vietnam war and the American military role throughout Southeast Asia has been the most widely publicized and dramatic of the many issues raised by the new left. The left has expressed its opposition in a number of ways, among them protests against corporation and military recruiting on campus, massive civil disobedience, burning of draft cards, and even disruption of supply and troop trains. The issue has spun off a number of subsidiary issues such as the proper definition of conscientious objector and the rights of protest within the armed services. Often missed among all the protests is the fact that new left thinkers see the Vietnam war as only a symptom of the underlying decay of American society.

The new left's criticism of United States foreign policy, particularly as it affects the Third World, predates the Vietnam war; the war focused and expanded the left's critique but did not originate it. Nor will the critique end with the conclusion of the war. For the left, the war is a horrible but entirely predictable phenomenon in that it is an application of the same destructive market values that

---

[26] Tom Hayden, "Two, Three, Many Columbias," in Teodori, ed., *op. cit.*, p. 186.

dominate domestic life. Let us look first at the new left's general analysis of U.S. foreign policy, and then to its specific analysis of the Vietnam war.

At least since the 1950s, the new left argues, U.S. foreign policy has been guided principally by a concern for profitability and foreign investments rather than by a desire to insure world peace and promote the development of independence in other nations. The image of the U.S. foreign policy as designed to protect and foster freedom is fundamentally misleading. Most new left thinkers concede that the U.S.S.R. is hostile and aggressive, but, they contend, the American postwar policy of containment and the fervent anti-Communism of western diplomacy regularly force her to extreme stands. But it is with regard to the Third World nations of Asia, Africa, and Latin America that American foreign policy is seen as most destructive and mistaken.

Although couched in the language of freedom and progress, in reality, the foreign policy of the United States with regard to the Third World has been an aggressive neocolonialism. New left writers point to both the growth of U.S. corporate investment in the Third World and the disproportionately profitable character of these investments. They claim U.S. corporations are draining the Third World countries of their resources and returning nothing. Capitalist writers' boast that U.S. economic strength may be measured by its share of the world consumption market becomes an indictment from the new left thinkers' perspective. In the words of Carl Ogelsby, "With about 5% of the world's people we consume about half the world's goods. We take a richness that is in good part not our own, and we put it in our pockets, our garages, our split-levels, our bellies and our futures." [27]

Further, the new left argues, the American corporate state demands not only the economic dependency of the Third World countries, but also their political subservience. The result is that genuinely nationalistic uprisings can be as great a threat as an externally conducted communist takeover. All political movements or regimes that genuinely seek independence for Third World nations are a potential danger to U.S. economic interests and are therefore suppressed by methods ranging from rightist coups to mass murders. The new left writers have alleged that a string of CIA

---

[27] Carl Ogelsby, "Trapped in a System," in Teodori, ed., *op. cit.*, p. 186.

coups or direct military interventions have maintained or established undemocratic but private enterprise-oriented regimes in a number of Third World countries. Clearly the criteria for U.S. support cannot be the democratic nature of the regime since the U.S. supports blatantly undemocratic governments such as those in Spain and South Africa. Always, when analyzed, the touchstone of American foreign policy is found to be protection and extension of corporate capitalism.

Although the majority of new left thinkers find communism as practiced in the U.S.S.R. distasteful, they uphold the right of other nations to choose their own form of government and find it comprehensible that they might choose a communistic form. Moreover, they are convinced that the anti-Communist ideology of the U.S. is the rationale, rather than the reason, for many of its foreign policy decisions. The real reasons, the need to maintain dominant and exploitative interests, are wrapped in the imagery of a crusade for freedom. The people of the United States are taught to interpret the natural fury and turmoil of a movement for independence and development as inexplicable and mysterious or as inevitably communist inspired. They remain uninformed about the connections between the conditions of misery in Third World countries and the popular support for development of socialist and other movements. They are led to ignore the brutality and disorder that accompanied the American struggle for freedom and prevented from seeing Third World struggles as manifestations of the same desires. The manipulative aspects of their own existences, the condition of powerlessness and apathy, renders them incapable of believing that men still fight and die for freedom.

New left thinkers reject the assertion that the Vietnam war is a war between two nations, one communist and the other free. They see it as a civil war in which an indigenous but foreign-originated elite, aided by the United States, is attempting to suppress a genuine and authentic national revolution. Again in the words of Carl Ogelsby,

> What the National Liberation Front is fighting in Vietnam is a complex and vicious war. This war is also a revolution, as honest a revolution as you can find anywhere in history.[28]

---

[28] *Ibid.*, p. 183.

The U.S. government claims that our policy in Vietnam, as in other Third World countries, aids a free government in its fight against an undemocratic one; new left thinkers argue that the credibility of these claims is particularly weak in the case of Vietnam. In 1954, they point out, the U.S. government helped cancel the scheduled elections and install the Diem regime, which proceeded to repress all opposition, noncommunist as well as communist. At the time, President Eisenhower was quoted as saying that if elections had been held, Ho Chi Minh would have been the overwhelming choice of the Vietnamese people. Since that time, the U.S. government has supported, and indeed created, a string of brutal and repressive dictators who would clearly have fallen without massive U.S. military aid.

The Vietnam war is distinctive, in the eyes of the new left, chiefly for exposing on an unprecedented scale the consequences for Third World peoples of American foreign policy. In Vietnam, an entire nation, civilians included, has been declared the enemy. Old men, women and children are confined and killed. The entire cultural life of a nation has been destroyed. As one thinker puts it, "We have uprooted the people from the land and imprisoned them in concentration camps called 'sunrise villages.' Through conscription and direct political intervention and control, we have broken or destroyed local custom and traditions, trampled upon those things of value which give dignity and purpose to life." [29] The Vietnam example leads the new left to conclude that there is no destruction that the U.S. government will not sanction to insure profitability and stability.

The domestic consequences of the war have also been clear. Thousands of Americans have been killed and hundreds of thousands of lives disrupted. Defense spending has increased drastically while social welfare needs have been ignored. From the new left perspective, the erosion of individual freedom is of even greater significance. The tendencies toward total control and manipulation already present in the warfare state are intensified by the pursuit of an extended war. Ironically, the war being fought for "freedom" in Vietnam leads to contraction of American freedom. Government officials consciously distort information and block attempts to reveal the truth. War propaganda has reinforced and exploited the nationalism, racism, and irrational anti-Communism of the American public.

---

[29] Paul Potter, "The Incredible War," in Teodori, ed., *op. cit.*, p. 246.

The war has revealed the extent to which dehumanization has progressed in capitalist society, when brutality such as that practiced in Vietnam is allowed and even condoned.

Thus, for new left thinkers, the Vietnam war has revealed the tremendous destructiveness of the American system—as a system. The war is the natural outcome of the market values that have replaced humanistic values in U.S. society. It's full horror is expressed by the fact that it was begun and is continued not by evil men, but by good men acting in a perverted and destructive system. Thus, the new left argues, we must not only end the war, but transform the system.

At the same time that the Vietnam war has exposed the worst in U.S. society and the enormity of the task of changing it, it has also inspired the thinkers of the new left to hope that change is possible. They point out that despite the nearly limitless technological power the U.S. has at its disposal, it has proved incapable of winning the war. New left writers see the Vietnamese people as exemplifying the determination of Third World peoples to be free whatever the cost. Like the most militant black thinkers, they look upon the Third World as a potential ally, a repository of values and beliefs that the United States needs badly and of the physical courage to create the world they desire. Paul Potter summed up this sense of hope at an antiwar demonstration in Washington:

> In a strange way the people of Vietnam and the people on this demonstration are united in much more than a common concern that the war be ended. In both countries there are people struggling to build a movement that has the power to change their condition. The system that frustrates those movements is the same. All our lives, our destinies, our very hopes to live depend on our ability to overcome that system.[30]

These are not the only issue areas in which the new left has been deeply engaged. They are, however, two in which the new left's characteristic process of both *applying* and *developing* premises, values, and goals are especially visible. In both cases, the new left began with some basic assumptions and aspirations and concluded that the prob-

---

[30] *Ibid.*, p. 290.

lems of American society were even deeper, more fundamental, and more pressing than they had realized. In the process of coming to grips with these concrete issues, the new left has refined its world view and added to its values and goals. The same process takes place as new left thinkers confront other issues; thus, the ideology is constantly growing and evolving new dimensions.

This built-in capacity for generation of new components of world view and of new values and goals is one of the distinguishing features of the new left. Another distinguishing characteristic is the prevalence of a fundamental level of analysis and prescription. Problems are not the result of wrong decisions by individuals, of faulty information, or of readily modified erroneous popular beliefs. Instead, they are caused by the basic structures of power and values and by the economic system that gave rise to those patterns. Both of these important characteristics of new left ideology may be illustrated in reactions to two issues that became publicly visible in the early 1970s—concern for the quality of the environment and women's liberation. For some, improvement of the environment required only new controls on pollution of the air and water and greater emphasis on conservation. For the new left, however, the issue became one of inevitable destructiveness and exploitation of both natural and human resources as a result of continuing materialist values and a profit-oriented economic system. Similarly, for some, the women's movement meant merely new legal rights and equal pay. But for the new left, women were as fully exploited in as institutionalized a manner as blacks, and their true liberation would require overhaul of dominant societal values and the economic relationships that sustain them. Tensions from liberal, system-preserving approaches and the more radical new left understanding of these two problems seem inevitable.

Social Change and Tactics

As the preceding sections make clear, new left thinkers are committed to sweeping and basic social changes. The creation of a community and participatory democracy are the general goals, and the new left sees a vast disparity between these goals and the present bureaucratized and stratified society. Unlike reform liberals, new left thinkers do not accept the economic and social system as given. While not explicitly socialist, they are opposed to capitalism and the market values they see it imposing upon human life. Nor do they accept the necessity of working with present political institutions since they regard them as inflexible and incapable of transformation. Thus, they are revolutionary both in terms of the goals they espouse and in their rejection of "working within the system."

The problems of social change for the new left begin, rather than end, with the articulation of these very general principles. In addition to the decision not to work within the system, one must decide (upon the level of strategy and tactics) what specific positive activities will promote change. Like the most militant black leaders, the new left has opted for revolutionary change but has not yet articulated a comprehensive theory of social change. In this area too, the new left's approach has been consciously experimental and eclectic, as suits an evolving ideology.

Many different processes of social change appear to have revolutionary results; these range from the elitist coup d'etat to a mass-based participatory movement. In general, the thinkers and activists of the new left appear to be committed to a mass-based popular revolution as both the most desirable and practical in a post-industrial society. They are inclined to view participatory democracy as a means as well as a goal, and to conceptualize the revolutionary process as the swelling up of change from the grass roots. As they put it, they have attempted to build a movement where everybody is a leader. There appears also to be consensus that any revolution in the United States must occur as part of the worldwide revolutionary movement led by the nations of the Third World. The movement must be both anticapitalist and anti-imperialist. But even with these general orienting principles established, a number of questions remain unanswered.

On a more specific level, the new left has had to face many of the same tactical issues as have the writers and activists of Black Liberation. They have had to consider with whom, and under what conditions, to form coalitions. They have discussed both the justifiability and the efficacy of violent as opposed to nonviolent tactics. And they have argued the merits of slow and patient organizing techniques as opposed to dramatic direct action techniques. But, again as in the black movement, no decision or broadly shared answers have as yet emerged.

In addition, the new left has had to face a problem that does not arise in the same form for black militants: the question of what group to organize. Much new left thinking about social change is devoted to the search for what is often labeled the "historical agency of change." In simplest terms, this means seeking the group or groups within the society that are capable of acting to fundamentally change the social order.

The new left's understanding of oppression encourages eclecticism and experimentation along this dimension of social change, as it does on the question of means. Because (in terms of new left analysis) almost all groups in the society belong to the oppressed, almost all groups are potentially organizable. The problem for the new left is not so much in identifying oppression as in identifying the conditions under which people can be brought to *perceive* themselves as deprived and oppressed. This brings up the question of which of the large number of issues, ranging from the Vietnam war to the character of welfare and the existence of unemployment, can trigger perceptions of oppression. Again, no decisive answer has been forthcoming.

In practice, new left groups have focused their organizing attempts around a variety of groups in the society and attempted to organize them with various means and issues. Often, these disparate attempts have led to bitter and damaging disputes within the ranks of new left activists. For instance, there has been a constant tension between new leftists who focused on the college campuses and tended to use dramatic action techniques and community organizers who identified the poor as the primary target and attempted to use the slower community organizing techniques. A second example occurred in 1968, when the SDS, the largest national new left organization, split into three groups because they were unable to agree on such questions as the role of blacks in the movement, the organizational potential of the working class, and the efficacy of violence.

It would be impossible in this short chapter to reproduce all of the debates concerning social change and tactics which have engaged new left thinkers. We have chosen instead to focus on the question of the historical agency both because it has given rise to much thoughtful new left writing and because many of the other arguments are similar to those discussed in the chapter on black liberation. In the discussion that follows, we describe the major groups identified by new left thinkers as potential agents of change and the rationale for the choices. We also indicate the methods used by new left activists in approaching each group. We hope, thereby, to provide some notion of the scope of new left tactical thinking and the disputes to which it has given rise.

THE POOR

The poor have been a major target for new left organizing efforts. Initially, new left efforts were directed at both blacks and whites, but with the development of the black power movement in 1965, the focus shifted to poor whites, particularly in urban areas. New left thinkers identified the poor as a potential agency of change for several reasons. First, and most obvious, they are a clearly powerless and materially deprived segment of the society. Having little stake in the status quo, they might be expected to welcome opportunities to mobilize and act for change. In Todd Gitlin's words, "The poor know they are poor and don't like it; hence they can be organized to demand an end to poverty and the construction of a decent social order." [31]

A second rationale emphasizes not what the poor lack, but what they have. New left analysis hypothesized that since they were excluded from the mainstream of society, the poor were less steeped in its dominant values, the individualism, materialism and competitiveness that are viewed as pervading middle-class America. The poor were thought to possess communal and cooperative values and goals. Thus, the activists hoped to find in the poor a set of values and beliefs that would guide the revolutionary movement. As Staughton Lynd expresses it, "There is an unstated assumption that the poor, when they find voice, will produce a truer, sounder radicalism than any which alienated intellectuals might prescribe." [32]

---

[31] Todd Gitlin, "The Battlefields and the War," in Cohen and Hale, eds., *op. cit.*, p. 126.
[32] Staughton Lynd, "The New Radical and 'Participatory Democracy,'" in Teodori, ed., *op. cit.*, p. 229.

New left activists believed that slow, patient community organizing techniques were most appropriate in attempting to organize the poor. This meant that organizers should move into the community and, as far as possible, share the life of the people. There were attempts to form neighborhood groups around relevant issues, such as unemployment, welfare, urban renewal, and the police behavior. The groups raised demands concerning these problems on the level of local administration and city government. Occasionally, direct action techniques such as sit-ins and rent strikes were employed.

Organizers, while beginning with local issues, constantly kept in mind the need for raising local reform issues to more far-reaching structural demands. In Todd Gitlin's words, "The special quality of *radical* issue-organizing is the intertwining of two different kinds of demands: demands for tangible concessions which can be granted by existing institutions, and demands for control and substantial restructuring of these institutions." [33] The move toward more radical demands on the part of the poor was expected to grow naturally out of confrontations on the local level, which would make clear that more far-reaching change was necessary. For example, it was expected that an issue such as the size of welfare payments would evolve into an issue over grass-roots control of the welfare bureaucracy, leading to an analysis of the causes and necessities of welfare, the overall structure of the economy, etc. In this manner, the poor would begin to connect the conditions of their own lives with the questions of participatory democracy and community organization that the new left thinkers felt were essential.

These issues were also expected to arise through the participation of the poor in the day-by-day activities of the community organization they had founded. The organizers were determined to establish participatory democracy not only as a goal, but also as a means, which meant building participatory democracy into the grass-roots movement from the start. Therefore, in the community organizations, formal structure was kept to a minimum, with decisions made on the basis of full discussion and consensus. When formal structure was found to be necessary, offices were to be elec-

---

[33] Todd Gitlin, "The Radical Potential of the Poor," in Teodori, eds., *op. cit.,* p. 139.

tive and frequently rotated. As soon as was feasible, initial new left organizers were expected to abdicate, rather than maintain control of organizational power. Although this method of organizing was conceded to be somewhat inefficient, it was thought to have the virtue of allowing many to share in a real decision-making process, thereby eliminating feelings of inadequacy, incompetency and powerlessness that the poor might harbor. It was expected, in the words of Staughton Lynd to result in "the building of a brotherly way of life in the jaws of Leviathan." [34]

Thus, the predominant approach to mobilization of the poor was the slow community organizing style. Direct-action techniques were to be used only after a strong organizational base had been established. These techniques (it was hoped) would result in a confirmation of the efficacy of group action as well as lead to concrete improvement in the life of the community. The emphasis was on the long-run building of constituency through restraint and patience.

These principles of organization were the subject of a series of interesting evaluations by members of the community organizing groups themselves. The general conclusion seems to be that the new left had initially underestimated the difficulty of its task. Many of the assumptions in the initial rationale of the poor as a viable agency of change were questioned. These justify a brief review, for they have analogies in other areas, and they help to explain the new left's shifting tactics.

Some writers raised questions as to the effectiveness of organizing only the deprived. The poor, although a large segment of the society, are far from a majority. The need for allies arose, creating problems such as the advisability of cooperating with liberals and reform liberals. Further, the poor, particularly poor whites, were difficult to locate in a geographic community. Unlike blacks, poor whites were diffused throughout the city in a series of small concentrations. Also, there were splits within the poor that prevented their acting as a unified force. The most obvious and often discussed was the split between blacks and whites. The new left confronted, first, white racism and, then, black power as formidable obstacles to an effective interracial movement of the poor. There were also, however, differences of age, ethnic identification and employment

---

[34] Staughton Lynd, quoted by Todd Gitlin, *ibid.*, p. 139.

status among whites, which gave rise to problems in organizing whites alone. In short, many new left thinkers felt that they had overestimated the extent to which the problems of the poor were common problems; perhaps it is more accurate to say that they had underestimated the difficulty of revealing the common root of these problems.

The second major challenged assumption was the ability of the poor to generate counter values. Organizers found that resentment toward the system existed side-by-side with a feeling that poor people, because of laziness or lack of competence, had only themselves to blame for their problems. It was more difficult than originally anticipated to bring people to see problems as structurally caused and collectively shared. In addition to racism, there was often a vehement anti-Communism that made the discussion of socialist-like alternatives difficult. The poor were found to share the values of materialism and competitiveness that the new left was seeking to destroy to a considerable extent. The organizers found themselves in the position of having to distinguish "real" and "manipulated" needs, a distinction clouded by elitist counter-democratic implications.

This type of problem led some activists to experiment with new approaches to organizing the poor. Some turned to other groups as potentially more fruitful for initial organizing efforts. The debate within the new left over "the radical potential of the poor" continues, as do various attempts to organize them.

THE "NEW WORKING CLASS"

As we have seen, the new left considers the middle class as deprived and powerless. Some new left thinkers have argued that this group could be a vehicle of social change, identifying it as the "new working class." The notion of the "new working class" as an agent of change probably originated with the observation that, in fact, it was the middle-class students on the college campuses who were originating demands for change. Indeed, it was from this group that the ranks of the new left were drawn. Despite this origin the "new working class" analysis emphasizes the structural position rather than the age composition of this group.

The rationale underlying the choice of this group as an agency of social change is as follows. The fastest growing and functionally most significant occupational category in the economy consists of technological experts, management, and other "mind workers" such as teachers, social workers, etc. Although absolutely necessary to the working of the corporate machine and compensated at a rate that categorizes them as middle class, they are subjected to many of the same structural strains described in the discussion of the university student. Despite the fact that they are highly educated, as specialized cogs in large bureaucracies, they are allowed little independence of thought or action. In fact, they lack the freedom that was a characteristic of middle-class life when this class was composed of small businessmen, independent farmers, and professionals. Potentially, therefore, they can be brought to recognize their lack of freedom and to act to recreate it.

Although, as noted, the concept of new working class refers to an occupational rather than an age category, actual attempts at organization have tended to take place in the universities. This focus makes sense in view of the new left's belief that "students are 'trainees' for the new working class and the factory-like multiversities are the institutions which prepare them for their slots in the bureaucratic machinery of corporate capitalism." [35] Similarly, many campus confrontation tactics are seen as valuable not only for what they may immediately achieve, but for their radicalizing effect on the future "new working class."

Campus organizational efforts, in contrast to the community organizing style, tend to lead very rapidly to direct confrontations such as sit-ins and, less frequently, to destruction and violence. A number of arguments underlie the use of such tactics. To some extent, they are motivated by a moral imperative to "put your body on the line" in protest of the present societal structure. But more pragmatic reasons can be found to justify their use. Concrete concessions are often won from university administrations in response to such tactics. Armed forces and corporation recruiters have been forced off campuses, and ROTC programs and war-oriented research operations have been eliminated. In addition, sit-ins and similar tactics have the effect of dramatizing issues that might be ignored by both the college community and the public. During

---

[35] Gregory Calvert, in Teodori, ed., *op. cit.*, p. 417.

demonstrations, university classes tend to lose their character of irrelevance and become forums in which issues are hotly debated. Wide television coverage of the more dramatic elements of a protest brings the issue before large audiences, though in somewhat distorted form. This is in line with the new left's emphasis upon the media as an important manipulative force. Through dramatic direct-action techniques, new left activists have found themselves able to raise issues of public policy that the media would otherwise ignore or cover only in passing.

Finally, in confrontations and in the demand for power, the demonstrators and those who are drawn in with them break with the acquiescent attitudes that the new left believes so necessary to corporate bureaucracy. This prepares the ground for a transformed "new working class" capable of independent action. As Greg Calvert puts it, "We have organized them (students) out of their alienation from the multiversity and have raised the demand for 'student control' that is important because that is precisely the demand that the new working class must raise when it is functioning as the new working class in the economic system." [36]

While much of the organization of the new working class focuses on the colleges and universities and follows the patterns outlined above, there are other areas of activity and methods in which new left activists have engaged in attempts to organize this group. Members of the middle class have been organized by raising particular issues such as the fight to end the Vietnam war. In addition, professional groups, such as social workers and teachers, and other occupational units that raise a variety of issues, have begun to organize. This extension of organization of groups of the new working class beyond the college campuses is still a tentative but nonetheless significant area of new left organizing attempts.

THE YOUTH

New left thinkers have also explored the possibility that youth, as a group in itself, is a potential agent of social change. New left thinkers point out that in post-industrial society, adolescence is prolonged because the economy is unable to employ the large number of individuals available. This leads to the formulation of a sep-

[36] *Ibid.*

arate youth culture with its own values and goals, often focused around drugs, rock music and communal living. The new left attitude toward youth culture, particularly the hippie variation, is somewhat ambivalent. While welcoming it as a partial rejection of capitalist morality and a strong expression of the drive for community, New left thinkers consider questionable its ability to create significant change without the interjection of more consciously political analyses and goals. New left organizing attempts are designed to help create this political consciousness.

New left thinkers point to the fact that the apparent freedom and leisure of the youth culture obscures the extent to which young people are uniquely subjected to strains and tensions. In occupational terms, the society is structured so that young men have little choice but to become students or soldiers during their young adult years. We have already discussed the new left's view of the alienating tendencies found in the role of student and need not repeat them here. The tensions of the soldier role are obvious. Young people, often of black, poor white, or working class origins are forced into the most bureaucratic and hierarchical of institutions. Their assigned tasks, directly or peripherally related to the Vietnam War, are the subject of controversy and dissent. The armed forces are organizations which naturally produce discontent and dissatisfaction. New left thinkers consider it their task to focus and channel this dissent.

The new left has utilized a number of tactics in attempting to organize youth. The relevance of campus organizing attempts is clear. There have also been attempts to engage non-student youth, particularly young people of draft age, by establishing draft counseling centers and picketing and leafleting induction centers. Groups in high schools have been organized around a variety of issues. Perhaps the most significant attempts being made are those to organize armed forces personnel on active duty, both through the establishment of G.I. coffee houses near army bases and the organization of G.I. rights groups within the services.

THE WORKING CLASS

New left theory, in its search for an agency of change, originally tended to ignore the working class (manual workers) except to the extent of including its members in other categories such as the poor or youth. This tendency can be attributed to the fact that the new left identified this class as the old lefts' traditional agency of social change—a group which, in the opinion of some new left commentators, had been "bought off" by capitalist materialism and a corrupt union bureaucracy. As a result of the new left's growing concern with classical Marxist theory and the events that shook France in the Spring of 1968, a reappraisal of the revolutionary potential of the working class appears to be under way. The French working class, catalyzed by a strike within the universities, conducted a general strike which came close to toppling the government.

A case for the working class as an agent of social change can easily be constructed from standard new left concepts. The general new left notion of oppression and powerlessness clearly apply to this group. Further, despite the fact that the working class is not increasing as a proportion of the population, they are and will continue for a long time to be the largest occupational group within the country. Any mass-based revolutionary movement would of necessity include members from these ranks. Finally, the increasing number of wildcat strikes in recent years attest to the growing restlessness and dissatisfaction of the working class with the compromise-oriented union bureaucracies.

New left activists have made beginning attempts to organize this group, primarily through the establishment of worker-student alliances on the campus. These campus groups attempt to act as resource groups for workers both in normal and in strike situations. The 1970 wave of campus protests against G.E. recruiters was conceived both as a protest against the Vietnam war and as an act of solidarity with striking G.E. workers. There has also been a small movement for students to quit the campuses and work in factories in order to participate directly in the life and struggles of the working class. Although the focus on organization of the working class is in its beginning stages, this movement shows signs of growing into a major concern of new left thinkers.

EXTERNAL SOURCES

In concluding this discussion of social change and tactics, we must consider another line of new left reasoning that represents a real departure. In essence, it suggests that there are no potential agencies of social change within the contemporary United States in the sense described above. This argument, put forward by a splinter group of SDS known as the "Weathermen," emphasizes the materialism and racism of *all* segments of white American society and the almost impossible task of wooing its members from these attitudes. They point out that on a worldwide scale, the masses of white Americans of whatever class represent a tiny and privileged sector. The only viable revolutionary force in the contemporary world is the Third World socialist nations such as Cuba and China. Within the United States, only blacks and other colored peoples (considered to be colonized Third World peoples) and a small number of young whites have any revolutionary potential. The Weathermen expect the decisive defeat of capitalism by these forces within the present generation.

This analysis of the sources of change leads on a tactical level to an almost total identification with Third World revolutionary movements and to an insistence on the necessity of using violence. Weathermen have organized for, and have engaged in, violence—primarily the destruction of property which they consider imperialist and racist. The rationale behind these activities is twofold. First, they concretely aid Third World Liberation movements, such as the struggle of the Vietnamese, by forcing the U.S. government to deploy troops and expand forces to quash internal turmoil—thus having the effect of tying its hands in the international sphere. Second, Weathermen admit the possibility that some whites, particularly the young, can be brought to a realization of the futility of their materialist and racist values. The technique that will succeed in making this point is not the community organizing or even direct action technique, but a confrontation with violence and fear. In the words of Shin'ya Ono:

> What Weatherman is about is breaking through the racism and chauvinism at its core by forcing white people to grapple with the existence of a white fighting force that understands that this imperialist mother country will come down, and actually fights on the sides of blacks, yellows and browns, of the world. If our action, struggle and words often put white working class people (and movement people, too) up against the wall forcing them to fight us, so be it.[37]

---

[37] Shin'ya Ono, "You Need a Weatherman . . . ." *Leviathan,* Dec. 1969, p .17.

All of the new left approaches to social change outlined above share with the Weathermen the conclusion that the Third World Revolutionary movements are of vital importance. But the Weathermen emphasis upon the intransigence of the masses of white Americans and the need to confront them violently represents a real departure from new left conceptions of mass-based revolution and perhaps even from some of the value and goal orientations which we have described as fundamental elements of new left thought. It is impossible, as well as beyond the scope of this book, to say to what extent this new perspective is shared within the new left movement and how widely it will be accepted in the future. If it came to prevail as the dominant ethos, however, much of the descriptive material in this chapter would require revision.

Annotated Bibliography

Berger, Peter and Richard J. Neuhaus. *Movement and Revolution.* New York: Vintage Books, 1970. Perhaps the most perspective work on the ethical issues involved in revolution, written from both conservative and radical perspectives—but with very little difference between the two conclusions.

Cohen, Mitchell and Dennis Hale, eds. *The New Student Left.* Boston: Beacon Press, 1966. Somewhat dated, but still a valuable collection.

Hayden, Tom. "The Trial." *Ramparts,* 9, No. 1, July 1970. Most recent work by the prolific and insightful founding member of SDS, viewing the Chicago Trial in the context of a pending revolutionary situation.

Marcuse, Herbert. *An Essay on Liberation.* Boston: Beacon Press, 1968. A short, direct statement summarizing his major arguments and projecting them toward programs of action.

————. *One Dimensional Man.* Boston: Beacon Press, 1964. The classic statement of contemporary unfreedom—a book with important impact on the left.

Mills, C. Wright. *The Power Elite.* New York: Oxford University Press, 1956. A full-scale analysis of the concentration of power in the United States.

Newfield, Jack. *The Prophetic Minority.* New York: New American Library, 1966. A sympathetic study of the issues and people who initiated the new left as a political movement.

Roszak, Theodore. *The Making of a Counter Culture.* New York: Doubleday Anchor, 1969. A good introduction to some of the cultural aspects of new left thinking not emphasized in our analysis.

Students for a Democratic Society. *The Port Huron Statement.* (Chicago: SDS, 1966). The seminal document.

Teodori, Massimo, ed. *The New Left: A Documentary History.* Indianapolis, Ind.: Bobbs-Merrill, 1969. Certainly the most comprehensive, and reasonably current, collection of new left writings.

7

American Marxism

American Marxism is becoming increasingly important among contemporary ideologies. In part, this may be because its analyses of the American political economy have strongly influenced many new left and some black liberation thinkers; it may also be due to the emphasis that contemporary Marxism places on capitalist foreign policy in relation to Third World nations. Though drawing its basic concepts from Karl Marx's nineteenth century writings, American Marxism is a thoroughly modern critique of the American system that offers concrete prescriptions for its revitalization.

We use the term Marxism as a comprehensive category embracing those American thinkers who (1) see the character of economic organization as the basic factor in shaping a society's value system, social class structure, and political institutions and practices; (2) see a capitalist economy as creating profit-oriented, materialist values and a class structure in which wealthy owners constitute a ruling class that uses the power of the state, both at home and abroad, in exploitative and selfish ways; and (3) believe that such a social system is unjust, unnecessary, inconsistent with man's nature, and should be eliminated—peacefully or, if necessary, by force. This is a more general definition than is sometimes employed. To be more faithful to the careful work of the many Marxist scholars and theoreticians would require a level of technical precision, a distinction of the competing interpretations, and an allocation of space that seem unjustifiable. We hope, in this way, to avoid some of the difficulties that have confronted Americans in understanding and evaluating Marx's analytical concepts. The latter are not necessarily to be found in the specialized work of any self-proclaimed interpreters (Marx himself once complained that he was not a Marxist), nor are they proved or disproved by the success or failure of century-old predictions; certainly, they are not illustrated in the practice of the Soviet Union. We are concerned here with the distinctive way in which some Americans interpret the American system, the hopes they have for its improvement, and how such a belief system may affect American politics. By exploring American Marxist ideology as we have defined it (and as it is voiced by American thinkers who fit this definition), we shall be best able to understand its substance and impact in the United States today.

World View

As implied above, Marxism begins with an economic analysis —one which challenges most of the fundamental assertions of capitalism. In broad terms, Marxism alleges that capitalism is unable to generate the kind of values and social system that is consistent with man's nature. Specifically, capitalism diverts socially produced goods and services from the workers who produce them to the profit of the owning (and ruling) oligarchy, thereby creating sharply conflicting class interests and an econopolitical exploitation process that, together, make for inherent instability. Where capitalism sees affluence, harmony, and stable progress, Marxism sees human misery, class conflict, deliberate waste, and unstable stagnation. Of the many components of the Marxist critique of capitalism, we shall focus on four major points: the nature of monopoly capitalism, imperialism, the role of government, and the character and prospects of the current economy.

MONOPOLY CAPITALISM

Capitalism and, to an even greater extent, reform liberalism have begun to acknowledge the concentration of economic power and its effects on the free market. Marxism, however, puts this insight at the center of its analysis of the contemporary economic and social systems, terming it "monopoly capitalism," and draws several distinctive implications from it.[1] Monopoly capitalism means that huge corporations dominate entire sectors of the market, rendering the economy bureaucratized, hierarchical, and totally controlled. More important, such dominance means that unprecedented levels of profit are generated and a constantly increasing economic surplus (the excess of money and products about what can be absorbed in investment or consumed) is created.[2] One major analysis, Baran and Sweezy's *Monopoly Capital,* describes the new situation in these terms:

> While competitive capitalism also generated economic surplus in substantial proportions, monopoly capital has produced it at an unprecedented level, both absolutely and as a share of total output.[3]

Moreover, under monopoly capitalism, surplus is generated at such a rate that what Marxism terms "normal" outlets, such as capital replacement, consumption by wealthy elites, and even technological innovation, are insufficient to absorb it.

The presence of this unabsorbable surplus is the key fact of contemporary American economic and political life, in the eyes of Marxists, and the main reason for the current pattern of governmental policies. In order to maximize profits, corporations continue to seek cuts in costs, control markets more effectively, and reduce competition. Thus, the surplus continues to rise, but under capitalist principles, there are only a few things that can legitimately be done with it. In itself, the tendency of the economic surplus to rise might be looked on as an indication of the essential well-being and richness of the economy. As Baran and Sweezy suggest, "The size of the surplus is an index of productivity and wealth, of how much freedom

---

[1] There are a number of formulations of the monopoly capital concept in current Marxist thinking. Here we draw primarily upon the one advanced by Paul A. Baran and Paul M. Sweezy in *Monopoly Capital* (New York: Modern Reader Paperbacks, 1968).

[2] This analysis is supported by a wealth of theoretical argument and the presentation of considerable evidence in several Marxists works, among them that of Baran and Sweezy drawn on here. But it is impossible to do justice to these complex and technical analyses, and we have been forced to telescope and summarize them briefly.

[3] Baran and Sweezy, *ibid.,* p. 79.

a society has to accomplish whatever goals it may set for itself." [4] Instead, Marxism holds, capitalism cannot absorb this surplus because it will not direct it toward social goals or toward the masses of workers. However, these attempts to absorb the surplus must somehow be made or the capitalist engine will slow and stop. The problem of disposing of the surplus thus becomes both the principal dynamic and the major contradiction of modern capitalism. The irony of this situation is that the capability of capitalism to produce such a surplus will ultimately be the cause of its stagnation and collapse. In Marxist analysis, the self-imposed standards of monopoly capitalism lead to a scarcity of acceptable means of absorbing this surplus and an abundance of those that cannot be allowed.

(a) *Forbidden channels: social uses.* Marxist thinkers see immense social needs in the United States for which the surplus might be used. Under a rational economic system oriented to serving human needs, demonstrable requirements for public housing, public transportation, health and educational facilities, etc. would prescribe the direction of surplus utilization. Under monopoly capitalism, the level of government expenditure for such purposes remains severely limited. This is because government is responsive to the preferences of the corporations, groups and individuals that comprise monopoly capitalism's ruling oligarchy, and their interests are not served by such government activity. They do not want government competition with private enterprise's opportunities in these areas, nor do they wish either to create expectations or undermine the present distribution of power in the society. Broader support for education, for example, might threaten the permanence of the existing class structure, make it difficult to obtain low-wage menial employees, and even create new political awareness among the lower classes. For these reasons, Baran and Sweezy argue, national support for education is kept unconscionably low and such government financing as is undertaken is channeled disproportionately to elite private schools and colleges.

(b) *Approved channels: defense, imperialism, and the "sales effort."* Marxism is quick to point out that the corporate oligarchy

---

[4] *Ibid.,* p. 9.

is not opposed to government spending as such. Government spending of a particular kind is a vital means of surplus disposal. Private enterprise can only gain from military contracts, and a strong military serves the further purpose of protecting the overseas involvement of monopoly capitalism—its markets, investments, and sources of raw materials. For Marxists, defense expenditures are doubly irrational. They are not only wasteful disposal of the economic surplus; they contribute to the essentially destructive impact of overseas corporate expansion, protect it against the justified wrath of exploited Third World peoples, and bolster immoral and fruitless efforts to oppose socialism in other nations. A less dangerous but equally irrational means of absorbing the surplus, is the "sales effort"—the unprecedented advertising and promotional efforts by which monopoly capitalism seeks to promote demand for its products. Marxist critics agree with others' distaste for such manipulative efforts to create artificial and unnatural "needs" and for the cultural debasement which results. But they add that the sales effort promotes unnecessary materialism and wasteful emphasis on consumer goods because it is a structural necessity of monopoly capitalism.

Two major points regarding monopoly capitalism may be made in summary. Marxism holds first that the capitalist economic system operates in such a way that only destructive and dehumanizing directions are possible for it. Waste is the typical mode of surplus utilization. Second, capitalist society is so structured that its operations automatically create the forces that will ultimately destroy it. The channels chosen for absorbing the surplus are both inadequate and dangerous. Foreign investment leads to conflict, and military armament increases the risk. Inevitably, capitalism must undergo a crisis of surplus absorption, and the depression, stagnation, and social conflict that result may lead to a complete restructuring of the society along more rational lines. This basic framework of analysis and expectation is the major building block of the American Marxist world view, from which flow all other images and interpretations. The remaining components of the Marxist world view are selected from among the many corollaries of the basic propositions of monopolistic capitalism on the grounds that they are among the more important and distinguishing features of the larger Marxist ideology.

IMPERIALISM

Probably no characteristic attributed to the American economic system is as much discussed by contemporary Marxists as imperialism. It is a fundamental tenet of Marxist ideology that capitalism is a world system rather than a system confined to national boundaries. The Marxist image of the United States as a major imperialist power contrasts sharply with the traditional ideologies' view of the self-sufficiency and insularity of the American economy. Marxism sees the economy and, therefore, the social structure of the United States as linked to, and dependent upon, its foreign operations. It holds that understanding of these links is vital to understanding the past growth and present state of our capitalist economy.

Marxists argue that exploitation of foreign nations, particularly those of the Third World, has historically been of major importance to capitalist development. Andre Gunder Frank and Paul Baran both argue that the rapid growth of the United States was aided by drawing capital and raw materials from undeveloped nations, particularly Latin America.[5] The result was destruction of local agriculture and other industries and conversion of such nations into dependent markets. Gunder Frank declares that it is fundamentally incorrect to view the development of advanced capitalist countries and the underdeveloped nations as two distinct processes. The capitalist system must be seen as developing as a whole, as a world system, rather than as developing in a particular nation. Thus, the achievements of the advanced capitalist nations were realized at the cost of the Third World, not because of the intrinsic superiority, capacity, or ingenuity of domestic capitalists. Marxist analysis is similar to that of the black liberation thinkers who call attention to the importance of the institution of slavery in the economic and social development of the United States. Both challenge the traditional image of an economic system based upon freedom and independently generating great wealth and plenty.

The importance of foreign economic links is generally considered by Marxists to be even greater for the contemporary economic system. Although certain of the most blatant manifestations

---

[5] Paul Baran, *The Political Economy of Growth* (New York: Modern Reader Paperbacks, 1968); Andre Gunder Frank, "The Development of Underdevelopment," *Monthly Review*, Sept. 1966.

of imperialism, such as direct political dominance of Third World countries, have been discontinued, imperialist practices continue unabated. Marxist ideology asserts that economic plundering of other nations has reached unprecedented levels in the twentieth century. The United States is described as operating a far-flung empire that grows every year. In particular, Marxism holds that, contrary to the claims of the traditional ideologies, American overseas involvement is (a) principally due to economic motivations, and (b) on balance, destructive to Third World nations.

(a) *The economic basis of American involvement.* Marxism takes direct aim at the claim that American involvement in the affairs of other nations is primarily attributable to philosophical or political motivations. It is often said, for example, that economic motivations are not important because American foreign trade represents a very small proportion of total gross national product. In *The Age of Imperialism,* Harry Magdoff argues that when the cumulative, rather than yearly, amount of foreign investment is considered and when its strategic, rather than gross, significance is examined, the American economic interest abroad is substantial.[6] Overseas investment is a major outlet for the surplus, according to both Victor Perlo and Paul Baran.[7] Others have noted the need to acquire raw materials, strategic materials, cheap labor, and assured markets.

Probably the most sophisticated argument regarding motivations is that of Magdoff, who asserts that large corporations have a general need to assure themselves of as controlled an environment as possible. This need encompasses all the specific motivations that might or might not be operative at a given time and in a particular situation. In his words,

> The urge to dominate is integral to business. Risks abound in the business world. Internal and external competition, rapid technological changes, depression, to name but a few, threaten not only the rate of profit but the capital investment

---

[6] Harry Magdoff, *The Age of Imperialism* (New York: Modern Reader Paperbacks, 1969).

[7] Baran, *op. cit.*; and Victor Perlo, "Relevance of Marxist Economics to U.S. Conditions," *Political Affairs,* Feb. 1969.

itself. Business therefore is always on the lookout for ways
of controlling its environment, to eliminate as much risk as
possible.[8]

One implication drawn by Magdoff from this analysis is that it is
incorrect to look for a specific economic explanation for every act
of U.S. foreign policy. The need to expand and protect economic
interests and the sanctity of the profit motive is a general guiding
principle. Resources and markets must be protected for their future
and potential value as much as for their present use. For instance,
areas such as Vietnam are critical not because of their direct and
specific economic importance, but because the general principle is
threatened by the attempt of a Third World people to establish independence, especially when accompanied by a socialist economic
perspective. Thus, Magdoff sees a general U.S. scheme of domination in which even economically marginal countries are of importance.[9]

Marxists do not claim that political and philosophical motives
play no part in American foreign policy. In a sense, some Marxists
would assert, freedom is a goal of overseas policies. Historian William A. Williams declares,

> Certain freedoms and liberties are essential to capitalists,
> even though capitalism is not essential to freedom and lib-
> erty. There is no discrepancy, therefore, in going to war for a
> free marketplace and going to war to defend, secure, and
> even extend the political freedoms and liberties associated
> with such a marketplace political economy.[10]

Freedom then may be considered a goal of U.S. foreign policy, if the
term is understood in a limited and culturally specific way. Political
freedom can mean only the Western style of democracy, and economic freedom means only a capitalist market economy. These are
encouraged because they complement rather than contradict the basic
interests of the corporations in profitable foreign relations. Other

---

[8] Magdoff, *op. cit.,* p. 35.
[9] *Ibid.*
[10] William Applemau Williams, *The Great Evasion* (Chicago: Quadrangle Paperbacks, 1968), p. 46.

freedoms, such as freedom to create a truly planned economy, freedom to control the country's economic resources internally, and freedom to make a socialist revolution, are a danger to U.S. corporate domination and cannot be tolerated.

(b) *The destructiveness of American involvement.* Marxism denies that the consequences of American economic engagement in Third World nations are benign. In particular, it denies that Third World nations develop significantly from American investments and, instead, asserts that capital is withdrawn, one-crop economies established, and the rate of growth slowed by American involvement. The original process of extracting capital and raw materials is continued today under only slightly changed terms. American capital is invested only at very high rates of return to its American owners, and control of the investment remains in the hands of Americans who are motivated only by the prospect of maximizing their profits. The independence of the Third World nation's economy is neither encouraged nor tolerated, because it would endanger markets and profits.

Considerable attention has been paid by Marxist economists to developing evidence about the impact of American involvement, particularly in Latin America. Three points make up this argument: First, isolation from the advanced capitalist nations appears to promote economic progress; second, those nations subject to capitalist intervention developed faster during periods when ties were temporarily weakened; and third, Cuba has progressed far more rapidly alone than have those nations that remain within the American orbit.[11]
This argument amounts to a nearly complete reversal of the images held by the traditional ideologies.

Marxists do not allege that no beneficial results occur from American involvement. They concede that some industry has been built and some workers employed at improved wages. But they see this development as superficial. Capital is still extracted, because the high profits generated are returned to the United States and/or

---

[11] For the first two points, see Andre Gunder Frank, *op. cit.* For the last, see Leo Huberman and Paul M. Sweezy, *Socialism in Cuba* (New York: Monthly Review Press, 1969).

the raw materials devoted to American use. Between such extractive operations and the insistence upon one-crop economies for the benefit of American interests, the underdeveloped nation may end up worse off then it would have been without any contact with the advanced American economy. Gunder Frank comments about formerly prosperous regions of Latin America:

> These regions' participation in the development of the world capitalist market gave them, already in their golden age, the typical structure of underdevelopment of a capitalist export economy. When the market for their sugar or the wealth of their mines disappeared and the metropolis abandoned them to their own devices, the already existing economic, political, and social structure of these regions prohibited autonomous generation of economic development, and left them no alternative but to turn in upon themselves and to degenerate into the ultra-underdevelopment we find there today.[12]

Further, when the growth of non-extractive local industry *has* been fostered, it is constructed in the image of the monopoly capitalism of the advanced countries and therefore fails to generate sustained growth in other areas of economic activity. Paul Baran declares:

> In most undeveloped countries capitalism had a peculiarly twisted career; it never experienced the vigor and exuberance of youth, and began displaying at an early age all the grievous features of senility and decadence. To the dead weight of stagnation characteristic of pre-industrial society was added the entire restrictive impact of monopoly capital.[13]

Thus, Marxism argues that, in its monopoly stage, capitalism is inherently incapable of generating true economic development, i.e., economic development that ultimately sustains itself. The major need of Third World nations to develop viable, balanced, and ultimately independent economies contradicts the need of capitalist countries to control and dominate. Monopoly capitalism dictates a

---

[12] Andre Gunder Frank, *op. cit.,* p. 28.
[13] Paul Baran, *op. cit.,* p. 177.

process in which the world metropolis continues to develop and the backward areas sink deeper into underdevelopment. In harsher terms, the rich get richer and the poor get poorer. The only remedy lies in development outside the monopoly capital processes.

THE ROLE OF GOVERNMENT

We have seen that capitalism has come to accept certain supportive state functions, and that reform liberalism has evolved to the point of viewing government as an effective manager of economic stability and growth. Both of these ideologies, however, assume that the natural relationship between economy and state is one of private initiative supplemented by government action in situations where the economy or individuals subject to it need help. Marxism, on the other hand, holds that the state has always been and still remains the agent of the corporate ruling class. Often, but not always, this implies positive direct intervention on the part of the state in the service of that class. Under conditions of competitive capitalism, for instance, corporate interests were in fact served by minimal governmental activity, and the relationship between government and business approximated that of the capitalist image. But the powerful forces that shaped the development of monopoly capital also transformed the relationship between the state and the corporate economy, making the former into the willing agent of the latter.

The positive use of the state by the corporate oligarchy is seen by most Marxists as predating the Depression of the 1930s by a half century. The research of several Marxist historians suggests that since the late 19th century, the ruling class used the state to regulate the damaging and anarchistic behavior of the corporations themselves and the relationship between capital and labor. The United States government, in this view, has never been a neutral arbiter between classes but has always been the instrument of the wealthy oligarchy.[14]

Since the second World War and the immense expansion of the federal government, the symbiotic relationship between state and

---

[14] For a summary of this research, see James O'Connor, "The Fiscal Crises of the State, Part I," *Socialist Revolution*, Jan.–Feb. 1970.

corporation has taken on even greater importance.[15] This relation-ship goes well beyond anything contemplated in Keynesian eco-nomics under monopoly capitalism; the state becomes a major channel through which economic activities are carried out and prof-its obtained. One Marxist analysis holds that the national budget has been transformed into a powerful instrument of national eco-nomic planning in accordance with the needs of national capital.[16] Moreover, the state supports the defense establishment which, in turn, serves both as a source of profits and as protection for over-seas adventures. Government subsidies for research and develop-ment, as well as for highways, shipping, and other transportation facilities developed by private enterprise, also serve the needs of the ruling class.

One of the primary consequences, and indeed aims, of this increased role of the state is that the costs of profit making are increasingly socialized. This is, they are supported by general tax revenues—while profits, of course, remain private. As William A. Williams characterizes it,

> The private use of public money has been and continues to be a central element in the success of American capitalism, which nevertheless attributes its achievements to the creative powers of private property and individual enterprise.[17]

THE CHARACTER AND PROSPECTS
OF THE CURRENT ECONOMY

In the course of its continuing challenge to the basic assump-tions of capitalism, Marxism also denies that the present economic situation in the United States can fairly be termed affluence. It ar-gues further that the true nature of the American system is unstable and crisis-prone, so that future prospects are by no means good.

---

[15] Some Marxist thinkers, like James O'Connor, suggest that the con-temporary relationship between state and capital represents a qualitative as well as quantitative break with the past, *ibid*. Others, like Baran and Sweezy, view it as a significant intensification of an established trend.

[16] O'Connor, *op. cit.*

[17] Williams, *op. cit.*, p. 75.

(a) *Affluence vs. inequality.* Marxism denies that the existing economic system produces steadily increasing affluence for the average man, challenging both the perspective from which such claims are made and definitions of affluence that are restricted to materialist dimensions. Claims that credit capitalism with creating affluence are, in Marxist eyes, narrow-minded chauvinism; growth rates in the Third World are declining, and in world terms, the capitalist economies are generating not affluence, but poverty. With the proper frame of reference, therefore, capitalism is *not* generating affluence. The orthodox claim is on sounder grounds when it is applied exclusively to the United States, but even in this context, it is subject to challenge. Workers' real wages have increased over the long term, but the pattern of distribution has remained constant. Workers are neither "affluent" nor "middle class." Like other social critics, Marxists point to the large segment of the population that lives below the poverty level, in absolute deprivation and misery. Some Marxist thinkers claim that even for the average employed individual, affluence and even moderate comfort are not always attainable. Victor Perlo draws on official government figures to point out that:

> The wages of American workers fall far below the U.S. labor department estimates of what is needed for a "moderate" living standard; 65 percent of workers—including white collar and blue collar, white as well as black—are able to consume much less than the so-called affluent American standard of living.[18]

Finally, Marxist thinkers argue, the material progress that has been made by workers under capitalism is constantly threatened. The last three years have been a period in which the real wages of workers in general have declined. Inflation caused by the Vietnam war has destabilized the economy and led to government policies that raise the level of unemployment. Even if the application of Keynesian policies prevents a recession, workers will continue to slip backwards for some time. The prospect of a depression is always present in a capitalist economy and could wipe out the gains of decades in a very brief period.

---

[18] Perlo, *op. cit.,* p. 43.

The second strand of Marxist ideology disputes the claims to affluence by suggesting that any viable definition of the term must include noneconomic dimensions. If affluence be held to include such nonmaterial aspects as the capacity to live a fully human and creative life (or, in the words of William A. Williams, "to establish an environment which supports human beings in their search for integration and wholeness" [19]), a great gap between true affluence and the capitalist performance is revealed. Many Marxist arguments in this category parallel those of the New Left, citing alienation, bureaucracy, and authoritarianism as barriers to human development. The nature of the profit-oriented capitalist workplace, in Marxist eyes, makes for alienation, subjection to machines, and meaninglessness. To the lack of control over conditions and products of work and the hardships of speedups and automation is added the lack of choice as a political man, as consumer, and as leisure man. In terms of all of these dimensions, Marxists assert, monopoly capital is destructive. To cite Williams again,

> The essential meaning of wealth has to do with an individual's participation and influence within his society. The great majority of Americans do not possess or exercise that kind of share or stake in contemporary society.[20]

(b) *Instability and crisis.* As we have seen, the dominant ideologies and even reform liberalism present a picture of capitalism as an economic system immunized against severe crisis. The picture is one of steady growth and expanding affluence. This is attributed to the efficiency and rationality of market processes, supplemented by the steadying hand of government's new Keynesian tool. From the Marxist perspective, however, the picture looks quite different. Marxists see instead a hesitant and uncertain mechanism maintained only by constant patchwork. They contend that when studied empirically, the economic history of the United States is one of constantly threatening recession and depression coupled with general underutilization of industrial capacity. In particular, the depression of the 1930s and 1940s is of considerable interest to Marxists because it is thought to have been curbed by the new Keynesian tools

---

[19] Williams, *op. cit.,* p. 108.
[20] *Ibid.,* p. 24.

of government management. Marxists contend that the crisis was resolved not by the success of deliberate manipulation of the economy by government but by the entry of the United States into World War II. This war and the boom which followed did create a period of prosperity, but Marxists point out that prosperity was dependent on the use of surplus to rebuild Europe and pursue the cold war. This prosperity has been accompanied by steadily increasing inflation, which undercuts the world trade position of the United States, increases the domestic cost of living, and undercuts real wages.

Marxists concede that the vast increase in the public sector may add to the potential effectiveness of Keynesian policies, but see indications that this may not prove to be the case. Attempts to apply Keynesian methods to curb inflation in mid-1966 threatened to bring the economy into a recession in 1967 and had to be discontinued, with the result that inflation returned at higher levels. Marxists watch with interest the efforts of the Nixon administration to "cool" the war-caused inflation of the early 1970s through policies that promote unemployment and lead toward recession. These Keynesian policies, they point out, can be successful only at great cost to the workers, costs which mean drops in living standards and rises in unemployment.

Further, Keynesian policies do not offer any possibility of basically restructuring the economy. They serve only to bolster an economy that is based upon the continued military spending, the maintenance of an overseas empire, and (as a last resort) war. Williams alleges,

> American capitalism has never since 1861 functioned effectively enough to decrease economic misery over any significant period of time, save as it has been stimulated by war or cold war.[21]

Thus, Marxist ideology contends that the notion of crises as an exceptional rather than a typical state of the capitalist economy is fundamentally incorrect. Baran and Sweezy say,

> The Great Depression is not the Great Exception but is the normal outcome of the workings of the American economic

---

[21] *Ibid.*, p. 83.

system. . . . Here for the first time we get a crystal clear view of the system operating with minimum external stimuli for an extended period of time, laying bare what Marx called its "law of motion" for all to see.[22]

Mature capitalism naturally tends toward stagnation, depression, and, therefore, crises; military spending, imperialism, and war can counter this tendency, but ultimately produce crises of the same dimensions. Marxism raises questions as to whether the capitalist economy can continue to function, even as badly as it does, for an indefinite period. The nearly unanimous answer is, of course, negative. The only point of dispute is the way in which this self-destruction will be accomplished.

Values and Goals

Capitalist and liberal ideologies assume a complementary relationship between man's nature and the processes of the capitalist economy. The competition of the market is seen as mirroring the competitive nature of man. The institution of private property follows from and supports his individualistic quest for freedom. Marxists, like new left thinkers, stress the cooperative and social aspects of man's nature, his search for fulfillment in relationships with others, his propensity for communal and cooperative efforts, and his ability to perform work as art or as a good in itself. Thus capitalism is seen as a perversion rather than an expression of man's real and essential nature.

Marxism focuses on the cooperative nature of the work that produces most goods in an advanced industrial society, pointing particularly to the contrast between the social nature of the productive processes and the private appropriation of the goods and profits as a major contradiction in capitalist society. It seeks to create a society in which this contradiction is resolved and production, ownership, and distribution of goods are social processes. Such an economic system is termed "communist" or "socialist." [23] These terms take on

---

[22] Baran and Sweezy, *op. cit.*, p. 24.

[23] While a distinction that describes socialism as a phase in the development of communism is sometimes made, it is unnecessary, for our purposes here, to distinguish the two.

specialized meanings as used by different Marxist thinkers but, at minimum, they refer to a society in which private ownership of the means of production is abolished and replaced by social ownership[24] and equal distribution of goods. That is, the entire wage system and the most fundamental structural relations underlying capitalism are eliminated. This change establishes the basis for the fundamental social and political changes that reorient human life entirely. While this change from private to social ownership may be identified as the most basic component of the transition to socialism, there is general agreement among Marxists on additional characteristics of a socialist society.

Under socialism, the unplanned and anarchic character of the capitalist production process is replaced by some system of planned economy. In some way, socialist societies must make a collective decision on general economic and social goals and organize the society to implement them. In such a system, Marxists argue, waste and irrationality would be eliminated and resources used to maximum advantage. The instability and cyclical crises that are characteristic of capitalism would disappear. Of equal importance to Marxists is the goal of reorienting the productive processes of the society from production for profit to production for use. In a socialist state, under conditions of abundance, production would be freed from the limiting criteria of profitability and would be directed instead by the needs and opportunities for human use. Capitalist economic "needs," such as the need to destroy food and keep land out of production, would be eliminated. Technological innovations held back or abandoned because they did not seem profitable could be introduced. Resources could be directed into "unprofitable" projects such as parks, education and other cultural activities. Finally, in a socialist society, the need for productivity would be balanced against the need for creative work opportunities and for abundant and well used leisure.

In addition to these characteristics of the socialist economic goal, Marxist thinkers see it as making possible a truly democratic political system. Mass participation in various forms would enable

---

[24] It should be noted that we are using the term *social* ownership rather than *state* ownership. Although, in practice, the countries usually referred to as "socialist" as characterized by state ownership of the means of production, Marxist theory speaks in general terms of communal or social ownership. State ownership may or may not operate as social ownership.

citizens to share in the crucial decisions over matters of economic planning and in resolving other issues concerning fundamental direction of the society. Marxists do not see such goals as utopian in the pejorative sense. They contend that capitalism has already created the material preconditions for the existence of socialist societies in the advanced industrial nations; their present productivity is huge, and it need only be redirected away from waste and inequality. But Marxists acknowledge that the political and social obstacles are formidable. Even assuming a socialist revolution, the process of building a true community would take decades; according to Paul Baran, "decades in which a new generation of human beings will be educated as members of a socialist society, rather than as competitive wolves in the jungle of the capitalist market." [25]

Marxism also acknowledges the additional difficulties of establishing socialism in the underdeveloped nations where the industrial base and abundance does not exist. They argue, however, that the establishment of socialism in the United States would have profound effects upon the development of the Third World. The elimination of capitalism and the profit motive would remove the structural pressures for imperialism, freeing nations to engage in real cooperation and perhaps move toward elimination of nationalism.

In regard to such a general level of values and goals, Marxists concur. But they begin to disagree when more specific details of the future socialist society are discussed. It is of great importance to contemporary Marxist ideology that there are several nations in the world (the Soviet Union, China, Cuba, the Eastern European countries, etc.) that claim to be socialist or, at least, on the road to socialism. The legitimacy of these claims is a matter of intense dispute. The Progressive Labor Party, for example, recognizes only China and Albania as worthy of the Socialist designation and denounces the Soviet Union and other Eastern European nations as "revisionist." The Communist Party of the United States contends that the Soviet Union remains the first and most advanced socialist state. To other Marxist organizations, such as the Young Socialist Alliance, Cuba seems the most firmly established and promising model of genuine socialism.

Underlying these disagreements are complicated questions con-

---

[25] Baran, *op. cit.*, p. 296.

cerning the nature of socialism and the proper means of establishing it, many with roots in the Russian revolution of 1917. Many of these questions focus around the internal development of nations attempting to establish socialism. Marxist thinkers disagree over the extent to which bureaucratization, undemocratic practices and even repression must be tolerated in the initial stages of socialist development. There is also disagreement concerning the legitimacy and necessity of maintaining or reintroducing certain capitalist economic structures such as the market, or the use of monetary instead of moral incentives.

A second general area of disagreement concerns the proper character of a socialist foreign policy, and the responsibilities of socialist nations to struggle against capitalism and imperialism. Some Marxist thinkers and groups maintain that any accommodation with capitalist countries is incorrect. The only responsible foreign policy for a socialist state would be directed at expansion of socialism. At the other pole, there are those who applaud the Soviet Union's policy of peaceful coexistence with capitalism. These and other questions have caused further splits between Marxists over issues of social change and tactics.

Social Change and Tactics

Marxism calls for far-reaching change in the American social system; as we have seen, its goals contrast almost completely with those of capitalism and liberalism. Marxism's image of the scope of change required is probably the most radical of all the change-oriented ideologies we have examined, and its theory of how change may come about is the most comprehensive. When black liberation thinkers dispute questions of social change, they are usually concerned primarily with questions of tactics. Similarly, new left thinkers tend to focus on very concrete and specific issues. In contrast, Marxism attempts to set up general principles about the dynamics of change in any society and to apply them to the contemporary United States. Although we can do little more than present the bare outlines of this theory, it should be enough to show its comparative depth and comprehensiveness.

At the basis of the Marxist theory of change is the principle that capitalism, like all economic systems before it, is developing toward its own destruction because of unsolvable strains and contradictions from within. Analysis reveals dynamic processes that are inherent in the system and create the conditions that will inevitably lead to socialism. More specifically, groups in the society are constantly led by their own self-interest to oppose the policies of the ruling class and ultimately to stand in opposition to capitalism itself. Monopoly capitalism is not just powerful and static, but steadily generates internal strains and develops class conflict.

The strains and contradictions exist at many levels of the society. The American monopoly capital system generates tremendous productivity and creates great wealth but must waste and destroy that wealth. Poverty and deprivation exist side by side with waste and frivolous consumption; the misery-ending and work-saving potential of automation, for example, is experienced as actual or threatened unemployment. Imperialism is an imperative, but its effect is to unite the Third World and a portion of the domestic population against the United States. Vast increases in the national budget socialize the costs and risks of production, but the profits are still privately appropriated; meanwhile, revenue demands provoke taxpayer revolts and general political unrest. In these and other ways, monopoly capitalism inevitably generates conflict and paves the way for its own transformation.

Marxists argue that while contradictions themselves will not establish socialism, they give rise to social conflict between classes in the society which can eventually culminate in the socialist revolution. The traditional revolutionary class of Marxist analysis is the working class or proletariat who do not own the means of production and can exist only by selling their labor. But contemporary Marxists see the question of the revolutionary class as more problematic. They are confronted by the seeming indifference of the American working class to socialist ideology. Their varying response to this problem constitute another dimension of difference among them. Some, such as Baran and Sweezy, have come close to abandoning the concept of the working class as an agent of revolutionary change. They see the working class under monopoly capitalism as oriented toward middle-class materialism and divided by racism. They argue that the major forces in opposition to capitalism are the Third World liberation movements. Sweezy says, "I believe that it is this revolutionary movement in the Third world, with its roots in centuries of exploitation and bitterness, which is the primary engine of change in the world today." [26] In this view, though the principle of internal contradictions is not abandoned, the primary instrument of the destruction of U.S. capitalism is external.

A second position, and the one which is endorsed by what is probably a majority of Marxist thinkers, is considerably more optimistic concerning the revolutionary potential of the American working class. The worker's alienating circumstances and his inability to share in the returns from productivity remain unchanged or are heightened under monopoly capitalism. Further, the conditions of work of some groups not usually thought of as part of the traditional working class (semi-professionals, white-collar workers, agricultural workers) are coming to resemble those of the other workers. Monopoly capitalism operates to increasingly "proletarianize" masses of people. Thus, the working class remains a major target of Marxist organizing efforts which focus on the factory and other work places. Often, their activities, especially of youth groups, are indistinguishable from or integrated with those of new left groups—demonstrations against the Vietnam war, attempts to organize students and servicemen, etc.

On the tactical side, Marxist ideology experiences the same internal disagreements that mark the black liberation and new left ideologies. Some groups, such as the Communist Party, engage in electoral politics, and generally advocate evolutionary and peaceful transition to socialism. Others work only for immediate and violent revolutionary change. Some support black nationalism as a revolutionary force, others denounce it as diversionary. Mutual denunciations regularly occur between factions in continuing testimony to diversity.

---

[26] Paul Sweezy, *Monthly Review,* October 1968, p. 47.

Annotated Bibliography

Baran, Paul A. *The Political Economy of Growth.* New York: Modern Reader Paperbacks, 1968. A good statement of the Marxist argument concerning the cause of U.S. imperialist policy and its consequences for underdeveloped countries.

Baran, Paul A. and Paul M. Sweezy. *Monopoly Capital.* New York: Modern Reader Paperbacks, 1968. A detailed presentation of the theory of rising surplus under monopoly capital.

Frank, Andre Gunder. "The Development of Underdevelopment," *Monthly Review,* Sept., 1966. Another analysis of the consequences of U.S. imperialism, with particular attention to Latin America.

Huberman, Leo and Paul M. Sweezy. *Socialism in Cuba.* New York: Monthly Review Press, 1969. An appraisal of the socialist revolution in Cuba which touches on some of the points of contention among American Marxists.

Magdoff, Harry. *The Age of Imperialism.* New York: Modern Reader Paperbacks, 1968. An argument for the economic motivation analysis of U.S. foreign policy.

Mandel, Ernest. *An Introduction to Marxist Economic Theory.* New York: Merit Publishers, 1969. A brief introduction to the basic principles of Marx's economic thinking.

Mills, C. Wright. *The Marxists.* New York: Delta Publishing Co., 1962. A good overview of the historical development of Marxism. Contains both interpretive essays and documents.

O'Connor, James. "The Fiscal Crisis of the State, Part I" *Socialist Revolution,* February, 1970. A discussion of the present role of the state in American capitalism.

Perlo, Victor. "Relevance of Marxist Economics to U.S. Conditions" *Political Affairs,* February 1969. An argument for the continued application of Marx to the U.S.

Williams, William A. *The Great Evasion.* Chicago: Quadrangle Paperbacks, 1964. A discussion of the consequences for Americans of failing to come to grips with the Marxian notion of "community."

8

Conservatism

In taking up conservatism at this point, we may appear to be following the change-seeking ideologies with one that is change-resistant. In practical effect, conservatism in the United States must be so characterized. But in terms of its own beliefs and principles, and in the contemporary American context, conservatism is as change-oriented—though in a contrary direction—as the others, and it shares many of their perspectives on the present. It, too, sees American political thought and practice dominated by capitalism-liberalism as they have evolved. It too interprets current problems as the product of failures in the values of these ideologies and calls for their replacement by a new set of governing principles. In short, if properly understood, conservatism is far more than a convenient rationalization for inertia or mere resistance to change. It is, quite simply, a change-seeking ideology with a contrasting set of goals from those most often voiced in the American context.

Conservatism has many problems in the United States, not least of which is that of gaining a fair hearing. On many occasions, its principles are seized upon by reactionaries or by others who seek merely to defend a particular status quo that happens to serve them well at the moment. Without adopting its values or goals, and certainly without following its consistent principles or even appreciating its real qualities, those who so use conservatism as a rallying point do it a major disservice. But its principles themselves do lend themselves to this use and contribute to this effect because they run contrary to the mainstream of American egalitarianism, majoritarianism, and idealism.

In analyzing American conservatism, we are really dealing with two very distinct ideologies. They are alike in their apparent change-resisting effects and in the manner in which they are misunderstood —as we have just described. They also share a similar problem: they are consistent and firm in their opposition to many of the problem-solving politico-economic developments of the twentieth century and, thus, effectively cut themselves off from most potential business *and* popular support. They enjoy much less past or potential impact in American politics (in terms of achieving the goals they seek) than the space allocated to them in this book would suggest. But analysis of these two very different forms of conservatism will help to explain why capitalism and liberalism, and the ideologies that would *accept* and *extend* their principles more widely, have been so dominant in the United States.

One form that conservatism takes may be called *individualist-conservatism*. It is an ideology closely approximating early liberalism and classical economics in its emphasis upon individual self-fulfill-ment in material terms and pure laissez-faire limitations on govern-ment. It is frequently used in the most platitudinous defenses of fea-tures of contemporary capitalism or liberalism. If there were no more substance to the ideology than suggested by such usage, we would dismiss it from consideration. Or we would note in passing that, though much honored in rhetoric, it was abandoned in practice by governments throughout the United States. But deeper analysis shows that most rhetorical usage is without understanding of the humane concern for individual freedom which animates consistent efforts to create a setting in which men can indeed be free of restraints, from whatever source. It is individualist-conservatism at this latter level upon which we shall focus in this chapter.

The other form of conservatism may be called *organic conserva-tism,* in order to stress its sharply contrasting emphasis on the or-ganic unity of the society and its roots in the eighteenth century con-servatism. This ideology rejects individualism entirely as a basis for political thinking. Instead, it sets up the society as an ongoing inde-pendent entity with a life and needs of its own which should be served by those who happen to inhabit it at any given moment. Es-sentially irrational and emotional individuals must be provided order and guidance through the wise actions of talented men in government. The progress of the society depends on making the correct decisions (often involving physical hardship) for its defense or improvement, and not on individual material satisfactions or ultimately self-destructive egalitarianism or majoritarianism. In most cases, the correct decisions are those that draw upon the traditions and experience of the society and apply those principles to its future needs.

Although the premises and goals of these two categories of thought are very different, the confusion that leads to labeling both "conservative" is understandable. Both take the same stands on some continuing issues of American politics. They insist upon a hard line against communist expansion, tending to view communism as an integrated and very dangerous threat that can only be checked through decisive force. They share a special concern for the protection of private property and commensurate resistance to social welfare legislation, and they oppose any widening of popular control over or involvement in the process of government. In addition, the two lines of thought have very similar problems. As we shall see, they have real difficulty in formulating attractive, affirmative programs, either for acquiring power or for building popular support. There is relatively little in the American past that fulfills their standards, so a backward-looking approach to gaining guidance for present action is often unsuccessful. On the rare occasions when their adherents are in positions of power in government, they frequently find that the complex of forces and existing momentum to which government is subject prevents them from carrying out their principles. But despite these shared issue positions and problems, the two ideologies' basic premises, values and goals are widely separated—even diametrically opposed to each other. We shall consider the underlying principles of each in turn, and the differences will be readily evident.

Individualist-Conservatism

Our analysis of the individualist-conservative ideology can be brief, for it is essentially the same as that described as bedrock capitalism (pp. 24–33, above) together with the basic framework of liberalism, with a deeper sense of purpose. It is sometimes known as

Manchester Liberalism, after the writings of a group of classical capitalist-liberal thinkers of Manchester, England in the nineteenth century. Perhaps the leading exponent in the United States was William Graham Sumner, who joined laissez-faire capitalism, individualism, and Darwin's theory of evolution into the doctrine known as Social Darwinism. In its contemporary form, individualist-conservatism still draws heavily from the basic tenets of nineteenth century capitalism. It remains firmly committed to individual striving for self-satisfaction (conceived in chiefly material dimensions) as the principal dynamic of the society, and all other priorities and principles flow from that.

Individualist-conservatism does not represent simply a case of arrested development in which some people have managed to resist awareness of contemporary conditions or of the evolution of liberalism to more social uses of government. Instead, it reflects the considered judgment that the early principles of capitalism are still valid for the United States, if only they would be properly and consistently applied. Further, they would create a better world than now exists under today's "pragmatic" or "problem-solving" approach to politics and economics. Three related premises and values support and give impetus to this conviction.

(1) The market is a sufficient regulator and distributor, if only it is left truly free to do its work. Indeed, the market is both the *source* of *economic* freedom and a kind of *precondition* of *political* freedom. Milton Friedman, a professional economist and perhaps the leading modern exponent of laissez-faire capitalism, states this principle emphatically in his major work, *Capitalism and Freedom*:

> On the one hand, freedom in economic arrangements is itself a component of freedom broadly understood, so economic freedom is an end in itself. In the second place, economic freedom is also an indispensable means toward the achievement of political freedom. . . . I know of no example in time or place of a society that has been marked by a large measure of political freedom, that has not also used something comparable to a free market to organize the bulk of economic activity.[1]

---

[1] Milton Friedman, *Capitalism and Freedom* (Chicago: University of Chicago Press, 1962), pp. 8–9.

For individualist-conservatives, the principal problem of social life is coordinating the economic activities of a large number of people while at the same time maintaining freedom of choice and action for all individuals. The free market—voluntary exchanges among mutually benefitting individuals—is the only instrument that can assure simultaneous achievement of both goals.

(2) Coercion of every kind is to be avoided, and the principal source of coercion is government action. Freedom consists of the absence of coercion upon the individual. It can be assured only by avoiding or controlling the use of political power as much as possible. In particular, this means reducing the economic role of the government to that of enforcing contracts, maintaining law and order, and umpiring the rules of the game. An operating free market renders government organization or management of the economy unnecessary and thus reduces the prospect of coercion on individuals. Further, free market capitalism assures wide distribution of economic power and helps to prevent centralization of either economic or political power—thereby promoting political freedom. It also assures the availability of support for advocacy of varieties of change and provides protection against economic sanctions for political activities. Friedman makes this point through extended examples, and concludes:

> No one who buys bread knows whether the wheat from which it was made was grown by a Communist or a Republican, by a constitutionalist or a Fascist, or, for that matter, by a Negro or a white. This illustrates how an impersonal market separates economic activities from political views and protects men from being discriminated against in their economic activities for reasons that are irrelevant to their productivity—whether these reasons are associated with their views or their color. . . . The groups in our society that have the most at stake in the preservation and strengthening of competitive capitalism are those minority groups which can most easily become the object of the distrust and enmity of the majority—the Negroes, the Jews, the foreign-born, to mention only the most obvious.[2]

(3) There exists among individuals an ultimate harmony of in-

---

[2] *Ibid.*, p. 21.

terests, which will lead to satisfaction and fulfillment of all men if the conditions of freedom from coercion are realized. This ultimate harmony does not flow from a recognition of shared needs and community actions to serve them, but from the articulation of the infinitely different but interdependent needs and desires of millions of satisfaction-seeking individuals. Their varied interests, when permitted to mesh through independent pursuit of their personal goals, will form a harmonious social system. Individualist-conservatives visualize men as naturally competitive and self-seeking and see progress as dependent upon their freedom to follow such inclinations. Equality of opportunity, therefore, is to be sharply distinguished from equality of condition, which is a brake on progress and a block to freedom. Again, Friedman illustrates this point very nicely:

> The heart of the liberal philosophy is a belief in the dignity of the individual, in his freedom to make the most of his capacities and opportunities according to his own lights. . . . This implies a belief in the equality of men in one sense; in their inequality in another. Each man has an equal right to freedom. This is an important and fundamental right precisely because men are different, because one man will want to do different things with his freedom than another, and in the process can contribute more than another to the general culture of the society in which many men live.
>
> The liberal will therefore distinguish sharply between equality of rights and equality of opportunity, on the one hand, and material equality or equality of outcome on the other. . . . But [the egalitarian] will defend taking from some to give to others, not as a more effective means whereby the "some" can achieve an objective they want to achieve, but on grounds of "justice." At this point, equality comes sharply into conflict with freedom; one must choose. One cannot be both an egalitarian, in this sense, and a liberal.[3]

Individualist-conservatism is, thus, far from a crass rationalization for the existing pattern of distribution of wealth and power, although some may seek to use it as such. It rests on a principled foundation of commitment to a particular definition of freedom and how it may best be achieved. Its renascence in the post-World War

---

[3] *Ibid.,* p. 195.

II United States flowed in part from a conviction that European efforts at managing economies and societies through the use of government inevitably led to some form of totalitarian coercion and consequent elimination of freedom. The crucial definitional question to be asked is: does freedom consist of the absence of coercion exercised by other men through the instrument of government (but the possible presence of economic hardship or market-applied pressures), or does it consist of the absence or reduction of economic hardships (but the possible presence of political restraints)? The question is not factual, of course; it is a complex value problem that may depend on whether an observer identifies with the *haves* or the *have-nots*. The individualist-conservatives opt firmly for the first definition of freedom. Contemporary capitalist-liberals reach uncertainly toward the latter and end up vacillating between the two.

Individualist-conservatives see an inevitable intrusion upon individual freedom every time men undertake to act on behalf of others through the vehicle of the United States government. With the most benevolent of intentions and the most democratic of impulses, leaders can only institute one set of priorities or policies. Efforts to institute society-wide planning or to provide security against various economic and social hazards inevitably lead to coercion, diminution of freedom, and tyranny by those that dominate the party. The most sincere and public-spirited advocates of government help for the weak may be innocent totalitarians, but however humanitarian their motives, eventually, they impose their standards and preferences upon the lives of others. In one of the major works of individualist-conservatism, appropriately titled *The Road to Serfdom,* Friedrich Hayek argues for abandoning attempts at social engineering through government and making a new start at achieving the old goals of freedom:

> It is more important to clear away the obstacles with which human folly has encumbered our path and to release the creative energy of individuals than to devise further machinery for "guiding" and "directing" them—to create conditions favorable to progress rather than to "plan progress." . . . Though we can neither wish nor possess the power to go back to the reality of the nineteenth century, we have the opportunity to realize its ideals—and they were not mean. . . . If in the first attempt to create a world of free men we

have failed, we must try again. The guiding principle that a policy of freedom for the individual is the only truly progressive policy remains as true today as it was in the nineteenth century.[4]

As articulated by Friedman, Hayek, and others, individualist-conservatism is a consistent ideology resting upon concern for individual freedom (as here defined) and visualizing economic freedom (free-market capitalism) as the indispensable source of that freedom. This consistency means, for example, that government is not to be used for the private advantage of *any* sector of the economy and that trade should move freely across national boundaries. Subsidies, trade barriers, monopolies, collusion between management and labor, government regulation of rates or quality equally impair operation of the American free market and should be eliminated. Clearly, some who seek to ally themselves with the individualist-conservative position are not so consistent, and do so in an effort to rationalize the status quo, oppose government assistance to others, and preserve their advantages. Others adopt some portion of the individualist-conservative posture and avoid the reciprocal obligations or implications for their own behavior. Because of such propensities, confusion and uncertainty about the nature of this variant of conservatism is probably inevitable.

There are also variants of individualist-conservatism that contribute to the blurring of the ideology. U.S. Senator Barry Goldwater, for example, in a much-read book entitled *The Conscience of a Conservative,*[5] argues that continued freedom requires vigorous efforts in defense of freedom, i.e., a powerful stance against the spread of communism. The potential conflict with the consistent laissez-faire-limited government principles of individualist-conservatism should be clear. Preservation of military strength requires that a large sector of the economy be dependent upon the government and independent of all market forces. A society mobilized around nationalism and anticommunism is unlikely to eliminate trade barriers or grant internal individual freedoms. In other respects, Goldwater is much the

---

[4] Friedrich Hayek, *The Road to Serfdom* (Chicago: University of Chicago Press, 1944).

[5] Barry Goldwater, *The Conscience of a Conservative* (Shepherdsville, Ky.: Victor Publishing Company, 1960).

consistent individualist-conservative. Even at the cost of appearing unsympathetic to racial discrimination, he insisted that government legislation to force people not to discriminate was an undesirable infringement upon individual freedom.

Perhaps the best-known variant of individualist-conservatism is that of Ayn Rand, whose many writings revolve around the principle of absolute individual entitlement to gain and hold all that he can in the way of material goods. Miss Rand maintains that capitalism is "an unknown ideal" which if actually instituted would fulfill all of the highest needs and goals of individuals, properly conceived. Titling one of her books "The Virtue of Selfishness," [6] she argued for frank avowal of the efficacy and propriety of self-seeking. She maintains that the individual has the right to compete and to retain all the fruits of that competition and that enforcement and preservation of those rights are the government's function. Evil in the United States and the world, she believes, stems largely from the exercise of government power—particularly from the acts (however well intentioned) of those who hold such power. Only a rigidly enforced emphasis on individual self-service and the utter absence of government interference with the free market can eliminate the prospect of war, coercion, and limits on self-fulfillment.

But these variants merely serve to demonstrate the scope and appeal of the basic ideology of individualist-conservatism. It is deeply sunk into the capitalist-liberal origins of American thinking. In its pure and consistent form, as we have described it here, it touches strongly held values of freedom and individual independence. Whether it is truly *conservative* in the sense of preserving and extending values or traditions of the past is less clear, and perhaps not important. Individualist-conservatism is a distinct ideology, and in its general resistance to most contemporary changes in the status quo, its effects are conservative.

Organic Conservatism

The concern for the *real* or *true* nature of conservatism is, in part, generated by the distinctiveness of organic conservatism. This

---

[6] Ayn Rand, *The Virtue of Selfishness* (New York: New American Library, 1966).

brand of conservatism explicitly lays claim to being "conservative" in the sense of deliberately seeking to conform contemporary change to perceived fundamental traditions and principles of the society. It is also totally different from all other American ideologies in that it conceives of the society as an entity *distinct from* and *superior in importance to* the individuals who happen to make it up at any given moment. Organic conservatism, as the name suggests, views the society as an intangible unit or organ, proceeding semimystically through time and having needs and goals independent of the ever-transitory group of people who temporarily live in it. Understanding the premises and approaches of this form of conservatism requires a substantial wrench out of the standard forms of thinking that characterize other American ideologies. Let us revert to our three-stage analytical framework.

WORLD VIEW

Organic conservatism begins with the society, not with the individual. The society, having evolved out of the dim past, contains within its traditions and practices the accumulated culture and wisdom of generations that guide an individual's life and give it meaning, making civilized existence possible. Organic conservatism is both pessimistic and fatalistic about man, collectively and individually. Men are born with talents, interests, and propensities that are inherently unequal. They are irrational, self-serving, and fated to struggle with each other unproductively. In effect, they are touched with original sin. Only the firm guidance of well considered principles can create the order and conditions of civilization within which men can realize some happiness and fulfillment. "Freedom" implies the presence of such order, within which at least some of the more talented men can develop and not only carry forward the culture and other qualities of the society, but by contributing to its betterment, to their own contentment.

The principles that can bring order and civility amidst these propensities for evil are those that the society has generated over the centuries of its existence. As the society moves through time, a kind of partnership develops between those members now dead, the present incumbents, and generations as yet unborn. The duty of the living is to devote their talents to discerning and applying (with modifications if necessary) the principles from the past that are appropriate to the conditions of the present. Change is inevitable, and those who insist on preservation of any particular status quo do not understand the nature of the world. But precipitate change, change for which the society is unready or which is inconsistent with that long line of practice extending from the past through the present and into the future, must be avoided.

Where are the necessary guiding principles to be found in actual practice? Organic conservatism finds them in history, in natural law, in religion, or in other standards that are external to any particular situation. In other words, organic conservatism denies that rational analysis can generate plans capable of achieving important long-term goals because such plans require assumptions about cause and effect relationships and the predictability of human behavior are at odds with all experience and the elements of chance and fate that shape events. Instead, guidance must be found in the principles of the American past that have been proved successful.

One prominent organic conservative, the author-columnist Walter Lippmann, terms his source of guidance (and his major book) *The Public Philosophy*.[7] He argues that there was once a distinct public philosophy, a set of moral standards for political action that man could deduce through logical process and to which all adhered. According to Lippmann, these principles have been forgotten and ignored in the United States until the prevailing view is that all positions on questions of purpose and moral standards in politics are equally valid. He insists that the public philosophy must be revived to guide man in determining what is right and proper and in the general interest. He describes the principles of this "public philosophy" in this way:

> They are the laws of a rational order of human society —in the sense that all men, when they are sincerely and lucidly rational, will regard them as self-evident.
>
> When we speak of these principles as natural laws, we must be careful. They are not scientific "laws" like the laws of the motions of the heavenly bodies. They do not describe human behavior as it is. They prescribe what it should be. They do not enable us to predict what men will actually do.

---

[7] Walter Lippmann, *The Public Philosophy* (Boston: Little, Brown, 1955).

> They are the principles of right behavior in the good society,
> governed by the Western traditions of civility.[8]

In the next section, we will explore the specific content of these
natural laws or public philosophy. The point to be noted here is that
organic conservatism firmly subscribes to the belief that *somewhere*
there is a fixed set of principles by which man should be guided.
Measured by these principles, the United States is a patchwork
melange of ad hoc actions and superficial rationalizations.

The existence of such a fixed and eternal guiding standard is
both confirmed and made necessary by the evil nature of man and
the wretched conditions of his stay on earth. No principles of action
devised on the spot by such men could lay claim to moral validity,
so there must be firm and transcendental standards somewhere that
can point the way toward civility. Lippmann reaches this conclusion
by positing a "confusion of two realms"—two conceptions of the
human condition. One is the state that is attainable on earth, the other
is the condition that is theoretically possible and for which men yearn.
The predicament of modern man, Lippmann says, is that "the harder
they try to make earth into heaven, the more they make it into a
hell." [9] The way out is to recognize the difference between the "two
realms" and reduce worldly aspirations accordingly:

> The radical error of the modern democratic gospel is that it
> promises, not the good life of this world, but the perfect life
> of heaven. The root of the error is the confusion of the two
> realms—that of this world where the human condition is to
> be born, to live, to work, to struggle, to die, and that of the
> transcendent world in which men's souls can be regenerated
> and at peace. The confusion of these two realms is an ulti-
> mate disorder. It inhibits the good life in this world. It falsi-
> fies the life of the spirit.[10]

This excerpt is characteristic of organic conservatism not only
in its pessimistic view of man and his terrestrial prospects, but in its
explicit contrast of the spiritual and material worlds. Organic conser-

---

[8] *Ibid.*, pp. 95–96.
[9] *Ibid.*, p. 109.
[10] *Ibid.*, p. 110.

vatism's denial of capacity in men leads to reliance on religion as a means of obtaining guidance and developing faith that can light man's ways in the darkness of the world. There must be some way of divining the truth, and some justification for finding it in a particular way; the necessarily mystical dimensions of this act naturally converge for some organic conservatives with religious faiths. The act of governing thus acquires some of the moral glow associated with religion and requires very special talents. Clearly, the necessary skills and wisdom are not the same as those that lead to success in other fields of endeavor.

The distinctiveness of the moral insight and culturally generated sense of public needs that are requisite to governing mean that only a few persons within the society are likely to be candidates fit for administering the public responsibility. Neither election, self-selection, nor appointment has proved satisfactory, and the few true conservatives who have acquired power in the United States have done so almost by accident. In particular, businessmen—with their exclusively materialistic and profit-seeking orientation—are ill-suited for governmental responsibility. Though many serve in American government, particularly in the executive and legislative branches, they are short-sighted, likely to avoid hard decisions that might cost immediate profit or support, and unwilling to sacrifice profit and materialism to protect and improve the society. Peter Viereck, one of the most prolific of modern conservatives, dismisses the business community in this fashion:

> Our distinction between rooted conservatives and rootless, counter-revolutionary doctrinaires is the measure of the difference between two different groups in contemporary America: the humanistic value-conservers and the materialistic old-guard Republicans. The latter are what a wrong and temporary journalistic usage often calls "conservative." It is more accurate to call them nineteenth-century Manchester liberals with roots no deeper than the relatively recent post-Civil War "gilded age." [11]

Organic conservatism, tracing its origins to the founders of the Republic and back through them to earlier English, Roman and

---

[11] Peter Viereck, "The Philosophical 'New Conservatism,'" in Daniel Bell, ed., *The Radical Right* (Garden City, N.Y.: Doubleday Anchor, 1964).

Greek principles, has little patience for short-sighted or self-saving behavior. Only those whose sense of the society's needs is finely developed and whose vision is informed by understanding of its future needs are capable of charting its course. That this is a relatively small number of persons with unique characteristics seems clear; identifying them within a society at any given time is not so easy, however.

VALUES AND GOALS

Organic conservatism's highest values are freedom and authority. From the proper definition and arrangement of freedom and authority flow such goals as societal order, individual achievement, and the kind of progress that succeeds in improving the culture. Property plays a vital role in sustaining freedom and permitting societal improvement and is, in effect, a subsidiary value.

Freedom is a general condition in which men are guided and encouraged to do that which they ought to do. It is nearly the opposite of the individual's exercise of free choice, which constitutes the essence of the liberal definition. It is what results from willing acceptance of authority, and the two must be understood together. The essence of organic conservatism's definition of freedom is captured by a single paragraph from Viereck:

> Liberties versus "liberty." Concrete liberties, preserved by the chains of ethics, versus abstract liberty-in-quotes, betrayed by messianic sloganizing, betrayed into the far grimmer chains of totalitarianism. "Man was born free" (said Rousseau, with his faith in the natural goodness of man) "but is everywhere in chains." "In chains, so he ought to be," replies the thoughtful conservative, defending the good and wise and necessary chains of rooted tradition and historical continuity, upon which depend the civil liberties, the shared civil liberties of modern liberals and conservatives, and parliamentary monarchists, and democratic socialists. Without the chaos-chaining, the id-chaining heritage of rooted values, what is to keep man from becoming Eichmann or Nechayev—what is to save freedom from "freedom?" [12]

---

[12] *Ibid.*

By thus embracing Rousseau's famous image of man in chains, Viereck points to the central theme of organic conservatism's view of freedom: structure, order, and guidance. The appetites of man must be controlled somehow, and until they are, he is not free. Thus, freedom involves not the *absence,* but the *presence,* of restraint. Such restraints, however, must be consistent (not arbitrary), purposeful (not whimsical), and in the public interest (appropriate to the *society's* needs, that is.) Restraints of this kind, it is argued, are not really restraints at all, for they merely prevent man from giving in to his baser instincts and release his creative capacities to proceed in productive directions. In this sense, they are *freeing* chains. They do not just permit, but affirmatively lead men toward, the kinds of activities that are most likely to produce societal advancement. And they create the conditions that make individual existence reasonably tolerable. As Lippmann says, "We are free if we have the faculty of knowing what we *ought* to do and the will to do it." [13]

Authority is essential to social existence; without it, there can be no organized continuing relationships among men, no order, and hence no freedom. Organic conservatism charges liberalism with undermining respect for authority by misusing it, turning it into the mere instrument of temporarily dominant groups of men—and thus robbing it of its majesty. The nature of man is to rebel against the people and institutions to which he owes most, and to cast off authority wherever possible. When liberalism encourages self-serving behavior on the part of individuals and asserts that majorities can by rational determinations employ government to serve their mutual needs, it creates the prospect of whimsical or aggrandizing action by men holding political power and the belief that all are equally capable of deciding what should be done—or equally *incapable* of doing so. If a man sees no greater claim to determine government policies in others than he does in himself, he is not likely to obey except through the application of force. In this way, the authority of the government becomes eroded, a condition that organic conservatives allege now exists in the United States.

Where is authority to be found, once it has been lost, as in the United States? Russell Kirk, a major conservative thinker, de-

---

[13] Lippmann, *op. cit.,* p. 111.

clares that the sources are prescription and tradition. Prescription means "those ways and institutions and rights prescribed by long —sometimes immemorial—usage." Tradition means "received opinions, convictions religious and moral and political and aesthetic passed down from generation to generation, so that they are accepted by most men as a matter of course." These twin sources are apparently to be applied through firm use of government, and in this way restored to the level of habitual acceptance. Kirk concludes,

> It is through respect for tradition and prescription, and recourse to those sources of knowledge, that the great mass of men acquire a tolerable understanding of norms and conventions, of the rules by which private and social existence is made tolerable.[14]

Once authority has been established, order and freedom again become possible.

The concept of order held by organic conservatism involves not just obedience to established legal requirements, but an order of things among people. Those who are more talented should be able to acquire and hold material possessions and other perquisites according to their success in amassing them. Whatever inequalities among men are natural should be permitted to run their course. If the more energetic are *not* allowed to develop and apply their skills to the fullest, some form of tyranny over them is threatened; in effect, it is to enforce mediocrity, which is what organic conservatives see occurring in the United States. When this natural order of relationships among people has been institutionalized, firm enforcement of necessary and just laws regulating individual behavior completes the imperative of order.

Contributing to several aspects of the freedom-authority-order pattern is the role of private property. Property has a moral validity all its own because it provides the base that assures independence and frees some individuals to devote their time and energy to developing understanding of the needs of the society. It fulfills natural human aspirations and marks the differences in capabilities among men. Its unequal distribution is thus part of the natural order of

---

[14] Russell Kirk, "Prescription, Authority, and Ordered Freedom," in Frank S. Meyer, ed., *What Is Conservatism?* (New York: Holt, Rinehart, and Winston, 1958).

things, and its protection, therefore, a part of government's function. Property promotes freedom, helps to project the wisdom of
the past into the present, and conforms to the needs and wants of
men—and is therefore a building block of a well-ordered society.

The goals of organic conservatism center on the creation of a
society in which these major values can be served, but they go
beyond that. One continuing goal is the development of a process
of change that respects the past and succeeds in fitting new policies
and programs into forms that are consistent with it. Organic conservatism recognizes change as inevitable and frequently desirable,
given the propensity of environmental conditions to change in sometimes drastic ways. Too much of value has been learned in the past
(or should have been), however, to permit idle or hasty—and particularly abrupt—change which departs sharply from earlier ways.
At the same time, not to change when there is need to do so is also
dangerous. Kirk declares, "We possess tested political institutions;
but for those institutions to endure, now and then reform is essential, lest the institutions atrophy." [15] This is why, for example,
organic conservatives often part company with individualist-conservatives on specific issues, such as the reform of rules in the Congress.

Once the conditions of freedom, authority, and order have been
established, individuals will be able to pursue their personal goals
freely and fulfill their potentialities consistent with their capabilities.
By doing so, they may be expected to contribute to the moral, intellectual, and material progress of the society. This is perhaps the
highest mission to which any generation can aspire; to each is given
the opportunity to add an increment of wisdom or of culture to the
ongoing heritage, but not all make good on that chance.

The goals of organic conservatism must of necessity appear
attractive to only a relative few. Nor will the route to achieving
these goals be at all an easy one. This realism is a part of the understanding that organic conservatism has of the self-limiting nature of
its leading principles. Lippmann sums up this realization aptly:

> The public philosophy is addressed to the government of our
> appetites and passions by the reason of a second, civilized,
> and, therefore, acquired nature. Therefore, the public phi-

---

[15] *Ibid.*

losophy cannot be popular. For it aims to resist and to regulate those very desires and opinions which are most popular. The warrant of the public philosophy is that while the regime it imposes is hard, the results of rational and disciplined government will be good. And so, while the right but hard decisions are not likely to be popular when they are taken, the wrong and soft decisions will, if they are frequent and big enough, bring on a disorder in which freedom and democracy are destroyed.[16]

The Logical and Tactical Dilemmas of the Two Conservatisms

Analysis of images of change and tactics on the part of organic conservatism alone would leave us with only a partial understanding of the nature of conservative ideology. Instead, we shall start from a broader focus and examine the self-limiting consequences of conservative principles as they affect tactics. Because individualist conservatism faces many of the same problems, we will include that version in the analysis also. Although the premises and values of the two conservatisms are very different, they end up approaching the question of accomplishing their goals in much the same manner.

The two conservatisms face a dual problem. First, there is the task of developing an affirmative program of social and political action. But the values and goals of the two ideologies call either for *inaction,* in favor of letting individual striving run its course, or for particular types of guidance that amount to *unattractive restraints* on many individuals. In both cases, an affirmative program would call for the repeal or drastic revision of much of the social and economic legislation of the last forty years. Further, the two ideologies agree that there is now too much popular control over the power of government and that this power is being used unwisely—sometimes for the aggrandizement and special advantage of particular businesses, and sometimes for social purposes that are destructive of the talent and will of capable individuals. Thus, the two conservatisms have inherent, principle-based limitations on what they can stand *for,* and similar imperatives concerning what they must be *against.* It is

---

[16] Lippmann, *op. cit.,* p. 124.

very difficult to fashion an affirmative program of government action out of such principles and highly unlikely that it would be a very attractive one in the eyes of either business, entrenched politicians, or the people generally. These are the groups that are viewed as dominant in government. They must somehow be converted to new principles that run sharply contrary to their immediate economic interests, but the more they learn about the practical implications of such conservative principles, the more they are likely to see their interests threatened.

Second, there is the task of acquiring power. The conservative perspective (i.e., that government is now dominated by private aggrandizers, whether they be particular corporations or the masses and their perhaps innocently totalitarian leaders) simply does not harmonize with the basic tactical implications of conservative principles. Both versions of conservatism are essentially prescriptions for "inside" or already-established elites to follow in governing. They tell how a government should be conducted, and why, but do not envision being out of power and having to acquire power in some way before the principles can be put into operation. Nor can conservatives consistently turn to a popular appeal as a means of acquiring power. Not only would their program be unattractive, as we have seen above, but, by definition, the people are likely to err and to follow their short-range interests to the exclusion of the less attractive long-range needs of the society. Only a talented few are capable of governing, and majoritarian control is wrong; but the talented few are not holding power in government now, and only something like a majority can put them there. Conservatism, an elite-centered, tradition-oriented ideology, thus finds it both inherently and practically difficult to appeal for majority support for imposing new restraints and disciplines upon the society.

The dilemmas are troubling, but not disabling. Both versions of conservatism insist upon maintenance and promotion of the established social, economic, and political structures, and their principles are generally acceptable to many men who hold power in government or elsewhere. Neither ideology is mass-based. As a consequence of these factors, the two conservatisms—even though rarely represented by officeholders—enjoy access to men of power. They provide useful rationales for *not* taking contemplated or proposed government actions, and public notice of both forms of conservatism usually is achieved in this negative sense. Their real problem is thus one of bringing men of power to acceptance of consistent, principled applications of their power in conformity with one of the two ideologies, instead of merely using the ideologies as rationalizations for opposition to particular changes in the status quo.

The tactic of rational argument in opposition to contemplated or proposed change is thus the main characterizing tactic of both forms of conservatism. This opposition provides the best chance of acquiring converts among men of power, and realistically the most that conservatism can hope for in the present world is to prevent the worsening of conditions as much as possible. For these reasons, both forms of conservatism oppose extension of government regulation, broadening of popular impact on policy, and centralization of power. At the same time, they both call for increased emphasis on maintaining order and enforcing rules of conduct, and for a firm military posture against communism. They both view government policies at present as insufficiently concerned with the protection of property rights and too ready to attempt to serve social ends. The increasing coercion visited upon the more talented individuals in this way, and the sapping of the will of the masses to improve themselves, diverts progress from its normal course and substitutes a kind of popular mania for unattainable earthly rewards that can only end in totalitarianism or societal fragmentation. Failure to make sufficiently determined efforts to preserve domestic peace and enforce obedience to necessary standards of behavior will continue the process of undermining the authority and capability of the government, to the point where (again) fragmentation will ensure. Survival requires constant military preparedness to counter communist expansionism.

Thus, both by action and inaction, contemporary government policies endanger the future of the society. To correct such errors, however, rational appeals must be directed, first, at men of power and, second, at potential supporters among the general public. But under all circumstances, the laws and practices of the established systems must be followed; anti-traditional actions are not employed, and violence or disruption is not even considered within the framework of these ideologies.

Annotated Bibliography

Barzun, Jacques. *The American University: How It Runs, Where It Is Going.* New York: Harper & Row, 1968. The problems of the university, from the conservative perspective of the need to train only an elite.

Buckley, William F. *Up from Liberalism.* New York: Honor Books, 1959. A stinging critique of liberalism by one of the most incisive of contemporary conservative commentators.

Friedman, Milton. *Capitalism and Freedom.* Chicago: University of Chicago Press, 1962. A short but important explanation of the relationship between capitalism and individualist conservative style freedom.

Goldwater, Barry. *The Conscience of a Conservative.* Shepherdsville, Ky.: Victor Publishing Company, 1960. Brief but much-read tract by the 1964 Presidential candidate.

Kirk, Russell. *A Program for Conservatives.* Chicago: H. Regnery Co., 1954. A good statement of the classic position.

Lippmann, Walter. *The Public Philosophy.* Boston: Little, Brown, 1955. One of the most important writings by organic conservative thinkers.

Lowi, Theodore. *The End of Liberalism.* Chicago: W.W. Norton, 1969. A perceptive modern conservative critique of liberalism, urging a return to "juridical democracy" as an alternative.

Rand, Ayn. *Capitalism: The Unknown Ideal.* New York: Signet Books, 1966. Marks the extreme individualist position.

Rossiter, Clinton. *Conservatism in America.* New York: Knopf, 1965. Perhaps the best single source tracing conservatism from its early manifestations to the present; reflects discouragement, but not unsympathetically.

Viereck, Peter. *Conservatism Revisited and the New Conservatives: What Went Wrong.* New York: Free Press, 1965. Critique of traditional or classic conservatism, from a "modern" perspective.

9

Competing Ideologies:
The Basic Distinctions

Although we have concentrated on analysis of each contemporary ideology as an independent belief system, we have also compared them with each other in several respects. In this chapter, we use our standard framework to summarize the major contrasts, both among the change-seeking ideologies and between them as a group and the two dominant ideologies. Our purpose is to draw some implications for American politics from the analyses made earlier. In particular, we will explore the extent and nature of the gap between established ideologies and the various change-seekers and try to see what this situation suggests for the future. The current conflict may be no more than a stage of political adaptation in which new conditions are creating pressures for modifications that will naturally occur. Or it may be another in the recurring series of reform efforts familiar in American history in which the dominant ideologies flexibly incorporate some new demands and thereby preserve themselves and the established economic and political systems. Or, as we believe, today's conflicts may be more fundamental and more serious than either of these interpretations would suggest.

Contrasting Images of the American System

Perhaps the most crucial difference between the various ide-ologies' world views lies in *the images they hold of where power is located* in the American system, and *the nature of the political process* to which that pattern of power distribution gives rise. An important cause of these contrasting images, however, is found in the concepts held by each ideology about the relationship between the economy and political power. We will first sketch the conceptual alternatives and then turn specifically to each ideology's conceptual approach and the images to which it contributes.

One can view politics as if it were a separate, compartmental-ized area of human activity. From this perspective, neither economic resources nor social settings are relevant to the power or purposes of individuals when they engage in political activity. Because of the division of labor in society and the specialization of knowledge with-in academic disciplines, businessmen, politicians, social scientists, and citizens alike may come to view economics and politics as dis-tinct and unrelated fields. Or, in sharp contrast, one may view social life as an integrated whole in which people acquire political power and purposes directly from their economic and social situations. In this view, power flows from economic resources and social class structures as well as from the possession of legitimacy under es-tablished social and political traditions; the latter, of course, may be seen as little more than the residue of *past* economic and social realities. From this perspective, men who possess or control aggre-gates of power must use the machinery of government to defend their achieved status and to further their current goals. To under-stand such a world, one cannot treat political activities in isolation, as if the influence of men were equal or the purposes of government neutral.

Capitalism and liberalism see economics and politics as two separate areas. Economic life occupies primary status because it involves the individual's natural self-serving needs and aspirations; it thus generates the primary shaping forces in the society. Politics is secondary, but it is an independent and open process analogous to the market economy. Acting as equivalent consumer units, in-dividuals select among products that compete for their support until majorities are developed.

Consistent with these premises, capitalism and liberalism see the American economic engine producing impressively, proof that the individuals involved are achieving their real goals. They see a distribution of wealth in which practically everyone enjoys some share of American abundance. Although some are very wealthy, as a result of their special capabilities, most Americans are at a reasonably comfortable middle-class level—with the highest standard of living the world has ever known. There *are* pockets of poverty, resulting from cultural deprivation and/or personal inadequacies, but the poor are steadily moving up into the middle class. Large corporations have recently created aggregates of economic resources, but these remain subject to the general control of the state and their managers are, in any event, sensitive and responsive to public preferences and needs.

Because each individual has one vote, the political process is also seen as working well. Power is distributed broadly. The organization of the population into interest groups both reflects social reality and provides further equalized representation. In short, the many benefits of pluralist democracy are being realized through American politics. And a variety of individual and social functions are being served, perhaps chief among which is the political system's service as the supportive agent of the economy. Capitalism sees the state increasingly as the agent for promotion of its growth and stability, and liberalism accepts responsibility for furthering the needs of the technological economy.

To varying degrees, however, the other ideologies conceive social reality in more integrated terms. Some make the link between economics and politics in quite direct fashion. They focus explicitly on the economic and social sources of political power. Marxism, for example, rests on the basic postulate that the character of economic organization shapes the social class structure and strongly affects political power and purposes. Organic conservatism has long recognized the same relationship and sought to guard the property and prerogatives of the upper classes in order that their talents might be applied to governing.

For a variety of reasons, the dominant American ideologies have never come to a direct confrontation with this unexceptional observation about social reality. In recent years, however, the change-seeking ideologies' concern for the tangible characteristics of human conditions and the actual consequences of government actions has brought about greater sensitivity to the integrated nature of economic, social and political affairs. Black liberationists first showed the many different dimensions of racism and the alternative means by which it was perpetuated. They then showed, at least to their own satisfaction, how myopic it was to argue that government had only limited powers, that due procedures prevented the kind of remedies sought, or that these matters were economic, social, or moral issues unfit for political action.

The new left also began by emphasizing the substance of government actions and the multiple dimensions of problems. It denied that government could avoid responsibility for the conditions of life in the United States or for the effects of policies it sponsored or permitted overseas. In search of explanations for what was perceived as intransigence and persistence in such policies, the new left moved to an analysis that, increasingly, found a web of economic and social power controlling government in the selfish interest of a relative few. The challenge raised by the various change-seeking ideologies may lead to a much franker and comprehensive frame of reference for political analysis, a "political economy" approach that reflects the integrated nature of modern society.

Reform liberalism too, at least as represented by Galbraith and other economists, has also begun to see connections between the economic and social order and the nature of the political process. For example, reform liberals dispute the generally contented image held by capitalism and liberalism in several ways, some of which are based on perceived links between economic status and political power. They see greater inequality between economic levels and a more permanent poverty status for some. Corporate concentrations appear to create a more serious problem and threaten uncontrolled technological domination of peoples' wants and opportunities. Political power follows such accumulation of economic resources in the hands of the giant corporation and poses a threat to the real independence of the state. In addition, modern developments have placed far too much real power in the hands of the military and the oligarchs in the Congress. The normal channels of political representation are not working well, with the result that disproportionate power is in the hands of those with outdated or dangerous ideas.

Conservatism departs from the capitalist-liberal image in quite the opposite direction, seeing an excessive and unjust leveling in the society. Personal incentives are kept artificially low, so that men are not as unequal as their talents warrant. Political power either lies with, or is responsive to, the desires of masses of people, resulting in frequent and unwise government intervention in the economy and insufficient firmness in other matters.

The three principal change-seeking ideologies hold even more sharply variant images. Black liberationists see wealth either in the hands of or at least available to whites generally—but denied to all but a very few individual blacks, and as a group. They do not go beyond this group-based differentiation to analyze the distribution of wealth within white society except in a few instances; for the most part, they accept the capitalist-liberal image of middle class distribution as correct. Political power is perceived in much the same way. While they recognize that it is not evenly distributed among whites, they think of white groups as being able to achieve their goals in accordance with the liberal image. But when it comes to blacks seeking their special goals, all of white society coalesces and, in effect, forms a unified power structure to oppose them.

The new left sees many illustrations of poverty, inequality, and racism and, unlike reform liberalism, finds them caused by basic structural features of the American system and the values that accompany it. Corporate concentrations are uncontrolled, and arrogantly shaping, the social and political conditions of the United States as their profit-seeking needs require. Political power has been effectively removed from the people by bureaucratization and institutional imperviousness as well as by the determination of the establishment to effectuate its special version of economic and political necessity. The established political processes not only are not working, but they are essentially diversionary means of preventing people from gaining their desired ends.

Marxism sees even more structurally caused class divisions, with an inevitable worsening of inequalities between rich and poor. Political power lies with the economically based ruling class, which uses the state exclusively for its selfish purposes.

It should be clear from this comparison of world views that

there is a further distinction to be drawn concerning the approaches taken by the various ideologies. This is the *level of causation* or the *frame of reference* with which the ideology understands events and processes. Capitalism and liberalism, perhaps because of their compartmentalized approach and their focus on the individual, tend to find such explanations in the decisions of individuals. If certain corporations prosper, or particular policies are followed by the government, the causes lie in the decisions made by a few people, or by many people together. Analysis of their interests, personalities, and interaction would probably explain why they acted that way.

Reform liberalism is somewhat more sensitive to regular patterns in such decisions, which recur over time regardless of the people who make them. It therefore begins to look for characteristics shared among such people, or aspects of the institutions in which the decisions are made, which might explain their consistent actions. It finds such explanations in the ideology held by key individuals or the circumstances in which they operate, such as the tendency of subordinates to report what superiors want to hear, the difficulty of getting accurate information to the President, his dependence on military advisers, the impotency of Congress and apathy of the people, etc.

The other ideologies move even further from an individual focus toward a still deeper, more structural analysis. They do not believe that mistakes, faulty information, or inefficient institutional arrangements are the causes of today's deplorable situation. They look for explanations in the basic values of the society or in the imperatives of the economic system because they see the political system as functioning entirely in accord with those fundamental forces. Regardless of the individuals or institutions involved, policies and practices would be essentially the same. They disagree as to whether the economic system is the first cause (Marxism) or whether self-perpetuating cultural values are an independent factor (black liberation, the early new left). But they share the conviction that one cannot explain the American system and its actions by looking at the behavior of individuals abstracted from the broad total context in which they act. By implication, neither would it be possible to correct the ills of the society without reaching to such basic causes.

Contending Values

In earlier chapters, we have made much of the tension within the dominant ideologies over definitions of equality and the relative priority to be given (among the several natural rights) to property rights and to civil rights (and particularly, among them, to equality). This property-equality tension is often seen as the principal dynamic of American political development, and it is clearly the cutting edge of controversy today between reform liberalism, liberalism, and capitalism.

The latter would define equality principally in terms of formal opportunities, such as the availability of university education if a youth were qualified and motivated. Though placing property at the top of its priorities, it would acknowledge obligations to contribute to the support of those who were less successful. Liberalism grants broader scope to the definition of equality, extending it to cover more of the reality of opportunity. It would recognize, for example, that there are cultural, social, *and* financial obstacles that prevent university education from being truly available to large proportions of the population. Despite its commitment to property rights, it would try to serve the needs of equality wherever practical.

Reform liberalism, operating with a broader and more contextual sensitivity to problems, might define equality in this case in terms of the actual mixture of students attending universities. If the wealthier strata are disproportionately represented, inequality of opportunity is demonstrated. To the extent that it is possible under established procedures, reform liberalism would say, equality (defined as equality of condition or "human rights") should be given coequal status with the still valid principle or property rights.

By contrast, black liberation would accept no other claim as legitimate if it prevented realization of the long delayed goal of (racial) equality. And the new left and Marxism would deny the possibility of actually realizing either racial equality or their communitarian, humanistic versions of equality as long as individualism and property rights continued as major contending values. All three of these ideologies deliberately pose the ideal of community against the traditional commitment to individualism. They insist that man has higher, ethically superior goals than mere material satisfaction and infinite self-aggrandizement. Among these goals are aesthetic enjoyment, creative use of leisure time, awakening to new dimensions of interpersonal relationships, and the fulfillment that comes from sharing and helping others. With pressures removed, the human personality might develop new emotional and creative capacity and ultimately reach new levels of social achievement. In short, life could be converted from struggle to serenity.

Clearly, some sharp differences in assumptions concerning the nature of man lie behind this basic contrast of values and goals. Is man, by nature, egoistic, competitive, and aggressive—as assumed by conservatism, capitalism, liberalism, and reform liberalism? Or is he, by nature, cooperative and rendered competitive only by the teachings of a capitalist value system and its artificial scarcities—as assumed by the new left and Marxism? In either case, could his circumstances be so modified and his growth so encouraged as to develop a truly fraternal community where freedom, justice and equality might be realized? The revival of a sense of utopianism in the latter ideologies has challenged the "realism" of the dominant ideologies, asserting that their pessimistic view of the nature of man is no more than a component of their ideology, one intended to justify the economic system and political constraints that they favor. The rise of this challenge explains the recent convergence between libertarian individualists (and some individualist-conservatives) and the new left. Both deny the validity of centralization, bureaucratization, and greater power in the corporate state, arguing that man's true nature can only be realized when external restraints and pressures are lifted from him. With a touch of philosophical anarchism, it is argued that the fewer the rules, the more human and cooperative man will become.

Related to this divergence is a less visible one about the nature of rulership in modern society. Is man inevitably to be ruled by some elite, either because of societal complexity or the need for expertise or the sheer problem of scale? If this is unavoidable, as most capitalists, liberals, organic conservatives, and reform liberals would say, then the question becomes one of which elite is best under all the circumstances. A number of fairly technical and familiar issues arise, and much institutional tinkering ensues. But if genuine mass-based democracy is held to be possible, as black liberation, the new left, and Marxism argue, a whole new range of questions is opened. What are the conditions, the size and character of organizations, the protections against elite dominance, etc., that make this possible? Even more crucial—how can masses be persuaded of this possibility, then enabled to achieve it? In the eyes of most change-oriented ideologies, masses are now managed by elites and are subject to their ideological and physical dominance. What tactics are justified in order to make possible a genuine mass-based democracy? Specifically, should (must) masses be "forced to be free" by some vanguard group in view of their inability to realize real freedom from their currently deprived and repressed conditions? If so, can such an action be honestly distinguished from the masses' prior capitivity by some other elite? The issue of whether a believer in mass-based democracy can justify elite-accomplished change to such a system is of course, one of the enduring dilemmas of politics. Much evil has been done in the name of laudable ends, and most are alert to this danger. Much evil is done under present conditions, they note, and the calculus as to which route would be better for the mass of the population may be very close.

Change: How Much, and How?

Many conflicting prescriptions for the kind of change required and the manner in which it should be brought about are embodied in these ideologies. At first, it might seem that the more drastic the change sought, the more radical the measures that would be endorsed to do so. But this does not necessarily follow in all cases. Some ideologies may have internal inconsistencies, their world views may tell them that the conditions are not yet right for transformation of the society, or their values may prevent them from taking steps that might seem logically implied in their world views and goals. As a means of exploring the complexity of prescriptions concerning change, we will first return to our distinction between reform and revolution and then employ other means of contrast and evaluation.

Reform involves modest extensions or adjustments of the basic values of the society and is carried out within the general political framework and without substantially altering established patterns of wealth, status, and power. Revolution implies major alteration or outright replacement of basic values and fundamental change in economic, social and political structures. Such sweeping changes may occur more or less peacefully, but often require sustained violent upheaval; the timing of such upheaval, however, may be a matter of disagreement among revolutionaries. Thus, reform and revolution are distinguished in part by the scope of change sought, but also by the kind of process through which it is sought.

These two dimensions of difference serve to point up some of the crucial distinctions of change-seeking ideologies. Including reform liberalism for purposes of comparison, we find some sharp contrasts between the four ideologies. The new left and Marxism not only redefine and reorder priorities among familiar values, but also assess humanitarian and communitarian values as of first-priority and drop such standbys as property rights, individualism, and materialism. The steps they would take to expunge racism also imply severe reconstruction of values. The class structure, too, would be sharply altered in the direction of egalitarianism. The consequences of all changes for the character of the capitalist economic system are clear: it is to be replaced by some form of socialism.

Black liberation ideologies differ over the scope of change to be sought, and for whom. The integrationists and some other focus chiefly on racism and on the social and economic conditions of blacks in the context of the existing economy. The value change involved for whites would be the elimination of racism, presumably, and this would be less drastic for them than for blacks whose entire life situation is affected by racism. In this sense, the integrationists seek revolutionary change for blacks, but something less than that for whites. The Black Panthers and many black power and nationalist thinkers, by contrast, call for changes in both black and white values. They do not ask for the extension of the good things of white society to blacks, but for a radically reconstituted society. In many respects, the Panthers in particular seek the same changes endorsed by the new left and Marxism. Reform liberalism, on the other hand, justifies our characterization by seeking the solution to problems through implementing familiar values within the existing economic, social, and political systems. Neither it nor the integrationists can be called revolutionary.

Much the same pattern of distinction applies to the strategies of change endorsed by these ideologies, though in this regard there is greater diversity within each general category. Most components of the new left, the Panthers and some black groups, and many of the Marxists, believe that violent upheaval will be necessary to accomplish their goals. But they disagree sharply as to the timing, nature of alliances required, and method of accomplishing the upheaval. For some, immediate efforts are essential to incite repression, destroy complacency, and build support. Others, probably a majority, insist that a period of organizing among students, workers, blacks, and other deprived groups must precede any serious effort to seize power. Some elements of both the new left and Marxism still hold to an image of a relatively peaceful (though protest- and riot-studded) process of change, either through the drastic transformation of values or the collapse of capitalism because of its inherent problems. On the other hand, all reform liberals and integrationists and some other black subideologies believe that full-scale violent upheaval is unjustifiable, impossible, or ultimately self-defeating. They cling to the established procedures and a number of pressure-maximizing embellishments with varying degrees of reluctance. Once again, the distinction between reform and revolution is clear, though, here, in some cases it separates individuals within ideologies. Revolutionaries are those who have reached the point of believing that peaceful, within-the-system methods of change cannot achieve their essential goals and have therefore accepted the necessity of whatever level of force is required.

The point of this analysis is not to show that there are inconsistencies among individuals or divisions within ideologies—nor even that only some qualify for the label of "revolutionary" in both its dimensions—but to illustrate the normally close link between the level at which an ideology explains the nature of the political world, the character of its central value commitments, and its strategy of change. Inconsistencies among these components carry implications for the viability of the ideology itself. The attractiveness of reform liberalism, for example, is reduced for some (though, paradoxically, it is probably increased for others) by the fact that it accompanies a very critical and near-fundamental critique of American problems, practices, and values with a quite orthodox, self-limiting set of within-the-system prescriptions. One may feel justified in concluding that, in logic, either the problems are not as bad as described by reform liberalism or the remedies urged are incapable of solving them.

FURTHER CRITERIA FOR CONTRAST AND EVALUATION

The reform-revolution distinction establishes a basic comparison, but we can explore the differences between the change-seeking ideologies in more subtle fashion. We will consider ideologies' conceptions of the role of violence in the process of change and their relative commitments to elite versus mass action to bring about change. This analysis assumes, of course, that it is the thrust toward change that forms the principal dynamic of American ideological conflict, and that the methods by which change are sought are crucial to public response.

(1) *The role of violence in the process of change.* As we suggested earlier, violence is often a focusing agent for ideologies' value reactions. Dominant ideologies tend to view nonofficial violence, whatever the provocation or justification, as inherently wrong and always punishable. Change-seeking ideologies are more likely to see violence as justifiable counter-violence, a response to continuing official violence (in recent years, the Vietnam war, racism, or police repression). We have noted that dispassionate analysis and value judgment about the *propriety* of violence should be contextual rather than automatic. For example, value judgments about violence should consider the contending ideological perspectives from which participants view it, the human costs that violence carries with it, the current balance of equities (power, wealth, deprivation, etc.) between the parties, and the prospects that violence will render that balance any more justifiable afterwards. In this way, at least some greater rationality—and less ideological triggering—will be brought to bear on the judgment.

But in this section, our question is pragmatic and not value-oriented. We are concerned about the *utility* of violence, and about how ideologies resolve the question of whether (and if so, where and when) violence may be productive of desired results. Clearly, change is not likely to occur without *some* violence. Our history teaches that lesson well, from the Revolution and the Civil War to the labor and civil rights movements. Each ideology understands the utility of violence distinctively, however, some transcending it and others embracing it. Reform liberalism, for example, denies its utility under all circumstances. Perhaps this is the result of reform liberalism's strong commitment to the established procedures, but it also reflects the view that great danger lies in the powerful reaction from the right that violence is sure to provoke. This reaction is seen as inevitable, very powerful, and probably destructive of the many good qualities of the existing system; the veneer of civilization, in short, is very thin and easily removed.

Black liberation has a much more ambivalent view of violence. Even Martin Luther King's commitment to nonviolence was sorely tested and perhaps weakening at the time of his death. For that matter, one of the advantages of nonviolence as a direct action technique was in the way in which it played on the prospect of provoking violence. If white citizens employed or seemed about to employ violence, local authorities were forced to aid blacks and perhaps even grant their demands in order to avoid bloodshed. If the authorities themselves resorted to violence, nationwide public reaction to the spectacle was an incalculable aid to the black cause. In recent years, protests and demonstrations that carry the clear possibility of erupting to violence have seemed to be a means of both mobilizing black support and of persuading policy-makers that they must grant black demands. Unplanned ghetto riots have been used after the fact to bolster the force of black demands. For most black liberationists, the threat of black violence is a major tool for loosening the hold of white society upon black people.

Marxists are more likely to embrace violence in the indefinite future than in current practice. Most envision a period of violence at some point in the future, either when capitalism collapses in chaos or when the cohesive revolutionary movement succeeds in overthrowing it. In the first case, there will be a period when right-wing groups contend for power and must be thrust aside; in the latter, a more sustained period of revolutionary effort will be required to achieve control of the entire nation. But these occasions are not yet near, and for the moment, the task is to organize workers and other deprived groups and to prepare for the future struggle. Violence now, under current conditions of weakness, is usually seen as counter-productive in that it calls down severe repression, makes organizing more difficult, and creates unnecessary hysteria.

Some Marxists, along with some components of black liberation and the new left, reject violence completely. They view it much as do reform liberals; either as unjustifiable in the presence of civil liberties or inevitably counterproductive. Some individuals within each of these ideologies hold to a pacifist viewpoint, which precludes violence under any circumstances as immoral.

The remainder of the new left and the Black Panthers see violence as one of many potentially productive tactics in the current context, at least under certain conditions. Where there are no other effective ways to make opposition known or to apply pressure, it may be the only means available to attract public attention to existing evils. It may serve as a vehicle for radicalizing individual participants (few see the American system the same way after a police clubbing or a night in jail), for revealing the "true nature" of the (repressive) system, or for attracting wider support from liberals who react against excessive police actions. It may simply harass and soften officials or other elites, who may then be willing to change nonessential policies in order to prevent further conflict and/or social disintegration. For the Black Panthers, violence in the present is advocated exclusively for purposes of self-defense. As an expression of their determination to stand up to all manifestations of white repression of the black community, it also serves both as a means of mobilizing support in the black community and forcing whites to cease some of the more extreme forms of exploitation and repression of blacks. For the Weatherman faction of SDS, violence serves a more immediate political purpose—that of aiding the liberation struggle of Third World countries, particularly in Southeast Asia. By deliberate sabotage and mass confrontations with police, the United States may be forced to bring some of its troops home or expend energy and resources in fighting a domestic guerrilla war, to the detriment of its capabilities abroad. Potentially revolutionary white youth, who see other whites risking their lives and willingly battling the overwhelming force of the combined local, state, and national governments, may be induced to join the cause; workers may come to respect the otherwise incomprehensible middle-class college youth; and all other left groups may take heart.

In each of these cases, there is an attempt at rational calculation of the odds, in which the risks of repression, backlash, and misunderstanding are weighed against potential returns. (Often, of course, what is planned as a peaceful demonstration is converted into violence by a single provocative act or by the rigidity of officials.

We are speaking here only of *deliberate* uses of violence.) But, in the process of calculating the utility of deliberate violence, the lack of alternatives is an important factor. Where there is no intention of competing in elections and no hope of creating a favorable image through the mass media, there is no sense in considering the impact of violence except on the target populations—either public officials or, more often, potential allies in the path to revolution. Workers and blacks, the most likely allies, are the groups whose reactions are most important, and violence counter to their interests or understanding is usually avoided except under provocation. For the Black Panthers, police harassment is an automatic provocation. The Weatherman faction acknowledges no constraints except strategic opportunity and the availability of people who are ready to sacrifice themselves; the act of violence that provokes massive response is an end in itself and is more valuable if it produces great public outrage.

In seeking to understand the utility of violence in concrete situations, ideologies must estimate its consequences at various levels. Violence has obvious physical consequences, in which people are killed or injured and property destroyed. It has deeper effects as well, because death and destruction shift the world views, values, and political loyalties of people—perhaps moving the range of possibility sharply one way or the other. Over time, repeated violence may lead officials to far greater degrees of change than they would have otherwise considered or to the defensive surveillance, preventive detention, and harassment equivalent to a police state. In the latter case, it is often argued on the left, more people come to see the need for revolution; by that time, of course, their prospective leaders may all be dead, in jail, or underground.

The change-seeking ideologies, it should be noted, develop a calculus or balance of costs and benefits of any act of deliberate violence by weighing it objectively *from the perspective of a theory of revolution,* not in terms of probable success under the standards of orthodox American political practices. The new left rejects the established procedures and knows that its goals are not attainable within the American system as presently constituted. In its eyes, it is building a process of revolution that may take some time to reach fruition but that *will* happen at some future point. The only relevant questions to be asked under such conditions are whether new allies have been gained or made more open to persuasion; whether the resolve of existing members has been heightened; whether officials have lost confidence in their capacity to control events; and whether the general public has come to see a wider range of possibilities for the future—including, of course, sheer chaos. For the new left, it would be well worth converting two apathetic supporters into equally apathetic opponents if one strongly committed new recruit could be gained in the process.

The risks of building deliberate violence into the political process are, of course, very great. Many can take part in that type of politics, and throughout American history, they have—usually against those who sought change. The modern society is highly vulnerable to bombings, attacks on municipal facilities, assassinations, kidnappings, and other violent acts. Such acts appear to justify the surveillance and repression that fearful officials employ in response. Although repression probably does build consciousness of the need for change, in the ordinary course of events, it is more likely to eventuate in entrenched fascism than in the change desired. Thus, the stakes in the use of violence are high, and one may well come full circle back to reform liberalism's recognition of the purposes served by the established civil liberties and other procedures.

(2) *The relative parts played by elites and masses.* Neither ideologies nor movements spring fully formed from the minds of millions; at some point, they are always initiated by a small number of thinkers and activists. It is not the original source or the number of current advocates that characterizes an ideology as elite or mass based, but rather the substance of the ideology itself—the roles it allocates for elites and masses in various ways. Sometimes, the commitments are clear in the category of values and goals. The participatory democracy commitment of the new left is a clear illustration of a mass-oriented goal. In sharp contrast to, for example, conservatism, forms of participation from the grass roots play a major part in new left thinking. At other times, these commitments may become clear from the process of change that an ideology prescribes. Some images of the process of change are clearly more mass-based than others. Again, the new left component that sees change emerging from the broad dissemination of the values of the young "counter-culture," for example, is readily distinguishable from Galbraith's allocation of

responsibility for change to the scientific and technological experts.

In general, change-oriented ideologies are forced to become more mass-based than those that are dominant. This occurs for communitarians and democrats partly by definition: the reason why change is needed is that there are unfulfilled needs, recognized or unrecognized, on the part of numbers of people. It also rests on pragmatism: because the machinery of the state is controlled by *some* elite, which wants to retain its power and status, an opposing ideology is induced to turn to the masses as a means of mobilizing an alternative source of power. Dominant ideologies, firmly entrenched in power, may be primarily concerned with justifying their acts. Though they may do so on the grounds that such policies serve mass needs or preferences, they are likely to insist that their acts are correct or necessary in the absolute sense, and regardless of the masses' views.

But even granting this practical pressure to assert a mass basis, some ideologies are clearly more oriented toward mass decision-making and control than others. Among the change-seeking ideologies themselves, there are substantial differences in the respective roles assigned to elites and masses, both in the system of government that is their goal and in the process of change by which it is to be reached. In regard to the ultimate form of governing sought, for example, reform liberalism does not raise fundamental questions about the present relatively elite-centered system. The elaborate checks, balances, institutional independence, and hierarchical structure of American politics effectively insulates decision-makers from much popular pressure and removes real power from masses to relatively small set of elites. Reform liberalism either accepts this as inevitable or views it as desirable; essentially, its prescriptions call for better actions—wiser policies—on the part of responsible elites. Black liberation moves toward a larger role for mass preferences, at least as far as blacks are concerned. But it essentially asks for black participation on an equal basis with whites, i.e., that blacks and whites be fairly represented in the familiar and ongoing American governmental structure. Both the new left and Marxism, on the other hand, assert their commitment to a much broader role for masses in the ultimate economic, social, and political order to be created. Decentralization and popular control in both the workplace and the polity are fundamental elements of these ideologies, as they are for the Black Panthers.

In regard to the process of change by which such goals are to be attained, the distinctions become more particularized. Reform liberalism sees a crucial role for the nation's universities. Either through the quality of social analysis and prescription offered policy-makers by academics or through the values communicated by them to the rising managerial elite, new policies will be generated and, in time, the political preferences of the mass public will be reshaped toward better goals. Beginning with a relatively small elite focus, in other words, reform liberalism sees an ever-widening set of consequences emerging from the progressive values and goals generated by educators. Although it probably reaches this position more from a lack of alternatives than from any demonstrable basis for optimism in the present character of the American university, reform liberalism does thereby present a consistent image of elite-generated, mass-supported change. Black liberation, again, has a larger immediate role for (black) masses, who are to act in solidarity with their leaders in ways that will force the larger system's policy-makers and ultimately, the entire white society to grant blacks fully equal status.

For the new left and Marxism, the role of the masses in accomplishing change is more problematical. Although nearly all sub-ideologies agree that masses are to play a major role in the system of government ultimately erected, they disagree on the extent to which change should be mass-based, and even more over the timing of mass participation. The concept of "mass" itself, it should be noted, presents opportunities for differences. Clearly, it need not mean majorities, but distinguishing mass participation from that of a moderately large elite may amount essentially to a value judgment. Some components of both ideologies hold that no major efforts to acquire power can, or should be, made until the movement is strong enough to have a real chance for success, by which presumably is meant a substantial and strategically located mass base. Few advocates of either ideology adhere to coup d'etat theories of change or to seizure of power by any small group, except as an incitement to further action by many others. But there are many and bitter disagreements over the precise number and character of supporters necessary to begin the revolution and over the best means of organizing them for that purpose. Further, what begins as action by a miniscule elite may mushroom, under the right conditions, into a mass action—as nearly happened (in the eyes of these ideologies) in France in 1968. Again, most subideologies in these two categories believe that conditions are not yet right for such actions in the United States, but there is no consensus on what the necessary conditions are, when they will be reached, or how.

The change-seeking ideologies are thus faced with a very large and difficult problem: what route toward change (a) offers real chance of achieving essential goals, (b) is possible under contemporary conditions, *and* (c) is consistent with the ideology's value commitments? The dilemma can be cruel, and the temptation to suspend one or another value commitment *or* much-desired goal may become very strong. We may note, at least, that the definition of what is possible under contemporary conditions is a question that is continually subject to shifting answers. What looks impossible at one moment may seem routinely attainable the next; in many respects, the range of the possible is a product of one's imagination and intensity of desire to make something happen. The limits of the possible are not found exclusively in objective conditions, but also in the hopes—and fears—of people.

Some Implications

Throughout this chapter, we have been building toward consideration of the meaning of today's ideological conflict for the future of the United States. We have no doubt that profound social conflict is strongly indicated. Of course, many other factors, forces, events, and circumstances contribute to the dangerous dynamics of American politics in the 1970s. But the presence of persuasive— and widely divergent—political ideologies assures that no easy accommodation will be possible. Neither "communication" nor "reasonableness" can solve differences between people who hold drastically different images of how the American system operates and how it should be changed. Orthodox images of processes of negotiation and compromise leading to mutually acceptable settlements overlook the fact that such arrangements are possible only where the parties share basic assumptions, values, and goals. If the parties disagree, for example, about the validity of the basis on which the economy is organized or about the present distribution of social status and political power—and each cares strongly about achieving his vision of the good life—negotiation and settlement are far more difficult, if not impossible.

The polarization of politics achieved in part by contrasting ideological maps in peoples' minds is not likely to be reduced in the near future. Social problems appear likely to become more acute, while at the same time resistance to change will stiffen and advocates will be vigorously punished. The analysis conducted here suggests that capitalism-liberalism may be in the midst of a more severe crisis than it has previously experienced. Its collapse should not be lightly projected, given the flexibility that it has displayed over two centuries, the network of power and interest invested in the maintenance of the present economic and political systems that it rationalizes and justifies and the incalculable advantage of legitimacy and sheer coercive power it now enjoys. But contemporary conditions create some circumstances not previously faced by capitalism-liberalism, and suggest that the prospect must be taken seriously. In particular, two factors seem to create a distinctive quality to the present challenge to continued domination by capitalism-liberalism, at least in its current form.

THE CONTENDING IDEOLOGIES' COMPLETE REJECTION
OF THE MOST FUNDAMENTAL VALUES OF CAPITALISM—LIBERALISM:
PROPERTY, INDIVIDUALISM, AND MATERIALISM

The three major change-seeking ideologies seek to replace property, individualism, and self-seeking with a version of equality, community, and sharing. They do not merely seek a share of the established pattern of economic and social benefits for their members. This is not a set of claims for participation by an excluded group, but a demand for fundamental change of basic values on the part of the dominant group. Even integrationists, the most reformist of the subideologies in these three categories, seek goals that are fundamentally at odds with capitalism-liberalism. The demand for the elimination of racism, the most profoundly polarizing force in American history, is itself sufficient to create a crisis of drastic import. But the other black ideologies, the new left and Marxism, go much farther. They seek the end of the capitalist system itself. They do not want to participate in, or to reform, the present system of thought and practice; they want to replace it with values, structures, and policies wholly at odds with its current basis. They even draw some support for their rejection of the core values of capitalism-liberalism from the more moderate reform liberalism. The latter's analysis reaches many of the same conclusions about the current ills of American society and may serve as a bridge whereby people can be brought to see the need for more profound change, by whatever means are required.

THE CONTENDING IDEOLOGIES ARE NOT ISOLATED SYSTEMS
OF BELIEF, BUT ENJOY BROAD SUPPORT AT THE CRUCIAL
VALUE LEVEL

One important key to the viability of a political ideology is the extent to which it is grounded in the most basic personal values held by numbers of people. Individualism and materialism press people to accept ideologies consistent with the capitalist-liberal framework. Communitarian values would probably do the reverse. And there are major constituencies for the community-oriented ideologies today. More than twenty-five million black people, held subservient for centuries, have a group sense of identity and consciousness. Although many seek no more than participation on equal terms, the obvious and hardening resistance of whites appears to make growing numbers receptive to the call for rejection of the values of capitalism-liberalism and drastic change in the basic structures of American life.

Perhaps equally important, even larger numbers of young people are undergoing fundamental value changes away from the underpinnings of the capitalist-liberal system. In some cases, as in the hippie, drop-out, and yippie phenomenons, no explicit political content has been perceived. But these are profoundly significant shifts in basic values, as major yippie leaders have pointed out, and they have the most basic political implications. When values shift in this way, existing economic and political structures must experience severe tensions. Increasing numbers of young people appear to have made the connection between economic and political practices and basic value changes in quite explicit fashion already, as the general support for new left principles indicates.

These two factors must be seen in context, of course. This context includes powerful status-quo enforcing forces. But it also includes objective conditions likely to continue to create problems that are unsolvable within the capitalist-liberal framework, such as race tensions, urban and environmental decay, crime, international conflicts, needs for economic expansion amidst foreign resistance, etc. If American government power is employed ineptly or repressively by persons unperceptive about or rigidly resistant to the change seekers' ideologies, polarization will proceed and only chaos can ultimately ensue.

This brings us back to the questions posed in Chapter 1 about the ways in which ideologies evolve and the circumstances that lead individuals to modify their personal ideologies. We have seen how various ideologies have evolved through time. In most cases, certainly including capitalism and liberalism, they have adapted by fitting current conditions into a new or revised rationale that, nevertheless, maintains and affirms their basic values. Some, such as black liberationists and the new left, have been led by their analysis of current conditions to endorse values and goals that would support wholly different conditions of life. This is the heart of today's conflict, of course: capitalism-liberalism can adapt flexibly, but not at the cost of undermining individualism, property rights, and materialism; black liberation, the new left, and Marxism will accept nothing less than the replacement of those same values, and view all else as deliberate fraud or counterrevolutionary cooptation. In short, the conditions for ideological evolution may no longer exist. In their place, we may have only the prospect of conflict.

The evolution of an ideology, it should be clear, ultimately reduces to the question of whether individual adherents, in fact, experience change in their personal ideologies. So does the question of conflict among ideologies today—and the issue of the outcome of that conflict. As people become more and more alert to the conditions around them and more sensitive to the implications of political values, ideas, and practices, they may seek consciously to reshape their own thinking. Indeed, perceived necessity (national and/or personal) thus may well be a leading cause of individuals' change in their personal ideologies. No doubt this is happening for many people today. And it is probably necessary to the eventual attainment of change reflecting widespread popular preferences. We hope that this book may have contributed in some way to making this process more natural, rational, and purposeful.

It hardly seems necessary to add that ideology is neither distant nor impersonal. Men and women, individuals all, hold beliefs and seek goals. Readers of this book may well play a part in the process of ideological and political change. Although great men and women have moved the world through their writings and actions, we recognize that neither the skills, dedication, nor opportunity are given most of us to generate such impact. Isolated and insignificant, our individual efforts can have little or no importance. But the values and aspirations expressed through politics are extensions of the human experience. Man is not a complete person—thinking, feeling, experiencing, growing—unless he is reacting and expressing himself through politics as well as the other dimensions of his life. Thus, it is not out of civil duty or the prospect of particular rewards that man takes part in politics. It is for the completion of self, for his own growth and self-definition in relation to others, and as an expression of the nature of his concern for those others, that man must act politically. To avoid political commitment is not only to support the status quo; it is to deny oneself areas of experience and development and to deny others the support and human contact that they need for their progress. The political community of which we are a part is now producing a mixed set of effects upon its members and upon the rest of the world, some good, some evil. It has come to a major crossroads in its evolution, in which it simultaneously celebrates the 200th anniversary of its Declaration of Independence and hears echoes of the same demands from many sectors of its population. The crisis is real, the route uncertain, the stakes immense. In the nearly 200-year-old words of another citizen, "The sun never shined on a cause of greater worth. . . . 'Tis not the concern of a day, a year, or an age; posterity is virtually involved in the contest, and will be more or less affected even to the end time by the proceedings now." [1]

---

[1] Tom Paine, *Common Sense* (Philadelphia: 1776).

Annotated Bibliography

Brink, William, and Louis Harris. *Black and White.* New York: Simon and Schuster, 1968. Opinion studies of blacks and whites, showing stark differences.

Domhoff, William. *Who Rules America?* Englewood Cliffs, N.J.: Prentice-Hall, 1967. A brief analysis concluding that the United States is governed by a permanent upper class.

Free, Lloyd A. and Hadley Cantril. *The Political Beliefs of Americans.* New York: Simon and Schuster, 1968. Full-length analysis, though at a relatively superficial level, of the political attitudes of the general population.

Graham, Hugh Davis and Ted Robert Gurr. *Violence in America.* New York: Signet, 1969. Historical and comparative perspectives on violence in the United States, showing its continuing role.

Hoffman, Abbie. *Revolution for the Hell of It.* New York: Dial Press, 1968. Classic statement of the counter-culture form of value change with limited explicit political content.

Kolko, Gabriel. *Wealth and Power in America.* New York: Praeger, 1968. Empirical study showing degree of inequality and premanence of this pattern in the U.S.

Lane, Robert E. *Political Ideology: Why the Common Man Believes What He Does.* Glencoe, Ill.: Free Press, 1962. Depth study of fifteen working men, arguing that there is a "fear of equality" among ordinary people.

Lasch, Christopher. *The Agony of the American Left.* New York: Vintage Books, 1969. Excellent analysis, not unsympathetic, of the intellectual and other problems facing the radical in the United States.

Terkel, Studs. *Hard Times.* An excellent oral history, spoken by people who passed through the depression of the 1930s, about what that period was like and how they reacted politically.

Young, Alfred F., ed. *Dissent: The History of Radicalism in America.* DeKalb, Ill.: Northern Illinois University Press, 1962. Useful collection of articles and lectures about various radical movements and their problems in gaining their goals.